AFTER MODERNITY

After Modernity

*Archaeological Approaches to the
Contemporary Past*

RODNEY HARRISON
and
JOHN SCHOFIELD

OXFORD

UNIVERSITY PRESS

Great Clarendon Street, Oxford OX2 6DP
United Kingdom

Oxford University Press is a department of the University of Oxford.
It furthers the University's objective of excellence in research, scholarship,
and education by publishing worldwide. Oxford is a registered trade mark of
Oxford University Press in the UK and in certain other countries

British Library Cataloguing in Publication Data
Data available

Library of Congress Cataloging in Publication Data
Data available

ISBN 978-0-19-954808-8

For Vicky and Emily

Acknowledgements

Writing can be a drag. But it can also be a joy, and somehow collaborative works such as this are more likely to be positive and entertaining experiences than cumbersome endeavours. And so it was with this book, which was for us a co-operative effort thus far unmatched in our careers. We would like to acknowledge the influence of colleagues from the Contemporary and Historical Archaeology in Theory (CHAT) Group, who by way of annual conferences and comment on the CHAT listserv have made an important contribution to the themes and case studies covered in the book. J.S. would also like to take this opportunity to acknowledge, not for the first time, the two teams that have inspired and encouraged such interest in the contemporary past: the Characterization Team at English Heritage, of which he has been a part since 2002, and the Change and Creation team (or 'collective' perhaps) who have been meeting and discussing these matters for nearly as long. Apart from himself, Graham Fairclough is the one common denominator, and his influence and encouragement are particularly significant to the realization of this project. J.S. would also like to acknowledge the generous financial assistance of the British Academy and the Farsons Foundation (Malta) for sponsoring his work in Malta, which features at various points in the book; the Council for British Archaeology for supporting the work at Greenham; and English Heritage for allowing numerous other foreign trips that inspired or presented the opportunity for projects and insight.

We are both grateful for the care, time, and effort put into the publication by Hilary O'Shea at Oxford University Press, and the reader, Paul Graves-Brown, whose perceptive comments have helped improve the book's final shape, form, and content. The book has taken a good deal of time to compile and create, which has often meant time hidden away from our families. Vicky and Emily have borne the brunt of this, and for that reason, and many others, the book is dedicated to them.

Contents

List of Figures

1

Introduction

How can we use the methods of archaeology to explore contemporary social phenomena? In what ways can the approaches of a discipline that has been developed to explore the distant past be used to understand the present, and should we even try? How can the 'excavation' of the recent past bring to light new insights into what it means to be 'us'?

These are the questions that have absorbed a new generation of scholars who seek to draw on the skills of archaeology to study an increasingly contemporary past and attempt to make the familiar past 'unfamiliar' (cf. Graves-Brown 2000a) by exploring its hidden, forgotten, and abject qualities and utilizing the powerful rhetoric of archaeological recovery in the retrieval of recent memories through the study of present-day material culture. This book aims to explore what happens if we take an archaeological approach to contemporary, late modern, post-industrial societies. It acts as an introduction both to the ways in which archaeologists approach the study of the recent and contemporary past, and to the interdisciplinary field of modern material culture studies more generally. We hope it will be of interest not only to students and practitioners of archaeology, but also to scholars who work within the broad interdisciplinary field of modern material culture studies—anthropologists, sociologists, historians of technology and science, and psychologists—in developing a new agenda for the study of the materiality of late modern societies. Because knowing more about our own society and how it functions is an issue of broad public concern, we have also tried to write this book in such a way that the reader who is not a specialist, but who has a casual interest in the manner in which archaeologists and others study contemporary material culture, will also be engaged by it.

The book's principal focus is the archaeology of developed, post-industrial societies during the second half of the twentieth century and the beginning of the twenty-first. Our emphasis is the period after about 1950, though the examples in Part II deliberately focus on the years after *c.*1970, a time which for us is literally the contemporary past, the period of our own lives and experiences. This period encompasses the end of the Cold War and the beginning of the 'internet age', a period that sits firmly within what we would recognize to be one of 'lived and living memory'. This period is often seen as discrete in exhibiting distinct features relating to the growth of new communicative technologies and electronic media, the globalization of technology, and the rise of new modes of capitalism associated with a sense of alienation and 'haunting' by the past. While there will be many people who have lived memory of an era before this one, we focus on this epoch as a distinct period, which we denote using the label 'late modern'. In using this term, we seek to make a distinction between it and the modern period. The term 'modernity' is generally associated with the development of centralized nation-states and industrialization, capitalist and mercantile economies, urban and suburban modes of living, and the emergence of long-distance communication and trading networks (e.g. Giddens 1991). A number of scholars (e.g. Lyotard 1979; Harvey 1990; Jameson 1991; Augé 1995; Appadurai 1996) have argued that the late modern (or super-/post-modern) period should be seen as exhibiting distinct characteristics that separate it from the modern period, including

- the growth of new communicative technologies and electronic media;
- the globalization of technology, and its association with altered patterns of production and consumption;
- the widespread experience of mass migration and the associated rise of transnationalism (in terms of capital, technology, labour, and corporations);

- new modes of capitalism involving more flexible forms of capital accumulation and distribution; and
- further growth of availability of leisure time (see further discussion in Ch. 5).

This is the first fully authored book to focus on the archaeology of the late modern period. Nonetheless, in reviewing the field of the contemporary past as it has developed within archaeology, it has often been necessary for us to refer to the archaeology of earlier time periods—the First and Second World Wars, for example—because it has relevance to the development of the field over the past two decades. This does not dilute the importance or the urgency of developing late modernity as a specific area of focus for archaeology. On the contrary, it is important to trace the antecedents of this field of study so as to understand the circumstances of its emergence and its relationship with archaeology as a broader academic pursuit. For reasons we will discuss in more detail in Chapter 5, we have consciously chosen the term 'late modern' rather than 'postmodern' to attempt to emphasize some of the continuities between the modern and late modern periods. As Jameson (1984; cited in Thomas 2004: 3) notes, the use of such terms as 'modernity' and 'postmodernity' has the tendency to establish a sense of homogeneity within, and heterogeneity between those periods that may not exist. Like Thomas (2004: 3), we suggest the terms 'modernity' and 'late modernity' be thought of more as social and technological *processes* than as entirely distinct time periods, to avoid making too clear a distinction between them and erasing the sense of continuity in certain longer-term processes that run through both periods.

Throughout the book, we focus particularly on post-industrial societies, and the urban and suburban lives of the majority of their inhabitants. In this sense, our perspective is largely Western, and certainly does not include people still living in small-scale societies in the modern world. However, by doing this, we are not suggesting that such people are any less a part of the contemporary or late modern world. Instead, we want to focus on methods particular to this form of late modern lifestyle that has not been considered in detail by archaeologists, rather than other forms of modernity that might be studied using more conventional archaeological methods suitable for the study of small-scale societies. Nonetheless, the ways in which such groups are caught up in globalized webs and networks of trade, communication, and consumption means that they are equally implicated in the circulation of objects, images, and information that are most often associated with post-industrial societies, and that some aspects of the everyday lives of such groups might also be studied using the methods outlined in this book. Indeed, many of the methods we discuss here come from prehistoric archaeology, not surprisingly given that many of those who work in this field have come to it from the study of prehistory (see further discussion below).

ARCHAEOLOGIES OF THE CONTEMPORARY PAST

The idea for this book emerged from an important and comparatively recent initiative within the related fields of archaeology and heritage, being the archaeology of the recent and contemporary past, a field of study that has grown dramatically over the past decade. The term 'contemporary past' has come to have a specific meaning for practitioners in the field, and it is important to pause to consider it in more detail here. While it might appear to be an oxymoron, the term refers to the tendency within contemporary post-industrial societies for the present to become almost immediately historicized, for the past to be perceived as imminent within the present. For this reason, unlike other historic periods and thematic studies of interest to archaeologists, the contemporary past is a period for which precise definition requires constant review and updating; unlike earlier periods or epochs ('the Neolithic' for example), the contemporary past moves with us into the future. The contemporary past is that period with which we are most closely familiar: the present, the age that we live in and have lived through, whose fabric and landscapes we shape and that influences our everyday lives and actions. The contemporary past is the past of *our* generation, and the generations immediately before and after, of which memories and stories are first- or second-hand, as the period of time we can most closely and clearly envisage and recall. It is called contemporary not simply because it is 'now' and recent but because it is not 'closed' in interpretation nor emotional influence. Further, the contemporary past is about lived experience; about human life. In this sense, the archaeology of the contemporary past overlaps closely with heritage, which for us is more a social phenomenon than something physical. The study of the contemporary past allows older models of heritage to be updated to find meaning for new audiences, for example recent immigrant communities, and those disadvantaged by the power structures of post-industrial societies. It is about vernacular experience and everyday life, and how the lived experience of the present forms as heritage in the longer term. It is a critical part of the public understanding of history because it belongs to everyone and everyone has a view about it.

The 'contemporary' period cannot be fixed to a precise chronological bracket, and unusually it might be best to see this as a period defined in reverse, from the present day back to a time when the past seems (subjectively) no longer recent (2010–1950, as opposed to the more conventional form of 1950–2010). Traditionally, the end of this period has been viewed as the point at which living memory fades (as now, for example, for the Second World War), but clearly this framework is open to interpretation depending on the point of view of the observer. It is not just the date range that is unusually subjective. Because we have lived and experienced this period directly, it is inevitable that our opinions about the landscape, and the buildings and places within it, will be strongly held; and because they are predominantly personal views, they will also be multiple and diverse. Archaeological sites of the contemporary past are places that in some ways we know all about, but in others can seem almost as mysterious and 'distant' as sites of prehistory or of the medieval period. Archaeology once focused exclusively on these earlier remains largely because only its approaches could reach so far back. But recently archaeologists have realized that their distinctive approaches and perspectives also have relevance for understanding very recent and present-day material culture. Although some might argue that archaeology has always been perceived to be a methodology rather than a discipline, we argue that the word 'archaeology' has become more methodological in its meaning than one that defines a particular period of interest.

Academic research into the contemporary past is common to a range of academic fields—in history and literature, sociology, and increasingly now in archaeology, anthropology, heritage, cultural geography, and the arts. In this way, we might think of the term 'contemporary' as akin to 'landscape' (with which it shares a core of subjectivity and perception), in being an inherently all-embracing field of interdisciplinary study. In joining this broader community of interest, archaeology brings three specific (and arguably unique) perspectives: first, that archaeological investigations, whether of the contemporary past or of early prehistory, begin with material culture, the stuff that people leave behind; second, there is a time depth that characterizes archaeological studies—a recognition of longer-term processes in which only geologists share similar insight; and third, due to their long-term temporal purview, archaeologists recognize that change happens—and that it is generally better to work with the principle of change than trying to prevent it.

WHY STUDY THE ARCHAEOLOGY OF THE CONTEMPORARY PAST?

Despite all this, some may find the idea of an archaeology of the contemporary past ridiculous, or just contradictory, being an unacceptable departure from archaeology's literal definition of studying ancient things. There are those that question what there is to know about the contemporary past that we do not already know from other sources. Yet there are many reasons why the archaeology of the contemporary past has emerged as an area of public, as well as academic, concern over the past decade. In this book we consider a series of themes to account for the development of the archaeology of the contemporary past, exploring its emergence within a distinct set of social and technological circumstances. These themes have their genesis in the work of archaeologists who have been involved in setting an agenda for the field over the past decade (especially Graves-Brown 2000*a*; Buchli and Lucas 2001*a, b, c, d*; Olivier 2001; Shanks, Platt, and Rathje 2004; Buchli 2007; González-Ruibal 2008; Piccini and Holtorf 2009), but in developing them we have drawn equally on the insights of various perspectives on contemporary material culture from other disciplines. Here we briefly introduce these themes, before moving on to discuss the structure of the book in more detail.

Speed, Experienced as the Acceleration of Space and Time

We argue that the speed of technological and social change of late modern societies has meant that the recent past seems to recede more rapidly, and in this sense, becomes obscured at a rate not known before in human history. Paul Virilio (1994, 2000; see also Tomlinson 2007) comments on the ways in which the later twentieth century has experienced an acceleration of time, or a sense of speed, that leads to a situation in which humans are so overwhelmed by the reversal, acceleration, and simultaneous nature of time that space itself becomes an element of time. This produces a sense of 'time-in-flux' that comes to be experienced as a fundamental part of the late modern landscape (see also Harvey 1990). As Augé (1995: 26–30) notes,

We barely have time to reach maturity before our past has become history... the recent past—'the sixties', 'the seventies', now 'the eighties'—becomes history as soon as it is lived. History is on our heels, following us like shadows, like death... time overloaded with events that encumber the present as well as the recent past. This can only... make us more avid for meaning... it is our need to understand the whole of the present that makes it difficult for us to give meaning to the recent past.

It is this sense of rapid change that both justifies an archaeology of the recent past, and has led to it becoming a topic of broader public interest. As the past appears to recede at an ever-increasing pace, the recent past becomes increasingly distant from individual and collective memory. This means that even the recent past is easily overlooked and quickly forgotten (Connerton 2009). As part of the educative apparatus of the state through its place in heritage (Appadurai 2001), archaeology has a role in creating officially sanctioned histories of the recent past that nourish national histories. At an unofficial level, as a discipline firmly rooted in material evidence, archaeology has a role in both challenging these official histories, and bringing to light the aspects of recent history that they seek to overwrite. At the heart of the archaeology of the contemporary past lies a desire to reconcile ourselves with a recent history that moves at such great speed that we feel both remote from it and disoriented by its passage.

A Present Haunted by the Past

Late modern societies could be argued to exist in a present that seems *haunted* by the past (Huyssen 2003; Buchli 2007). This is often coupled with what we might consider to be its flip-side, retro, or a sense of nostalgia for the modern past (Guffey 2006). We see these two related phenomena as both the reason for the development of the archaeology of the contemporary past as a distinct field and an issue that the archaeology of the recent past should seek to address. We consider the rapid acceleration in official processes of heritage throughout the late twentieth century as a closely linked phenomenon (see also Harrison 2010*b*; Ferguson, Harrison and Weinbren 2010). Both archaeology and heritage are involved in a therapeutic process of retrieval and memorialization of the past. For this reason, the archaeology of the contemporary past cannot be perceived simply as another form of period study; instead, it needs to be viewed as a critical engagement with the spaces in which the past intervenes in the present. The palimpsest nature of the late modern period and its archaeology cautions against a narrow focus on the archaeological remains of late modernity. The archaeology of the contemporary past is an archaeology of all time periods and the way in which the material remains of the past are mobilized and help to create the present. The acknowledgement of late modern societies as haunted by the past leads us to a consideration of archaeology's redemptive potential.

Archaeology as Exorcism and Its Redemptive Potential in Creating Public Memory

The twentieth century was a period in which super-modern forms of conflict developed (González-Ruibal 2008), and which saw the rise of totalitarian states, many of which committed acts of atrocity against their citizens (Olivier 2001). This trend has continued into the late modern period, alongside the rise of globalised terrorism (Appadurai 2006). In such circumstances, the role of archaeology in the recovery and interpretation of artefacts and assemblages—the staple of archaeological endeavour—becomes a metaphor for the recovery of memory. Of course, archaeology is not an objective practice, but (like heritage) a creation of the past in the present through a process that draws on the material evidence it creates. This puts archaeology in a unique position to engage actively and creatively with the recovery of lost memory and the therapeutic process of reconciliation (Shanks 1992: 78; Buchli and Lucas 2001*a*: 16). These themes have been explored most thoroughly in relation to the forensic excavation of mass graves, crime scenes, and sites of natural and cultural disasters (e.g. Cox 2001; Doretti and Fondebrider 2001; Hunter and Cox 2005; Funari and Zarankin 2006; Ferllini 2007; Gould 2007; Ballbé and Steadman 2008; Cox et al. 2008; Steele 2008; Sterenberg 2008; Zarankin and Funari 2008; Bagwell 2009), but we can also think about the therapeutic process of remembering and memorializing the recent past in relation to other aspects of hidden memory, such as the archaeology of homelessness (Buchli and Lucas 2001*c*; Zimmerman and Welch 2006; Harrison 2009*b*). In this sense, archaeology has a particular obligation to those people whom society pushes to its margins—the abject, the poor and the subaltern. Archaeology can act as both a form of *exorcism*, by bringing to light and casting out those hidden and haunting aspects of the past, and a form of *redemption*, in reconciling communities and nations with their recent hidden histories.

Non-place: Isolation, Solitude, Melancholy and Nostalgia

Some of the most characteristic aspects of late modernity (or using Augé's term, 'supermodernity') are associated with the experiences of 'non-places' and their dissociative spatial elements that produce a sense of isolation, solitude, melancholy (cf. Buchli 2007), and nostalgia. The term 'non-place' was developed by Marc Augé (1995) to describe a whole series of types of space in contemporary societies—airport lounges, shopping malls, motorways—which he suggests are to be distinguished from 'places' in the sense in which these spaces are not relational, historical, or concerned with the establishment of a sense of identity (all those things which characterize the traditional social anthropological interest in 'place'). For Augé, these 'non-places' are primarily associated with the experience of travel or transit, and are characterized by a feeling of solitude and the emptying of the consciousness in response to their generic or formulaic nature.

As we discuss later in the book, archaeologists are in a unique position to explore non-places, as their constitution is primarily based on their materiality. They employ generic architectural design elements based around mass-produced objects and spaces and can be associated with processes of 'Disneyization', mass customization and 'McDonaldization'; all processes that we argue are based in the relationships between people and the material world. An archaeological exploration of non-places will allow us to understand not only their affect, but also the ways in which they are composed and their involvement in relationships between human and non-human agents within late modern societies. Our archaeological exploration of non-places is closely aligned to our exploration of another important late modern phenomenon, the increased use of 'theming' and the concentration within goods and service provision on selling 'experience' rather than 'product', which has been discussed as one of the organizing principles of an 'experience society' by Pine and Gilmore (1999). By exploring the archaeological manifestations of the post-industrial 'experience economy', we highlight the new role of the imagination in late modern societies (after Appadurai 1996) and the ways in which theming has begun to infiltrate all areas of contemporary life.

The Role of Archaeology in Presencing Absence

In their groundbreaking edited volume *Archaeologies of the Contemporary Past* Buchli and Lucas (2001*a, b, c*; see also Buchli 2007) mapped out a series of themes that they saw as characterizing the archaeology of the recent past, which have been very influential on the development of the field. They pointed to the linked themes of production/consumption, remembering/forgetting, disappearance/disclosure, and presence/absence, in which they emphasized the role of the archaeology of the contemporary past in 'bringing forward or indeed materialising that which is excessive, forgotten or concealed' (2001*b*: 171). They suggested that as a result of this role, 'this body of archaeological work begins to appear qualitatively different from more conventional archaeological projects and other disciplines working on the recent past' (ibid.). A theme that was very prominent throughout *Archaeologies of the Contemporary Past* was that of the subaltern, and the idea that archaeology has a major role to play in foregrounding those aspects of contemporary life at the margins that are constantly being overwritten by dominant narratives.

In this book, we place a great deal of emphasis on the quotidian, or 'everyday', traditionally the focus of archaeological endeavour. We do this because it is often the everyday which is most easily overlooked. By its very definition, it is ordinary, perhaps dull, and certainly not perceived to be worth detailed investigation. However, it is the quotidian aspects of life that are most important in defining who we are (de Certeau 1984; Perec 1997; Olivier 2000). If we overlook the everyday, we overlook what it means to be 'us', and run the risk of remembering only the noteworthy, or the unusual. We also place emphasis on the subaltern, and the marginal spaces in society that are easily overlooked. But we do not wish to emphasize the marginal as a space of binary opposition with the centre; instead, we are influenced by the work of Homi Bhabha in *The Location of Culture* (1994) and hope to establish an equality that emphasizes diversity and multi-vocality, even symmetry (Hicks 2005; Webmoor 2007; Webmoor and Witmore 2004, 2008; Witmore 2006) in archaeological practice. We see an important space in the archaeology of late modernity both for a focus on the 'great and important' as well as the everyday. Indeed, many of the events of the late twentieth and early twenty-first century have been shocking and profound—genocide, political killings, riot, and protest—but such things should not be emphasized at the expense of the quotidian, or the meaning of the archaeology of the contemporary past will be lost.

Now We Are All Archaeologists: A Note on Inclusivity and Autoarchaeology

The concept of multi-vocality is central to the archaeology of the contemporary past (Olivier 2001: 187), because it is the archaeology of 'us'. In many ways, we can all be archaeologists of the contemporary past, because it is a critical inquiry into what it means to be ourselves. We all have direct access to the field sites (our towns, cities, and neighbourhoods), and access to the tools with which to analyse them (free aerial photography using Google Earth, or whole catalogues of contemporary artefacts for sale on eBay for example). The point of an archaeology of the contemporary past is to decentre the underlying aspect of modernist archaeology and anthropology which is about producing a sense of an 'Other' to ourselves (Thomas 2004, see further discussion below); we make ourselves the subject of our research. In this book we consider specific archaeological investigations into our own lives under the title 'autoarchaeology', but we need to see the whole intellectual project of the archaeology of the contemporary past as relating to the breakdown of fundamental divisions between subject and object, researcher and 'other', us and them. The archaeology of the contemporary past is a new, inclusive archaeology for a multi-vocal, postmodern age. While the archaeology of earlier periods is typically undertaken by 'experts', the archaeology of the contemporary past can be more democratic, more participatory in nature. We can all be archaeologists if we choose to think of our subject matter, or our way of examining it, in this way. Some may prefer to think of themselves as artists or artist-archaeologists (like Boyle Family, see Ch. 4), and others as urban explorers. But despite these differences of emphasis, there is a strong element of 'contemporary archaeology' in all of us.

Archaeology as a Form of Material Witness

The nature of the media and its control by external forces means that late modern societies have rendered much of their recent past unknowable, either by processes of active concealment or passive forgetting. Rather then promoting multiple perspectives on the present, the saturation of media coverage and its 'plague of fantasies' (Žižec 1997) often leads to the rapid development of a dominant, authorized account which is difficult to challenge. As a discipline focused on material evidence and concerned with revealing and bringing to light that which has been hidden, archaeology has a distinct role to play in developing alternative perspectives on the recent and contemporary past as a form of material witness (e.g. Buchli and Lucas 2001*d*). We have already mentioned the role of archaeological forensics in the legal system, but we can think more broadly here of archaeology as a form of documentation, like documentary photography, for example, which has a role in bringing forward those things that are hidden from view and placing them before the public (e.g. Boulton 2006, 2007). Once again, this aim of a contemporary archaeology relates to its desire to establish a fair, multi-vocal, inclusive history of the recent past and its present.

The Politics of Contemporary Archaeology

It remains for us to make some brief observations here on the politics of the archaeology of the contemporary past. Clearly, given the discussion above, the archaeology of the contemporary past must be political (González-Ruibal 2008: 256). Many archaeologists working on aspects of the recent and contemporary past would understand their work to be part of a broader, critical practice that seeks to engage with larger political issues (e.g. Buchli and Lucas 2001*a*; Buchli 2007; Steele 2008: 425). There are three, interlinked aspects to the politics of archaeologies of the contemporary past. The first of these relates to the politics of archaeology itself, as a discipline linked to the educative apparatus of the state, and that bases itself on a model whereby archaeologists are the expert arbitrators on the past, as they have privileged access to the materials with which to create stories about it. The second relates to the archaeological act, as a creative engagement with the past in which it is produced in the present. The third dimension involves the engagement of archaeologists with forms of activism through their research practices, and through the topics on which they choose to focus their attentions.

As González-Ruibal (2008: 259) notes, 'How can we survey a concentration camp, excavate a trench or a mass grave, or study a derelict ghetto without getting involved in politics? By focusing on the destructive operations of supermodernity (war, failed development projects, mass emigration and displacement, industrialization and deindustrialization) archaeology can be an original critical voice in the social sciences.' The three interlinked dimensions of an archaeological politics will be considered throughout the book in relation to the role and significance of an archaeology of late modernity and the present past.

ARCHAEOLOGY AND POSTMODERNITY

Julian Thomas (2004, see also 2009; Schnapp, Shanks, and Tiews 2004; Shanks, Platt, and Rathje 2004) has recently argued that archaeology is intimately connected with modernism, indeed, that archaeology could only have emerged as a distinct discipline under the particular social and intellectual conditions of modernity. He points not only to the connection between archaeology and the foundation stories of modern nation-states, but the reliance within archaeological thought on distinctively modern perceptions of the relationship between new knowledge and material things. He also notes the ways in which archaeology (and 'excavation' in particular) has continually been drawn upon by other modern disciplines as a metaphor for understanding the relationship between knowledge and its intellectual pursuit, through a string of linked images relating to concealment and discovery. He sees archaeology and modernity as connected by a series of preoccupations, including the ordering of time, the idea of a normative with which to contrast a non-normative (or 'Other'), with ideas of human development, the relationship between historical change and human reason, and analytical and comparative perspectives (2004: 224–6). Thomas concludes by asking what place there is left in a postmodern world for archaeology if its existence is tied to a set of historical circumstances that could be said to be declining (p. 223). Similarly, a number of authors have begun to question the role of archaeology under the changing economic, social, and material circumstances of the late twentieth and early twenty-first century (e.g. Hodder 1999; Olsen 2001).

Thomas (2004: 223) suggests that rather than dismiss archaeology as modernity declines, we need to develop a 'counter-modern' perspective on archaeology for a new age. Within a counter-modern archaeology, politics and ethics would take a central place. The emphasis would lie in discussion and the promotion of diversity. Archaeology would come to embrace considerations of meaning and rhetoric. In beginning to chart an agenda for the archaeology of late modernity, we hope to take up Thomas's challenge. As we have discussed above, the fact that the archaeology of the contemporary past is about us, and not an 'Other', represents a major break with the relationship between archaeology and the project of modernism. The archaeology of the contemporary past is not about difference, but diversity, and the process of turning the archaeological lens on ourselves. Nonetheless, it is important, as Thomas notes, to be constantly aware of the origins of the archaeological approach in the philosophies of modernism, and to question the ethics and politics of archaeologies of late modernity. This is particularly the case when dealing with the intimate details and memories of individuals' recent histories and lives. Clearly, when dealing with recent history, the ethical questions that should be a part of all archaeological practice (Moshenska 2008) become even more urgent.

THE ARCHAEOLOGY OF THE RECENT AND CONTEMPORARY PAST IN PRACTICE

One thing to note at the outset is that at the present time, very few archaeologists have had training specific to this period and to the particular issues of investigating the archaeology of the contemporary past. Many of those 'specializing' in this area of archaeology have come to it from the study of earlier time periods, and many from studies and specialisms in prehistory or from historical archaeology. However, in the years ahead, this will change, and will probably bring with it fundamental changes both to archaeology as a discipline and to the nature of projects undertaken by archaeologists of the contemporary past. Another interesting point is the sheer number of practitioners who have embraced this late modern archaeology. Whether they work for agencies, local authorities, or commercial units, many have discovered the archaeology of the contemporary world and found it to be a worthwhile and captivating endeavour. Projects that explore the late modern period are popular and it seems increasingly so.

Alongside this enthusiasm has been a growing awareness of the importance of conserving archaeological sites relating to the recent past, in particular Cold War and other military sites, but also the remains of more quotidian life. Although this is not a book about heritage, we explore the influence of heritage on archaeological practice at various points owing to the important role that heritage management plays both in archaeological employment and as an indicator of broader relationships between our society and its past. These issues will be considered in more detail as part of the background history in Chapter 2 and again in Chapter 5.

One of the distinguishing features of the archaeology of the recent and contemporary past is its dual perspective on both places and material practices that are essentially extinct or have ceased to function, as well as on those places and practices that are still functioning. For example, within the book, we explore the archaeology of theming and the experience economy through Hall and Bombardella's (2007) exploration of the materiality of a functioning casino in Cape Town, South Africa, before moving on to look at the archaeology of an abandoned theme park in Derbyshire in England. This need to develop techniques appropriate both to the study of living, functioning places and objects as well as those that have been abandoned and have fallen out of use is one of the key challenges for an archaeology of the contemporary past. We suggest that it is this dual perspective on both living and extinct material practices that gives this area of study particular relevance. We explore these issues in more detail in the second part of the book.

STRUCTURE OF THE BOOK

The book falls into two parts. Part I, Surveying the Field: The Development of an Archaeology of the Recent and Contemporary Past, takes a look at the expansion of the field over the later part of the twentieth century, and its emergence as a recognizable subdiscipline after the new millennium, in an attempt to characterize it and provide some methodological and theoretical background to its development. Chapter 2 explores the history of archaeological approaches to the contemporary past, showing how it developed out of the interests of the New Archaeology in the 1960s and 1970s and post-processual archaeology in the 1980s and 1990s in the use of contemporary case studies to answer archaeological debates about the relationship between material culture and social behaviour. It shows how the archaeology of the recent past began with a focus on the First and Second World Wars, and then the Cold War, eventually to encompass a field concerned with the broader archaeology of 'now'. In Chapter 3, we explore the nature of the field methodologies applied by archaeologists of the recent and contemporary past, and consider whether they might be understood to be distinct to other forms of archaeology. In Chapter 4, we look at the relationship between archaeology and other disciplines that focus on contemporary material culture, in particular anthropology, contemporary material culture studies, and art. And in Chapter 5, we explore some reasons why archaeologists might have developed an interest in the contemporary world and the period of late modernity in particular, through an investigation of some of the conditions that make it distinct from the periods that preceded it. This discussion forms the background to the second part of the book, in which we explore the archaeology of some of these distinct features of late modern societies.

In Part II, Archaeological Approaches to Late Modern Societies, we look in more detail at how we might approach the archaeology of contemporary post-industrial societies, with reference to a series of case studies, the bulk of which relate to the archaeology of the period after c.1970. We have organized this part of the book around a series of traditional areas of archaeological focus—Artefacts (Ch. 6), Sites (Ch. 7), and Landscape (Ch. 8). Each chapter includes several core case studies in which we take an archaeological approach to the artefacts, sites, and landscape of the late modern period. Inevitably, given our particular experiences, there is some bias towards case studies that we have been directly involved with, predominantly in the UK, but also in the United States, Australia, and Europe. In Chapter 9, 'Non-Places and Virtual Worlds', we address some of the most distinctive features of late modernity—the new materialities of non-places; virtual worlds; experience economies and the work of the imagination; and hyperconsumerism and globalization. This chapter provides the groundwork that allows us to look forward in the book's Conclusion (Ch. 10) to explore some of the future research directions for the archaeology of the recent and contemporary past.

Part I

Surveying the Field: The Development of an Archaeology of the Recent and Contemporary Past

2

A Disciplinary (Pre)History

INTRODUCTION

Following the brief definition and discussion of the archaeology of the contemporary past provided in Chapter 1, this chapter will consider the academic context for the development of the archaeology of the contemporary past and its emergence in the years surrounding the Millennium. It then briefly surveys and summarizes the topics which have emerged as areas of focus amongst archaeologists working in the field over the past decade. It will chart the important role of commercial archaeology and developer funding in the emergence of the archaeology of the contemporary past, and look at the role of national heritage agencies and local authorities. Another major issue in this chapter is the ways in which the archaeology of the recent and contemporary past has developed as a means of addressing cultural diversity and recent migrant communities and their heritage, which is inevitably and by definition 'contemporary' albeit often with reference to other times and places. The chapter concludes with a consideration of the relationship between historical archaeology and the archaeology of the contemporary past, considering claims for and against seeing it as a discipline in its own right.

A (PRE)HISTORY OF THE ARCHAEOLOGY OF THE CONTEMPORARY PAST

It is now a decade since the publication of two key books which have been central to the establishment of the archaeology of the contemporary past as a specific area of study within the English speaking world—*Matter, Materiality and Modern Culture* edited by Paul Graves-Brown (2000*b*), and *Archaeologies of the Contemporary Past* edited by Victor Buchli and Gavin Lucas (2001*e*). As Buchli (2007: 115) points out however, archaeologists have had a long interest in studying contemporary material culture, dating back to the late nineteenth and early twentieth century and including Pitt-Rivers's studies of contemporary rifles while working as a military officer, and Kroeber's (1919) study of changes in contemporary women's dress lengths. Nonetheless, throughout most of the twentieth century, archaeology has concerned itself almost exclusively with the study of the distant past, accepting a conservative and literal definition of archaeology as something that should focus only on that which is ancient, or 'archaic'. Within the history of archaeological research throughout the course of the twentieth century, we can isolate two principal influences on the establishment of a field of archaeology concerned with the contemporary world—the ethnoarchaeological interests of the 'New Archaeology' which began in the 1960s, and the inversion of the archaeological lens to concentrate on the politics of archaeology that characterized the post-processual reaction to the New Archaeology in the 1980s and 1990s. Another important influence was the emergence of the more anthropologically focused field of material culture studies that re-emerged strongly, also during the 1980s and 1990s. Here we will briefly examine these antecedents to the archaeology of the contemporary past, before moving on to survey the field as it has developed since the beginning of the new millennium.

The term 'New Archaeology' describes a new theoretical and methodological turn in archaeology that developed in the late 1950s in North America, and that subsequently had a major influence on the theory and practice of archaeology throughout the anglophone world in the later part of the twentieth century. The New Archaeology arose out of a dissatisfaction with traditional culture-historical archaeology, which was seen to be largely descriptive in nature, and hence unable to tackle topics of universal human interest. Proponents of the New Archaeology suggested that archaeology was a social science and should be concerned with *explaining* change in the past rather than just *describing* it. The goal of archaeology would thus become the development of universal laws of human behaviour. The New Archaeology was influenced by systems theory, and was strongly functionalist and empirical in its approach. Central to the New Archaeology was the idea of linking past human behaviour with its material residues.

During the 1960s, New Archaeologists began to study contemporary peoples and material culture to generate analogies and models for understanding the archaeological record. This interest is exemplified by the work of Binford (eg. 1978, see also 1983), who studied the modern stone tool and bone assemblages of *Nunamiut* people to help interpret the remains of Palaeolithic archaeological sites, and Yellen (1977) who recorded the contemporary archaeology of *!Kung* people of the Kalahari in southern Africa. Further important studies were published by Gould (1980), an important figure in the development of the archaeology of the contemporary past, who described the seasonal round and contemporary archaeology of *Ngatatjara* people from the Western Desert of Australia in his book *Living Archaeology*. Similarly, Cribb (1991) examined the archaeological traces of contemporary nomadic peoples in Turkey and Iran, living amongst them and then returning to their abandoned settlements to record and analyse their material traces. This approach, which involves the study of the contemporary material residues of human activities to develop rules and associations between material culture and universal forms of human behaviour, became known as 'ethnoarchaeology' (David and Kramer 2001).

This interest in ethnoarchaeology within the New Archaeology formed the background to what are generally acknowledged (Graves-Brown 2000*a*: 2; Buchli and Lucas 2001*a*: 3; Buchli 2007: 115) to be the first formal publications on the archaeology of the contemporary past, titled 'Modern Material Culture Studies' (Rathje 1979) and *Modern Material Culture: The Archaeology of Us* (Gould and Schiffer 1981). These publications grew out of the research developed by Schiffer and Rathje at the University of Tucson, Arizona and separately by Gould at the University of Honolulu, Hawaii during the 1970s. Where most ethnoarchaeological research had been undertaken with communities who employed traditional technologies in a contemporary setting, the student programmes developed at Tucson and Hawaii, and the projects outlined by the authors of 'Modern Material Culture Studies' and papers in *Modern Material Culture* were largely concerned with the description and analysis of contemporary material cultures in modern, industrialized societies.

Rathje's provocative article 'Modern Material Culture Studies' (which also appeared in revised form in *Modern Material Culture*) outlined an ambitious agenda for the development of an archaeology of modern material culture. He suggested that archaeology should be defined as the study of 'the interaction between material culture and human behaviour or ideas, regardless of time or space' (Rathje 1979: 2), and as such, research on the recent or contemporary past was as much a part of the archaeological mission as research into the deep past. He suggested that 'the archaeology of today' (p. 4) could make contributions to the teaching and testing of archaeological principles and to the development of models that relate our own society to those of the past. Further, it should be seen as a sort of 'rescue archaeology' of contemporary life, helping to address what might become future gaps in knowledge as the material and archaeological record of contemporary life is destroyed around us. For Rathje, modern material culture studies represented 'a final step in the transformation of archaeology into a unified, holistic approach to the study of society and its material products' (p. 29).

The papers in *Modern Material Culture* covered a series of themes, from the study of traditional technologies in the present, to ethnoarchaeological, methodological, and theoretical approaches to understanding contemporary material culture. Of particular relevance were the papers in the section of the book brought together under the thematic heading 'Early and Late Americana'. Gould's introduction to the section noted the potential for such studies to contribute to developing 'a series of provisional inferences about the real nature of American materialism...involv[ing] both the debunking of commonly accepted ideas about American behaviour as well as discoveries, sometimes of an unexpected nature, of how Americans really behave' (Gould and Schiffer 1981: 57).

The papers included analyses of graffiti and racism in Hawaii (Blake 1981), studies of contemporary supermarkets (Bath 1981;

Cleghorn 1981), and research on patterns in the discard of modern pennies (Rothschild 1981). Gould's summary of the papers outlined the potential for the archaeology of contemporary America to contribute to an independent study of the nature of contemporary society:

Who are we? More than anything else, these modern material-culture studies show us that we are not always what we seem, even to ourselves. We rely more upon kinship and friendship in our economic dealings than we may have realised, and our economic relations are more often based upon nonmarket and even perhaps nonrational behaviour than we are aware. Factors like ethnicity and a willingness to re-use manufactured goods can be more decisive in our patterns of consumerism than media advertising and published economic indicators would suggest. Americans have a historic commitment to civil rights and racial equality, yet... greater racial or ethnic equality means increased conflict (with appropriate social controls), and graffiti in Hawaii are one expression of that conflict. Americans are... prone to re-write history... as shown by the omission of selected wars from the public exhibits at the National Air and Space Museum. We hoard, collect or lose pennies almost as much as we spend them, yet our marketing and merchandising system is remarkably flexible and able to respond to unusual and unlikely demands... one could go on in this vein, generating and testing observations about the realities of American life, and, indeed, that is exactly what this collection of chapters is intended to do.

(Gould and Schiffer 1981: 65)

Nonetheless, there was a lack of agreement, particularly amongst authors represented in the edited volume *Modern Material Culture*, over whether the archaeological study of contemporary material culture should be seen to be an end in itself, or whether the main aim of such a study was the generation of models for understanding past human behaviour. Rathje's own contribution to the field, which he had so challengingly sketched in 'Modern Material Culture Studies', was the Garbage Project, the archaeological study of contemporary rubbish dumps in Tucson, Arizona (and elsewhere) which began in 1973 and sought to:

demonstrate the utility of archaeological methods and theories for achieving a better understanding of issues of current public concern... including assessments of resource waste and proposed methods of waste minimization, measures of diet and nutrition, evaluations of household participation in recycling programs, identification of household-level sources of hazardous wastes, cross-validation of census counts of minority populations, and providing base data for the design of new 'environmentally friendly' packages.

(Rathje 2001: 63)

The Garbage Project is one of the longest running studies in the archaeology of the contemporary past, and has involved the meticulous excavation and documentation of garbage dumps and land fills, and the comparison of excavated data with questionnaire data and statistics on consumption and use of food and consumer goods. The project has provided data that have been used to interpret issues as diverse as diet and nutrition, social stratification, recycling, and waste management. The work of the Garbage Project has been the subject of numerous journal articles and book chapters (e.g. Rathje 1979, 1981, 2001) and a monograph (Rathje and Murphy 1992), which was reissued with a new preface in 2001 (Rathje and Murphy 2001).

Gould (1987) subsequently turned his archaeological gaze to the abandonment of northern Finnish farming communities, examining the way that fields and associated buildings change their use and decay during the gradual process of abandonment. He recorded the ways in which hay barns, for example, seem subject to a much wider range of uses than their original purpose, serving as storage areas or 'garages' as other areas of the farm were gradually abandoned. He recorded the breakdown of various distinct artefact categories: those related to resource extraction, maintenance of fields and structures, consumption activities and ephemeral activities with evidence here including graffiti and newspapers. As he noted (p. 149), 'ethno-archaeological observations of material residues in situations like this offer a potentially sensitive indicator of changing technoeconomic relations with the wider, industrial society'.

Nonetheless, for many years, work such as this remained an idiosyncrasy in terms of its archaeological focus on contemporary culture. This initial North American efflorescence of research on the archaeology of modern material culture was largely not followed up by the establishment of further research projects. While research by Rathje (e.g. Rathje and Murphy [1992] 2001; Rathje 2001), Gould (e.g. 2007) and Schiffer (e.g. 1991, 2000) continued, much ethnoarchaeological and modern material culture studies within archaeology throughout the 1980s and early 1990s remained focused on traditional forms of technology, and on the use of ethnoarchaeological models for the explanation of cultural change in the past. However, several British archaeologists who had begun to develop a new approach that would ultimately come to be known as post-processual archaeology, began to turn to contemporary material culture as case studies against which to test social archaeological models. 'Post-processual archaeology' is a term used to describe a raft of different approaches that were unified in their dissatisfaction with the New (or 'processual') Archaeology's functionalist, systems-oriented methodologies (Trigger 1996). These functionalist methods were considered to have drawn attention away from the contextual understanding of meaning and the social interpretation of the past in archaeology. Post-processual archaeology instead placed an emphasis on issues of power and ideology, and on understanding the social role of artefacts in past societies. For example, Hodder (1987) undertook a study of the social meaning of bow ties in a contemporary British pet food factory, as a case study for modelling the relationship between social practices, material culture, and meaning in human societies. He described the ways in which the management of a particular pet food factory introduced bow ties as symbols of social stratification within the work environment, and how they were subsequently removed in response to changing work practices including more egalitarian work environments and the transition from competition between *levels* within the organization to competition between *shifts* to increase productivity.

Shanks and Tilley ([1987] 1992), in what became an important manifesto for post-processual archaeology, also explored contemporary material culture through a study of the design of Swedish and English beer cans. They criticized the authors of the chapters in *Modern Material Culture* for being too empiricist in their approach, suggesting that they 'failed to realise the potential of the study of modern material culture as a critical intervention in contemporary society...with transformative intent' (ibid. 172). Their own approach was a detailed examination of the design of beer cans in England and Sweden, suggesting that differences existed in the degree of complexity and elaboration of designs. They began by noting that there is a contradiction in beer consumption in capitalist societies between the need to maintain the discipline of populations, and the expression of difference and self-identity through beer drinking and consumer choice in the purchase of beer. The designs on Swedish cans were found to be more elaborate than those in Britain, reflecting the greater need to mediate the ambiguous position of beer in Sweden, where it was more highly regulated when compared to other alcoholic drinks. In the case of both British and Swedish beer cans, the use of particular 'traditional' designs was seen to create a sense of the 'naturalness' of beer consumption, and to draw attention away from the sense of the danger in consuming alcohol (ibid. 240).

These changes in archaeology during the 1980s and 1990s were closely linked to changes within the field of ethnoarchaeology, which also came to have an important impact on the development of the field of the archaeology of the contemporary past. Work by French anthropologists on the 'anthropology of techniques' was introduced to an English-reading audience by an article written by anthropologist Pierre Lemonnier for the *Journal of Anthropological Archaeology* in 1986 (see also Lemonnier 1992). Similarly, the work of French archaeologist Valentine Roux and colleagues (e.g. 1985, 1989; Roux, Bril, and Dietrich 1995) had an impact across the channel on British archaeologists working on recent archaeological contexts. Various questions about ideology and style that were integral to post-processual perspectives on archaeology were generated within, or significantly extended by French (e.g. Audouze 1992), British (e.g. Hodder 1982), and North American (e.g. Moore 1986; David, Sterner, and Gavua 1988) ethnoarchaeological literature and research. The history of ethnoarchaeology and its relationship with archaeology in more general terms is discussed in detail by David and Kramer (2001: 14–31).

In addition to particular post-processual studies of contemporary material culture, another important aspect of post-processualism in the development of the archaeology of the contemporary past was the way in which it turned the archaeological lens on the process of 'doing' archaeology itself, particularly in terms of its political ramifications. The study of the political motivations of archaeology is sometimes known by the term 'critical archaeology' (see discussion in Wilkie and Bartoy 2000), as its proponents drew on the critical theory of the 'Frankfurt School', the Institute for Social Research of the University of Frankfurt in Germany, which was established in 1929 and came under the direction of the sociologist Max Horkheimer in 1930. Critical archaeologists (and indeed, many post-processual archaeologists) maintain that archaeology is a contemporary engagement with the past (however recent), and as such is part of a process of creating the past-in-the-present (Tilley 1989). Archaeology, through its connection with the processes of creating heritage, is also intimately caught up in the ideological work of creating a sense of nationhood (e.g. Kohl and Fawcett 1995; Appadurai 2001). For this reason, the archaeological act is a political one, worthy of investigation for its own sake. Shanks and Tilley's work ([1987] 1992) demonstrated the relationship between ideology and power in archaeology, drawing on the ideas of Michel Foucault to argue that archaeologists had an obligation to draw attention to inequalities from the past and their relationship with the politics of the present. This new focus on the social and political role of archaeology in the present developed at the same time as a wider critique of the role of archaeology in settler societies as a tool of the colonial project (e.g. see discussions in Smith 2004) and produced a large volume of writing focused on the social and political aspects of archaeology as a contemporary research practice (e.g. Leone, Potter, and Shackel 1987; Pinsky and Wylie 1989; Shanks 1992; Lucas 2001). This in turn led archaeologists to think increasingly about archaeology's relationship with the present. We argue that such thinking was a necessary precondition for the development of an archaeology of the contemporary past.

At the same time as these important developments in postprocessual archaeology in Britain and the US (as well as other countries such as Australia and South Africa, and in Latin America), an interest in modern material culture based on more anthropological methodologies was also gaining momentum in Britain, the US, and France. This field has subsequently come to be referred to as 'material culture studies'. While the interests of this field are diverse and include both modern material culture and collections of ancient material culture in the present, the reinvigoration of anthropological studies of material culture that it ignited was influential in stimulating a renewed interest amongst archaeologists in contemporary material culture. The interest in the social lives of objects (Appadurai 1986; Kopytoff 1986; Strathern 1988; Gell 1988, 1992, 1996, 1998), studies of consumption (e.g. Douglas and Isherwood 1979; Miller 1987, 1995, 1998b), the social aspects of the material world (e.g. Lemonnier 1986, 1992; Ingold 2000) and the material culture of the 'everyday' (e.g. Attfield 2000) have all been influential on the field of the archaeology of the contemporary past as it developed throughout the early 2000s. Anthropological approaches to modern material culture and the relationship of material culture studies to the archaeology of the contemporary past are explored further in Chapter 4.

ARCHAEOLOGIES OF THE CONTEMPORARY PAST

We have seen how the precedents for the archaeology of the contemporary past were developed out of early ethnoarchaeological studies in the US in the 1970s and early 1980s which were closely aligned to the New Archaeology. Following this early burst of activity, archaeologists turned to modern material culture in the 1980s to test new ideas about the relationships between people and material things deriving from the post-processual response to the New Archaeology. At the same time, archaeologists were influenced by the new anthropological focus on contemporary material culture within the emerging field of material culture studies. As we have seen, the turn of the century saw the publication of two key books that have been central to the establishment of the archaeology of the contemporary past as a specific discipline in the English-speaking world—*Matter, Materiality and Modern Culture* edited by Paul Graves-Brown (2000b) and *Archaeologies of the Contemporary Past* edited by Victor Buchli and Gavin Lucas (2001e). Both volumes were part of a significant shift in orientation away from the ethnoarchaeological focus of most of the earlier work on the archaeology of the contemporary past towards a more specific focus on contemporary life which now characterizes the field. Both edited volumes emerged within a specifically British archaeological context, while drawing together the work of archaeologists and other interested academics from Britain, North America, South Africa, and Europe. At this time too, significant early publications on archaeologies of the recent past began to emerge in France (e.g. Schnapp 1997; Olivier 2000), and Latin America (e.g. Freitas 1999; Crossland 2000). It is also worth mentioning here a significant literature on the archaeology of the contemporary past that subsequently developed in Sweden (e.g. Campbell and Ulin 2004; Karlsson 2004; Burström 2007, 2008; Burström, Gustafsson, and Karlsson 2006). Nonetheless, the edited volumes by Graves-Brown (2000*b*) and Buchli and Lucas (2001*e*) came to have the most lasting impression on the field as it has developed in the anglophone world.

There are several observations which are worth making about these two books. As noted above, both were influenced more or less comprehensively by work on contemporary material culture that was being carried out within the field of material culture studies (eg. Miller 1987, 1998*b*, see further discussion in Ch. 4). Where Graves-Brown (2000*a*: 3) was critical of material culture studies (and the work of Miller in particular) for being too focused on consumption and on the analysis of artefacts as texts rather than as material objects, Buchli and Lucas (2001*a*: 7–8) acknowledged the important contribution of material culture studies to the archaeology of the contemporary past, following Miller in seeing modern material culture as an 'inherently interdisciplinary space where a number of disciplines converge' (p. 7). Moreover, both books contained papers that were primarily concerned with the study of contemporary material culture in terms of what this study could tell us about contemporary culture itself, rather than as a means to generate models to assist with understanding the deeper past. Both books also raised a number of issues around the politics of 'doing' the archaeology of the contemporary past that have now come to dominate the field. While we will consider the significance of the timing of the emergence of the new archaeological focus on the recent and contemporary past in Chapter 5, we will summarize the main themes of each of these books here briefly so we can look at their influence on the development of the field in the subsequent decade.

Buchli and Lucas (2001*a, b, c, d*) and their contributors established several key themes that have come to characterize the archaeology of the contemporary past over the past decade, several of

which we have already mentioned in the Introduction. They pointed
to the linked themes of production/consumption, remembering/
forgetting, disappearance/disclosure, and presence/absence. A theme
very prominent throughout *Archaeologies of the Contemporary Past*
was that of the subaltern, and the idea that archaeology has a major
role to play in foregrounding those aspects of contemporary life at
the margins that are constantly being overwritten by dominant
narratives.

> In addressing the issue of the non-discursive realm the archaeological act
> comes directly into contact with the subaltern, the dispossessed and the
> abject. This is not simply in terms of the usual archaeological preoccupation
> with material remains, but the practical and social act of uncovering that
> which has once been hidden. The two converge here both literally and
> figuratively.   (Buchli and Lucas 2001*a*: 14)

Case studies included both conventional and unconventional archaeological concerns, ranging from the analysis of early twentieth-
century ceramics (Majewski and Schiffer 2001; Stevenson 2001), to
late twentieth-century garbage (Rathje 2001) and the archaeology
of an early twentieth-century fraternity house (Wilkie 2001). The
volume juxtaposed chapters that dealt with the archaeology of the
Second World War (Legendre 2001) with those on post-colonial
remembrance (Hart and Winter 2001) and North American labour
relations (The Ludlow Collective 2001), while establishing an
ongoing theme relating to forensic and human rights archaeology
(Doretti and Fondebrider 2001; Cox 2001). Perhaps the most
influential paper involved the archaeological recording of a contemporary abandoned council flat in England (Buchli and Lucas
2001*c*), in which the authors attempted to reconstruct some of the
occupants' motivations for becoming 'intentionally homeless' (and
hence legally unable to claim state housing benefits). They suggested that such a study had a potential role in understanding
processes of marginalization and alienation. Commentary by the
editors and Olivier (2001) convincingly argued the relevance of an
archaeology of the recent past, an area largely ignored by conventional archaeological studies, which were more concerned with
the 'oldest' and the 'best'. Instead, the authors emphasized the
importance of the archaeological investigation of the everyday,

charting a new critical agenda for archaeology at the beginning of the new millennium.

Papers in *Matter, Materiality and Modern Culture* mapped out a different series of themes. In part, this was because, although Graves-Brown was an archaeologist, his volume was explicitly interdisciplinary, and focused on the *materiality* of modern material culture (as a response to what he viewed as an emphasis on material objects *as texts* within conventional anthropological modern material culture studies), rather than its archaeology per se. Nonetheless, the volume contained a number of studies directly relevant to the archaeology of the contemporary past, and many of the ideas in the volume have influenced subsequent research in this field. Its authors stressed particularly the way in which the study of modern material culture can make the familiar unfamiliar, a theme that has subsequently been repeated by a number of contemporary archaeologists. This idea had previously been discussed by George Perec in *Species of Spaces* in terms of an 'anthropology of the endotic' (Perec 1997; see also Olivier 2000) which might rescue an understanding of the cultural and social workings of everyday life from the dustbin of history. The book also stressed the theme of mutuality—the idea that culture is an 'emergent property of the relationship between persons and things' (Graves-Brown 2000a: 4)—and the relationship between functionality and power. The focus on the material qualities of contemporary artefacts and the influence of material objects on contemporary culture was influential on later studies in the archaeology of the contemporary past, which have tended to foreground the human experience of technology and material things. Graves-Brown's book also included a contribution by Latour (2000), introducing many archaeologists to the work of Science and Technology Studies (STS; e.g. Latour and Woolgar 1979; Callon, Law, and Rip 1986; Latour 1987; 1993, 1996, 1999, 2005; Callon 1989; Bijker, Hughes, and Pinch 1989; Law 1992, 1993, 2002, 2004; Woolgar 1991; Law and Bijker 1992; Bijker 1995; Law and Hassard 1999), a field that has had a major influence on the archaeological work on the contemporary past (see further discussion in Ch. 4). The work of Latour on material agency, and that of Callon, Law, and Latour on Actor-Network Theory (ANT; see further discussion in Chs. 4 and 5) is worth mentioning, both areas having been particularly influential on the development of this emergent field of research and an associated turn away from the 'social' to a focus on 'things' (e.g. Webmoor and Witmore 2008).

A number of new studies emerged following these two key publications during the new millennium. A significant step was the establishment of the Contemporary and Historical Archaeology in Theory (CHAT) conference group in 2003 (see further discussion in Piccini and Holtorf 2009: 19). This group now hosts an annual conference that considers issues relating to both historical archaeology and the archaeology of the contemporary past, and has acted as a forum for the development and presentation of much of the UK and a significant proportion of the US-based research that has subsequently come to define this field. Papers from two of these conferences have been published (McAtackney et al. 2007) while another is in preparation (Frearson et al. forthcoming). Of equal significance has been the rise of a field of forensic archaeology in the US, UK, Europe, Australia, and Latin America that has seen archaeology develop as a way of documenting mass graves, war crimes, disappearances, and state-sponsored repression. We will explore how these influences have shaped the new field of the archaeology of the contemporary past later in this chapter. But for now we will turn to focus on another important influence on the development of the archaeology of the contemporary past as a distinct field of study: cultural heritage management and the broader interests of the general public in the archaeology and heritage of the supposedly familiar past.

MANAGING THE HERITAGE OF
THE CONTEMPORARY PAST

An important development since the 1990s has been the increased engagement of state-sponsored heritage management agencies, and indeed, the International Council on Monuments and Sites (ICOMOS), with twentieth-century heritage and archaeology (this section after Ferguson, Harrison, and Weinbren 2010). At the national and international level, 'recent' or 'twentieth century' heritage began to receive increasing official attention amongst architectural historians in the 1960s and 1970s. In Britain, for example, the Twentieth Century Society was originally established as the Thirties Society in 1979, in response to the Thirties exhibition of British art and design before the war organized by the Arts Council in conjunction with the Victoria & Albert Museum and held at the Hayward Gallery that same year (Stamp and Powers 2008). The society was established as a campaigning organization with the stated aim 'to protect architecture and design after 1914'. During the 1980s, they successfully campaigned for the removal of the year 1939 as the end point for the age of buildings to be listed in England, arguing instead for the use of a 'thirty-year rule' (which had already been passed in Scotland), that is, that buildings could be considered for designation once they were thirty years old or more. The society was renamed the Twentieth Century Society in the early 1990s to reflect the increasing number of campaigns that they were involved in relating to post-Second World War buildings. Another important international non-profit, non-government organization, the International Working Party for Documentation and Conservation of buildings, sites, and neighbourhoods of the Modern Movement (DoCoMoMo) was established in 1988 at the Technical University in Eindhoven, the Netherlands, its International secretariat moving to the Cité de l'Architecture et du Patrimoine in the Palais de Chaillot in Paris in 2002 (DoCoMoMo 2008). DoCoMoMo rapidly became an important force in the conservation of modern architecture, setting out its goals to conserve and educate the public about the architectural significance of the modern movement in its *Eindhoven Statement* in 1990. At the time of writing, DoCoMoMo has working parties in over thirty countries, each of which undertakes to work on developing a national register of modern movement buildings and runs campaigns to preserve what they perceive to be key works of architectural modernism in each country.

During the late 1990s, twentieth-century heritage became a major agenda item for ICOMOS. After a series of expert meetings held in 1995 in Helsinki, 1996 in Mexico, and national ICOMOS conferences in Helsinki and Adelaide in 2001, ICOMOS (2001) announced the Montreal Action Plan on 'recent' heritage (defined as heritage relating to the last 100–150 years). The Plan acknowledged the findings of the *Heritage at Risk* 2000 Report, which expressed 'concern over the fate of various heritage types associated with 19th and 20th century, such as residential or urban architecture, industrial complexes, landscape creations or new building types such as stadiums, airports, waterworks or large city parks'. On this basis, the Montreal Action Plan on 'recent' heritage was developed. The plan aimed to

- Understand the full diversity of twentieth-century heritage and of the issues related to its recognition and conservation. To that effect, ICOMOS, with the support of US/ICOMOS, [would conduct] a survey of illustrative cases, through all its National and International Committees. (The result of the survey would help ICOMOS identify needs for new international committees or further partnerships with other organizations.)
- Promote twentieth-century heritage by dedicating the International Monuments and Sites Day (18 April 2002) to twentieth-century heritage in all its diversity.
- Put a special emphasis on twentieth-century heritage in the 2002 edition of the *Heritage at Risk* Report, and invite partner organizations [including] DoCoMoMo to contribute substantially to its content.
- Co-operate fully with UNESCO and other partners to develop workshops and meetings on that theme.

The Montreal Action Plan was followed with a UNESCO Heritage at Risk conference on 'Preservation of 20th-Century Architecture and World Heritage' in April 2006 in Moscow and an ICOMOS 'International Scientific Committee meeting on 20th-Century Heritage' held in Berlin in 2007. The Berlin meeting found that twentieth-century heritage was underrepresented on the World Heritage List. According to the ICOMOS Report and Action Plan, *Filling the Gaps* (2004/5), in 2004 twentieth-century heritage made up less than 3 per cent of the (then) 800 world heritage sites, and nominations for twentieth-century sites were seldom on the tentative lists of the signatory countries of the World Heritage Convention.

ICOMOS responded to this flurry of recommendations with the widely publicized listing of several new twentieth-century world heritage sites during the early 2000s, as a result of its Modern Heritage Programme undertaken jointly with DoCoMoMo. For example, the city of Tel Aviv was inscribed on the World Heritage List in 2003. The listing description notes that

Tel Aviv was founded in 1909 and developed as a metropolitan city under the British Mandate in Palestine. The White City was constructed from the early 1930s until the 1950s, based on the urban plan by Sir Patrick Geddes, reflecting modern organic planning principles. The buildings were designed by architects who were trained in Europe where they practised their profession before immigrating. They created an outstanding architectural ensemble of the Modern Movement in a new cultural context. (UNESCO 2008)

What is interesting about this phenomenon of twentieth-century heritage is that it is, perhaps even more than other forms of contemporary Western heritage management, very narrowly focused on what were perceived to be key or seminal works of architecture, and in particular, architectural modernism. Indeed, it appeared to be focused on developing a new 'canon' of modernism. One might distinguish between the DoCoMoMo and ICOMOS campaigns in this regard, as the listing of places such as Tel Aviv depends on the quantity and consistency of the housing and planning, as Tel Aviv has few really 'important' buildings from an art historical perspective. Nonetheless, what we saw in the 1980s and 1990s was a shift in policy to conserve increasingly 'modern' buildings as heritage. Some of the issues that underlie this late twentieth-century nostalgia for modernism are discussed in more detail in Chapter 5. The important thing to note here is that such initiatives fundamentally shifted the landscape of heritage, to make it into something that embraces both the very old and the comparatively new.

While much of this international activity seemed focused on a new-found enthusiasm for architectural modernism, in the UK a more radical approach to understanding the heritage of the later twentieth century was launched. In 2003, a collaborative project called 'Change and Creation', involving partnership between a heritage agency (English Heritage), two universities, and a commercial consulting company, aimed to begin a process of characterizing, understanding, and managing the archaeology of later twentieth-century landscape (1950–2000), assessing the processes of change and creation in both urban and rural settings. Its influential discussion document of the same name (Bradley et al. 2004) asked members of the public to discuss what the heritage of the later part of the twentieth century 'meant to them' in terms of their sense of place, and the role of archaeology in informing that meaning. It was followed by *Images of Change: An Archaeology of England's Contemporary Landscape* (Penrose 2007), a popular typology of late twentieth-century English landscape elements. The fundamental issue at stake in both these documents was to encourage people (planners, the public) to think about the historic environment as something holistic, not selective and exclusive to certain places and things. In this sense, the document's approach was radically different to that of DoCoMoMo and ICOMOS, and the approach of architectural history in general, which instead were focused on the establishment of a 'canon' of heritage sites that represented the period.

The idea that something can be 'historic' only beyond a certain age defies the logic that time is continuous, and that something recent can be 'historic' alongside something ancient not least in terms of how people perceive and engage with it. In the past, those responsible for managing and curating the historic environment have tended to take this view, that anything old is important and valued, and that on the whole modern change will only serve to damage that which had persisted from the deeper past. Change and Creation made explicit the continuation of the past into very recent memory, and challenged the view that modern change only damages that which came before. Change creates as well as destroys, and it does so continuously, a process that introduces, alongside prehistoric and historic remains, the new archaeological sites of the present and of the future.

In the context of the increasingly transnational world in which we live, migrant communities, who need to build effective links with places that they have occupied over relatively short periods of time, have also been influential in the development of the idea of contemporary heritage (see further discussion in Ashworth, Graham, and Tunbridge 2007 and Harrison 2010*a*). It is worth pausing here to consider what a recent migrant from Ghana to the UK, for example, might think of an eighteenth-century English country house (see Ferguson, Harrison, and Weinbren 2010). Might she, for example, consider it to be a part of her heritage?

How could she relate to such a place? Returning home after her visit to one of the many cities in the UK in which émigrés from Ghana have formed vibrant communities, how could she be expected to use it to build a sense of herself and the space in which she lives? We could ask similar questions of a recent Asian migrant to a North American city, for example. What aspects of this historic environment will he find comforting, or will help him build a sense of his identity in a new environment? Many people are beginning to challenge the conventional forms of heritage that have been promoted throughout the later part of the twentieth century as they become increasingly remote from the needs of contemporary communities, and this challenge has contributed to the development of programmes such as Change and Creation, and the emergence of the field of the archaeology of the contemporary past (see further discussion in Chs. 4 and 5). It has been argued that heritage is in part motivated by the desire to root oneself in a particular place and a community. But once that community loses its association with place, for example, through the development of 'online' virtual communities, there is a challenge to the conventional role of heritage (e.g. Harrison 2009a). This has resulted in many heritage management agencies witnessing the broader community show an increased interest in contemporary and late twentieth-century heritage. In a study conducted for English Heritage in 2000, MORI asked 3,000 people a series of questions about the heritage. An interesting and positive response was noted for the recent past. The report stated:

The definition of what counts as heritage also revolves around the concept of *time*. In a society where things change more quickly, where technologies become obsolete more rapidly, and where trends become out-dated within weeks and months rather than years or decades, how will this affect our definition of heritage? The quantitative study found that most people disagree with the notion that anything after 1950 does not count as heritage, while they feel that it is important to preserve modern buildings for future generations. (In each case younger people are most likely to take a broader viewpoint. Age is therefore important—to those aged over 65, 1950 represents young adulthood, while to those under 20 it is effectively ancient history.) It seems that definitions of heritage are so personal that even if there were any benefit in trying to put a precise cut-off date on what is heritage and what is not, it would be extremely difficult to get two people to agree on a date and a reason for their choice.

(MORI 2000: 11; emphasis in original).

An example of widening access to heritage in this way, and encouraging people who may never have considered their participation with heritage in any sense, is the Liverpool Musicscapes project (Cohen, Lashua, and Schofield 2010; Schofield, Kiddey, and Lashua 2010). This study, funded by the Arts and Humanities Research Council and hosted by the School of Music at the University of Liverpool has engaged young hip-hop musicians from some of Liverpool's most problematic and socially deprived neighbourhoods in discussions and dialogue about their lives, and about the music they make, both the way they make it and its composition. They sing and rap about the things that shape their lives, and the places and landscape they frequent. It is their familiar ground, their home-turf and they do care about it, but often in understated ways. Their music reflects this, as do the experiential maps they have compiled. These are effectively landscape characterization maps of their neighbourhoods (the so-called 'hood'), and represent the only time these young people have ever been, and possibly ever will be, asked for their opinion on the place they inhabit. The project has proved enlightening, and a rare example of talking with troubled young people about their heritage, for that is what this is, even though it is not a term they would necessarily use to describe it. Projects such as this are in turn influencing archaeologists, by forcing them to engage with a contemporary past that seems increasingly distant to its interested stakeholders, and in which they are finding a role in opening up new perspectives on the lived experience and material worlds of everyday contemporary life. Such studies are also increasing the diverse range of methods and techniques that archaeologists might use to study the contemporary past, and with it expanding the very scope of archaeology.

THE ARCHAEOLOGY OF THE CONTEMPORARY PAST: SURVEYING THE FIELD

We will now turn to review the field of the archaeology of the contemporary past as it has developed in the decade following the publication of *Archaeologies of the Contemporary Past* and *Matter, Materiality and Modern Culture*, pointing to a series of topics that have characterized it. We include in this review material that, by definition, belongs to a field of contemporary or recent archaeology. We have chosen to do this by adopting a broad 'snapshot' of the field before focusing explicitly on the more specific definition of the contemporary past of late modernity that we develop in the second half of the book. Important areas of study that have emerged over the last decade include the archaeology of twentieth-century and later conflict, the archaeology of recent and contemporary urban environments, forensic archaeology (with a focus on war crimes and atrocity, as well as the archaeology of modern disasters), the archaeology of virtual environments, and the archaeology of contemporary post-colonialism. We will explore these topics here in an attempt to characterize the discipline as it has emerged. This will contribute to, and help to broaden, the definition of the archaeology of the contemporary past that we provided in Chapter 1 by way of a background to the rest of the first part of the book.

Twentieth-Century and Later Conflict

An important area of research for archaeologists working on the contemporary past has been the archaeology of 'supermodern' twentieth-century conflict (after González-Ruibal 2008; e.g. Schofield 2005; Schofield, Johnson, and Beck 2002; Schofield, Klausmeier, and Purbrick 2006; González-Ruibal 2005, 2006, 2007). The First World War has formed a major focus for this research (e.g. Saunders 2003, 2004, 2007; Robertson and Kenyon 2008). Most of this archaeological work has focused on the Western Front, with only limited investigations elsewhere, in Britain, northern Italy, and Gallipoli in Turkey (Saunders 2007: 201). For example, Saunders (2001, 2002) discusses the excavation of Pilckem Ridge on the Ypres Salient battlefield, undertaken by the Institute for the Archaeological Heritage of the Flemish Community (IAP). This ultimately led to the establishment of the first dedicated Department of First World War Archaeology as part of the IAP in Belgium in 2003 (Dewilde et al. 2004). Saunders (2007) summarizes the various phases of Great War archaeology, beginning with the work of the Imperial War Graves Commission and various amateur groups up to the beginning of professional archaeological research by French, Belgian, and, later, British archaeologists in the 1990s and early 2000s.

Another significant area of recent attention has been the impact of the Second World War in Britain, with a concentration of effort initially in documenting site distributions, typologies, and chronological frameworks through research undertaken in the National Archives (e.g. Dobinson, Lake, and Schofield 1997). This major and long-lasting study has laid the foundation for subsequent projects, many of which are developer-funded archaeological interventions on sites earmarked for future development. Other large-scale surveys have included English Heritage's National Mapping Programme (e.g. Hegarty and Newsome 2007), which is reviewing aerial photographic cover of the entire country, and many of the newly recorded sites are from this period, some surviving above ground and others below ground. English Heritage has also provided guidance for enthusiasts on such things as military aircraft crash sites and recording military wall art (accessible online at <www.english-heritage.org.uk/military>). Enthusiasts have been the mainstay of a national study of anti-invasion defences—the Defence of Britain Project. Work has continued apace in other countries and situations too. In Australasia the War in the Pacific has been the subject of ongoing research, while twentieth-century conflict has also been the subject of archaeological scrutiny in North America and many northwest European countries. It is interesting to note that much of this research was heavily influenced by two situations that arose in France, where little such work has thus far been undertaken (but see Legendre 2001). One was the fiftieth anniversary of the D-Day Landings and associated events and celebrations, prompting a wider awareness of the iconic value of surviving bunkers; and another was an archaeological study of those bunkers exhibited at the Museum of Decorative Arts in Paris and published in 1975 by a non-archaeologist, the urban theorist and philosopher Paul Virilio (the English language edition was published in 1994).

The Cold War period has also been the subject of significant academic attention within the higher education and heritage sectors. Major overview studies have been published on the archaeology and architecture of this period (Beck 2002; Johnson 2002; Cocroft and Thomas 2003). As with earlier overviews, these led to further more detailed studies, of particular places or thematic and topic-based research, such as wall art for example (Cocroft et al. 2006). Some of these studies are described more fully in Chapter 7. The archaeology of space and of space exploration and the Star Wars Programme of the Reagan Administration also has relevance here (Gorman and O'Leary 2007).

A further dimension of modern conflict is the evidence of those that opposed militarism, and in fact the archaeology of protest and opposition is clearly centred on military sites and those of the Cold War specifically. For example, work has been undertaken on the archaeology of the Greenham Common protest camps in West Berkshire, England (Schofield 2009a) and on the peace camps in Nevada, US (Beck, Drollinger, and Schofield 2007) (see also Schofield, Beck, and Drollinger 2003). Although these are discussed more fully in Chapter 7, it is worth stating here the intellectual arguments behind this work. The reasons for both the Greenham and Nevada studies involve an attempt to ensure symmetry and balance in the way we construct and analyse the archaeological record. Despite some considerable difficulties in striking this balance it was essential that this was achieved. How could the military occupation of Greenham Common, especially in the 1980s, be understood without an appreciation of the archaeological traces that existed beyond the fence, and of the materiality of protest? Equally in Nevada, the significance of archaeology of the nuclear testing programmes, described in Beck (2002), and discussed in Chapter 7, can only be fully appreciated alongside the remains of the peace camps, the settlements of those that opposed these tests. And here in particular the situation is further complicated by indigenous issues of ownership and colonization. There is a balance to be struck, in other words, and it is through attaining that balance that the most interesting issues and analyses begin to emerge.

The Archaeology of Urban Environments

The archaeology of recent and past urban environments has also received much recent attention (Finn 2001; Buchli and Lucas

2001c; Symonds 2004; Graves-Brown 2007b; Penrose 2007; Schofield and Morrissey 2007), a concern that archaeology shares
with cultural geography (see e.g. Hayden 2004 and Edensor
2005). Finn (2001) provides an archaeological commentary on
time spent in Silicon Valley, California in which she comments
on the material and cultural world of a community that upholds
the values of constant change and technological flux. Graves-
Brown (2007b) has undertaken a landscape archaeological study
of a modern retail park in Wales. Connected to this we have seen
work on twentieth-century industrial archaeology in the UK
(Stratton and Trinder 2000), US, and Australia; the archaeology
of buildings and standing structures, the archaeology of social
housing in the former USSR and the UK (Buchli 1999; Buchli
and Lucas 2001c; Harrison 2009b; see also Miller 1984a, b) and
the archaeology of zoos (e.g. Holtorf 2008). Archaeologists in
South Africa have undertaken work on the archaeology and
material meaning of District Six and other similar places in the
post-apartheid urban imagination (Hall 2000, 2001, 2006; Hart
and Winter 2001; Shepherd and Ernsten 2007), along with the
archaeology of contemporary tourism and heritage (Hall 2005;
Hall and Bombardella 2005). Another area of interest has been
that of urban interiors (e.g. Buchli 1999; Stevenson 2001), an
area of research that has received a significant impetus through
the establishment of the journal *Home Cultures* by founding
editors Victor Buchli, Alison Clarke, and Dell Upton in 2004.

One of the outcomes of English Heritage's Change and Creation programme (discussed above), *Images of Change* (Penrose
2007), has developed a typological approach to the contemporary
English urban and rural landscape in which it breaks the landscape features of contemporary England down into a number of
broad themes—people, politics, profit, and pleasure—before further isolating subthemes and site types below this. The themes
and subthemes employed by *Images of Change* are listed in
Table 2.1. While not intended to be definitive, this typology
has provided a structure for understanding and analysing aspects
of both rural and urban contemporary and recent archaeological
landscapes, and has begun to be used as a framework for late
twentieth-century archaeological research in the UK.

Table 2.1. Themes towards a typology for an archaeology of the post-1950 English landscape

People	Politics	Profit	Pleasure
Temporary housing	Hospitals	Forestry	Back gardens
Social housing	Mental health	Farming	Front gardens
Privatopia (private	Detention	Metals and industrial	National parks
housing and	Schools	minerals	Country parks
estates)	Higher and further	Industry	Heritage
New towns	education	Freight	Zoos
Edge towns	Defence research and	Brownfield	Television
(commuter	development	Materials of power	landscapes
satellite towns)	Defence	The national grid	Theme parks
Migration	infrastructure and	Energy	Swimming pools
Faith	support	Nuclear power	Leisure centres
Homelessness	Memorialization	Renewable energy	Sports stadia
Airspace	Cemeteries	Water	Artificial surfaces
Airports	Crematoria	The office	Golf courses
Motorways	Protest (e.g. places	Information	Cultural centres
Roads	associated with	(Internet, etc)	Art and place
Car parks	protest, even	Mobile phones	Holiday camps
Motorway service	where little	Out of town	The seaside
areas (roadside	material	commercial	
truck stops and	remains of this)	estates	
diners)		Town centre	
The rail network		shopping	
Railway stations		Shopping malls	

Source: Penrose (2007).

Twentieth-Century Technology

Although we see isolated examples of work on contemporary technology (Graves-Brown 2007*a*; Schiffer 1991, 2000), surprisingly this has received less attention compared to work that has occurred at a landscape or site level. Exceptions include the work on 'the van' by Schofield and others (Bailey et al. 2009; see Ch. 6) and Graves-Brown's work on the AK-47 (2007*a*). The area of technology and material culture is one in which there is significant overlap with other fields, for example material culture studies, cultural studies/sociology (e.g. Du Gay et al. 1997), and technology studies (e.g. Bijker, Hughes, and Pinch 1989; Bijker 1995) all of which have taken quite different trajectories in terms of their approaches to technology and material culture (see further discussion in Ch. 4).

The Archaeology of Contemporary Post-colonialism

Although it has not often been described as relating directly to archaeologies of the contemporary past, we have also seen the archaeology of post-colonialism and contemporary indigenous peoples emerge as an important concern over the past decade. In many countries, indigenous people maintained 'traditional' lifestyles in the wake of colonization until the very recent past. In others, the politics of decolonization is such that the archaeology of the mid to late twentieth century has become a key site for developing new national narratives. The archaeology of living indigenous memory and indigenous counter-mapping in Australia (Byrne and Nugent 2004; Harrison 2004), the relocation and government control of indigenous peoples over the course of the mid to late twentieth century (e.g. Paterson, Gill, and Kennedy 2003; Harrison 2003, 2004), and archaeology of mid–late twentieth-century indigenous protest seem relevant here. Archaeological work in South Africa relating to apartheid and its immediate demise (e.g. Hall 2000, 2001, 2005, 2006; Hall and Bombardella 2005; Hall and Lucas 2006; Shepherd 2002; Murray, Shepherd, and Hall 2007) would also seem to be closely related. Many of these studies draw on similar theoretical and political perspectives, and on techniques such as informant interviews, oral histories, and detailed site mapping that are common to other archaeologies of the contemporary past (see further discussion in Ch. 3). Similarly, much of this work has found a contemporary relevance, for example in the use of archaeological evidence in native title and other reparatory land claims in Australia (e.g. papers in Lilley 2000; and Harrison, McDonald, and Veth 2005) and its implication in debates around land restitution in South Africa (e.g. Shepherd 2002*a*; Meskell and Scheermeyer 2008).

Forensic, Human Rights and Disaster Archaeology

Gould (2007) defines a field of 'disaster' archaeology which deals with the urgent requirements of victim identification and scene investigation in the aftermath of mass fatality events. He distinguishes between disaster archaeology; human rights archaeology, which is concerned with the definition and investigation of mass graves and the sites of mass executions which result from genocide and political 'disappearances'; and forensic archaeology more generally, which is concerned with the investigation of crime scenes. We use the term 'forensic archaeology' in its most general sense to describe the application of archaeology to investigate questions of interest to the legal system, in particular criminal or civil law. In this sense, forensic archaeology might be linked in some ways to the work carried out by archaeologists working on land rights claims with indigenous peoples, discussed above.

Although linked with the archaeology of conflict, forensic archaeologies have developed along far more specialized lines and exist as part of a slightly divergent intellectual trajectory to other archaeologies of the contemporary past (see further discussion in Chs. 4 and 5). It is an area that has seen major growth since the 1990s and particularly in the wake of the World Trade Centre disaster in 2001. We have seen a major expansion of research in this field associated with the use of forensic archaeology in war crime and homicide trials (e.g. Doretti and Fondebrider 2001; Cox 2001; Hunter and Cox 2005; Ferllini 2007; Cox et al. 2008; Steele 2008; Sterenberg 2008), and the establishment of the Forensic Archaeology Recovery Group (FAR) (Gould 2007) and its role in the World Trade Centre disaster, the Station nightclub fire, and Hurricane Katrina (Dawdy 2006*a*, *b*; Bagwell 2009). In Latin America, we have seen the emergence of a whole field of archaeology concerned with revealing the repressive military dictatorships and the material remains of state-sponsored terror campaigns that occurred between 1960 and the early 1980s (e.g. Funari and Zarankin 2006; Zarankin and Funari 2008), which is connected closely with work in the field of forensic archaeology through its focus on the recovery of that which has been concealed and made forgotten, alongside the contemporary politics of memory. Similarly, Ballbé and Steadman (2008) describe the growth of forensic archaeology in Spain alongside human rights investigations associated with the Spanish Civil War (see also González-Ruibal 2007). The role of 'remembering' in the archaeology of the contemporary past will be discussed in more detail in Chapters 4 and 5.

WHEN WAS THE PAST 'CONTEMPORARY'?
UNDERSTANDING THE RELATIONSHIP BETWEEN
HISTORICAL ARCHAEOLOGY AND THE
ARCHAEOLOGY OF THE CONTEMPORARY PAST

Here we consider how practitioners have viewed the relationship between historical archaeology and the archaeology of the contemporary past. When does the one end and the other begin? Is the archaeology of the contemporary past simply an extension of historical archaeology into the present? Orser (2004: 6ff.) summarizes the various definitions of historical archaeology that have been put forward. In some instances, historical archaeology is defined as being of a particular period (defined as that period in which the society in question began keeping written records). In other circumstances, it is defined as a research method based on the combined use of historical and archaeological sources, or as the study of the 'modern world' (after Deetz who prioritized European colonial and imperial expansion as its main theme). Orser (p. 19) himself provides this definition: 'Historical archaeology is a multi-disciplinary field that shares a special relationship with the formal disciplines of anthropology and history, focuses its attention on the post-prehistoric past, and seeks to understand the global nature of modern life.' Despite the emphasis on modernity (as opposed to late modernity, see further discussion in Ch. 5), all the work discussed in this chapter would fall comfortably within this definition. However, the fact that the archaeology of the recent and contemporary past has distinguished itself from historical archaeology suggests that at least some authors consider there to be something 'special' or 'different' about this form of archaeology, and that difference might be related to the temporal proximity of the subject. Some clear themes emerge from a review of the literature. González-Ruibal (2008: 247–8), for instance, suggests that the archaeology of the recent past is there 'to fill the gap left by historical archaeologists', which he sees as coinciding with the beginning of the First World War. This view seems to be shared by others, Olivier (2001) for example. Yet others focus on those aspects of the archaeology of the recent past that engage with living memory as being most significant (e.g. Buchli and Lucas 2001*a*; Schofield 2000) which would tend to shift focus forward in time several decades, at the time of writing to somewhere around the 1940s. What is interesting here is the extent to which the archaeology of the contemporary past is viewed as distinct from historical archaeology per se. Most authors who comment on this issue do seek to make a distinction, although such a distinction is usually seen to relate to the themes under consideration, rather than temporal distance. Gavin Lucas (2006: 47), for example, asks:

> To what extent is there still a difference between such 'archaeologies of the contemporary past' and historical archaeology? From one perspective, the only difference is a chronological one, and therefore any boundary is as fluid or as tight as that between, say, post-medieval and medieval archaeology. However, a more radical position would argue that there is more than a chronological distinction here . . . while the temporal distance between the subject and object of study is preserved within mainstream historical archaeologies, it is no longer present when conducting archaeologies of the contemporary past . . . consequently any pretence of detachment . . . becomes implausible, and the role of archaeology as a cultural practice in the present is foregrounded.

However, Lucas goes on to add that 'none of this is any less true, of course, of the archaeology of the recent or distant pasts' (ibid.), suggesting this is more a matter of scale rather than any fundamental difference between historical archaeology and the archaeology of the contemporary past.

Burström (2007), by contrast, has argued that all archaeology that relates to the time period after 1850 should be defined as contemporary (Holtorf, pers comm.). An equally ambitious position, albeit one that harks back to the work of Shanks and Tilley ([1987] 1992) in the 1980s, is that of Funari, who states that archaeology should no longer be seen as being about the past, but simply 'the study of material culture and power relations' (in González-Ruibal 2008: 264; see also Zarankin and Funari 2008) in all its forms. Indeed, others have argued that it is the very palimpsest nature of the late twentieth century and the early twenty-first that makes disentangling the distant from more recent past impossible. 'There is no archaeology of the twenty-first century but only an archaeology of the twenty-first and all its pasts, mixed and entangled' (González-Ruibal 2008: 262). Readers will recall the influence of this position on our own definition of the archaeology of the contemporary past provided in Chapter 1.

Almost all commentators on the archaeology of the contemporary past emphasize the role of archaeology as a creative process of making anew previous time periods (e.g. Buchli and Lucas 2001a). Clearly the process of creating the past is easier when you have greater distance from the period under study, as there are fewer competing narratives. When you are dealing with the very recent past, archaeology becomes only one of a series of narratives competing with the living characters themselves in making stories about them and their pasts. This makes us more keenly aware of the ways in which archaeology constructs its particular representations of the past in the present.

If we are to see the archaeology of the contemporary past characterized more by the themes and issues it engages with rather than its temporal proximity to the present, we should consider which themes distinguish it from other forms of archaeology, and from the other academic disciplines with which it shares an interest in material culture and the recent past. This is an issue considered at length by González-Ruibal (2008), who suggests that the archaeology of the contemporary past should be an archaeology of 'supermodernity', that is, modernity 'become excessive', drawing on Marc Augé's discussion of supermodernity (1995; see further Ch. 5). He notes:

The archaeology of supermodernity... is different from any other archaeology... The particular character of the archaeology of supermodernity can be, nonetheless, reasonably argued: the traumatic nature of the recent past, our intimate implication in its events, and the disturbing nature of its record, whose historical proximity makes it so raw and traumatic... the archaeology of supermodernity is the archaeology of superdestruction of life and matter... a way of dealing with a traumatic past, bringing forward presence and managing conflicting memories.

(González-Ruibal 2008: 262)

His focus on destruction was queried by a number of commentators on his paper, who suggested that *diversity* might also be equally important a focus as destruction in the archaeology of the late twentieth century (a point he acknowledged as part of his own viewpoint in his reply).

One of the frequently cited notions to distinguish the archaeology of the contemporary past from other disciplines that share a concern with material culture and the recent past is its use of archaeological methodology (e.g. Holtorf 2008: 6–7; Schofield 2007; Piccini and Holtorf 2009), although it is difficult to see a unitary approach to the methodology that is applied across the breadth of the field (see further discussion in Ch. 3). Forensic archaeology is clearly an area where particular specialized techniques dominate. Other archaeologists, particularly those working within the area of archaeological heritage management, often use approaches that are more closely aligned to the detailed heritage recording of standing structures (e.g. Cocroft 2007b; Cocroft and Thomas 2003). On the other hand, the approach of some archaeologists seems to sit more comfortably within those more anthropological approaches of material culture studies (e.g. Graves-Brown 2007a; Buchli 1999). Excavation, perhaps the method that best characterizes the archaeological approach, appears to be reasonably rare, although it plays a role in some aspects of conflict archaeology (e.g. see Saunders 2007). Landscape approaches (e.g. Fairclough 2007) and description at the level of the 'site' and individual 'structures' (see further Ch. 7) largely dominate the field.

The connection between archaeology and other ways of representing and documenting the past, such as art and photography, is emphasized by Schofield (2007) and others (e.g. in Schofield and Cocroft 2007; Piccini and Holtorf 2009). Recognizing the relevance to archaeology of photographic documentation seems to be common to most authors. The apparent forensic qualities of photography and its connections with heritage practices have been discussed elsewhere (Harrison et al. 2008). In many ways we could characterize the approaches of archaeologists working on the contemporary past as perhaps far more diverse and certainly more interdisciplinary than on other archaeological time periods, although the extent to which this is simply a product of it being a

newly developing field is at present difficult to gauge. These issues
are discussed further in Chapter 4.

Whether we should consider the archaeology of the contemporary past as somehow 'separate' from historical archaeology
will be considered further in Chapter 5. For now, it is enough to
hold in mind the particular shades of difference that have been
discussed in this section—the focus on particular themes such as
the recovery of memory, the presencing of absence and the uncovering of the concealed, the abject and the subaltern (Buchli and
Lucas 2001a), the dissolution of the temporal distance between
subject and object, and the consideration of the contemporary
'surface' as an amalgam of all layers of history (rather than a focus
on particular aspects of the past to the detriment of others). We
argue that these specific areas of interest and shades of archaeological interpretation map out a particular agenda for the archaeology of the contemporary past that means it must be seen as
separate to historical archaeologies in general. We will return to
consider these issues at various points throughout the first part of
the book.

CONCLUSIONS

This chapter has charted the emergence of the archaeology of the
contemporary past as a distinct subfield. From its origins in
North America with the ethnoarchaeological studies aligned to
the New Archaeology, and the influence of British post-processual
archaeologists and the new field of material culture studies, it
emerged as a distinct area of study in the years around the turn of
the twenty-first century. Influences on the nature of the topics
explored by contemporary archaeologists include the close alignment of many working in the field with the heritage industry, and
the broad interest that has been noted in the general public for
contemporary and recent heritage. Authors working within the
field have sought to distinguish it from historical archaeology
through an emphasis on those aspects of the late twentieth
and early twenty-first century (or the late modern period) that

distinguish it from earlier periods—in particular the themes of deindustrialization and the influence of new communicative technologies. Some of these issues will be explored in more detail in Chapter 5. The next chapter considers methodologies appropriate to 'doing' archaeology on the contemporary past as a way of further defining it as a distinct subfield.

3

Field Methods

INTRODUCTION

In Chapter 1 we suggested that the archaeology of the contemporary past is a critical inquiry into the present using archaeological approaches originally developed to look at the past. But how, precisely, does one undertake an archaeological study of the contemporary past, and what do practitioners more familiar with earlier periods bring with them to this particular type of archaeological enquiry? Is this archaeology of the very recent past so different to that of earlier periods? Is it simply a matter of transferring skills from more familiar grounds of the deeper past? We suggest that to large extent it is, though recognizing at least one key difference: the degree to which our diverse cultural backgrounds and life experiences will influence the way we think about and interpret material remains that often seem closely familiar. In this chapter we look particularly at the ways in which an archaeology of the contemporary past is informed by oral accounts and living memories, and at approaches to recording and analysing complex and multi-layered contemporary landscapes in which the past is manifest as an integral part of the present.

ON THE NATURE OF THE CONTEMPORARY ARCHAEOLOGICAL RECORD

Following the work of Michael Schiffer (1987), most archaeologists are used to thinking about the archaeological record as the cumulative product of both cultural and natural forces over the full course of human existence, from the Lower Palaeolithic until the moment just passed. But there are obvious differences with the way human behaviour is constructed and transformed into an archaeological record. When considering the archaeology of the contemporary past, for example, many of the natural processes that lead to the decay and deterioration of traditional archaeological sites are not present. And in many ways, the cultural site formation processes are more varied, resulting in archaeological sites of the recent past being either extremely well or very poorly preserved. Comparatively few modern buildings simply deteriorate for example, the more likely outcome being a decision to renovate, modernize, upgrade, or demolish and replace. Those buildings and places that are just abandoned to their fate are interesting because they are often adopted for truly alternative uses, sometimes becoming the characteristic places of those at the margins of contemporary society, as squats for example, or places for play, or where drugs are taken and alcohol consumed. The nature of contemporary mass garbage removal means that, unlike in the past, domestic refuse will seldom be discarded in close proximity to the home. Activities that leave traces of 'the night before' in towns and cities all over the world are cleared away before most of us are even awake. We are more conscious of rubbish now than we were in the past—the 'leave as found' principle now being widely supported and practised. There are clear and obvious differences between how time has treated ancient and modern traces of human activity, but those factors pertinent to the contemporary past do make linking the archaeological record to its users more complex and more diverse, more challenging and—for us—more interesting. Another challenge for archaeologists of the contemporary past is often one not of too little information, but of too much. Understanding how to deal with the 'messy' (after Law 2004) nature of the material remains of the recent past emerges as a central concern for the field.

Artefact Analyses

Let us begin with artefacts. The broad types and categories of artefacts that relate to the contemporary past are largely the same now as they always have been. There is a predominance of domestic assemblages, and the traces of industry. But there is also a plethora of objects and categories related to religious activity, leisure and pleasure, and militarism, all of which certainly make modern assemblages more diverse than much of what exists for earlier periods. As we have seen, there are also commercial and discard practices that can make interpretation a more challenging business. We now have a more wasteful society, for example (e.g. Rathje 2001), and of course a consumer society. We love to shop (Miller 2007), and ultimately we throw away much of what we buy. In recent years recycling has become important and popular, first through charity and second-hand sales, including car boot sales, and now through internet auction sites such as eBay (see further discussion in Ch. 6). But nevertheless, much still gets discarded for archaeologists now and in the future. It is just the manner and locations of its discard that differ from earlier periods.

Studying these late modern artefacts can be fascinating, not least because of their (supposed) close familiarity. We may think we know all about these 'familiar' objects, but increasingly experience through archaeological investigations suggests otherwise. Taking a biographical view of almost any object can draw out a life history of extraordinary scale and complexity (e.g. Hoskins 1998; Joy 2002). At one level they can communicate family tensions and disputes, through inheritance and contested ownership for example. At the other extreme is the inevitable and clear evidence for globalization. For example, objects made in the Far East are imported by the West, before being sold, bought, used and stored, used again, passed down through generations, and then perhaps recycled through sale, gift, or loan. Eventually the object breaks or becomes worthless and is discarded, only to enter those great archaeological sites of the present and future, the land-fill (Rathje 2001). But even discard is complicated. For example, an increasingly elaborate system of domestic recycling means that raw materials are separated at various stages for reuse, with some materials often ending up in similar objects being manufactured once again at their first point of origin.

This precise situation is illustrated in a consideration of the car parts and objects in a Ford Transit van excavated in Bristol (England) in 2006. Not a conventional excavation so much as a forensic dissection of an everyday vehicle, albeit one used in archaeological projects, this project sought to investigate the archaeological potential of a contemporary and everyday object. The van was thus surveyed, artefacts were surface collected, and then the vehicle dissected piece by piece, with contexts and finds recorded according to conventional archaeological procedures and practices. A further discussion of this project, and the artefacts in particular, is in Chapter 6. Here though it is the recycling of modern material culture that is more relevant. As part of the analysis of the van's component parts, their points of origin and their destination following the van's destruction were established. Maps displaying these points of origin and destiny betray clear symmetries (Fig. 3.1) (Bailey et al. 2009). Of particular note is the importance of such places as Avonmouth (North Somerset, UK). Travellers on the M5 west of Bristol will notice thousands of parked cars here, imported from the Far East and awaiting redistribution within the UK. The more eagle-eyed or adventurous traveller will find, within the wider industrial landscape, a metal recycling plant, where cars and other large metal items are dismantled and shredded, the various separated raw materials then redistributed by ship, often back to their point of origin, for use in the construction of new cars, some of which are reimported to the UK through Avonmouth! Avonmouth then, like other similar places around the world, is a conduit: a place through which many of our most familiar objects repeatedly pass and repass.

Identifying artefacts has benefits for dating assemblages and for site interpretation, even on sites of recent date. A Smith's crisp packet recovered from the peace camps at Greenham Common was dated to 1983 by its advertising of the James Bond film *Octopussy,* released late that year. The camp at which this item was found opened in 1983 (Schofield 2009*a*). Often with modern artefacts it is not scientific analyses that are needed so much as simple internet research (increasingly referred to as 'Googling'), or the identification of items in catalogues and through archives and templates held by the original manufacturer. Nails and screws for example can be tightly defined to type and function, if not approximate date (e.g. Myers in Bailey et al. 2009, and Ch. 6). And meaningful analyses can certainly be conducted for modern and familiar material items, as Shanks and Tilley have demonstrated in their study of British and Swedish beer cans ([1987] 1992; see discussion in Ch. 2).

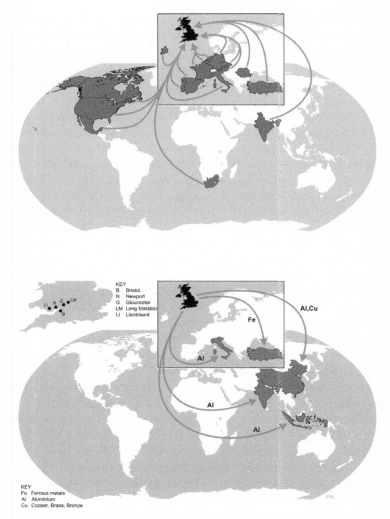

Figure 3.1. Point of origin (above) and destination (below) of component parts of the Ford Transit van. (Drawing: Eddie Lyons.)

We will see further examples of artefact studies in Chapter 6. For now though it is sufficient to emphasize that many categories of late modern artefact, and the component parts they incorporate, are well documented, unlike those relating to earlier periods. For these earlier objects, databases are the result of years of specialist research. Information about late modern artefacts can be found, usually online, and often identified with a name, place, and date of manufacture, and a description. On contemporary archaeological sites therefore, research is more likely to be internet-based, requiring 'Googling skills', rather than scientific analysis as traditionally used in archaeological investigations for dating and sourcing. As the Ford Transit van demonstrated, however, scientific analysis might still prove helpful, for example in determining patterns of use, as in more traditional forms of forensic inquiry.

SURVEY: LOCATING AND RECORDING SITES

What about contemporary sites? Are they just as 'archaeological' as Stone Age settlements and Roman forts? Certainly, sites of recent date can be investigated using the same techniques as for earlier periods. In the former USSR for example, forty years after they were acquired for intelligence purposes, declassified US photographs from the KH-7 GAMBIT photo reconnaissance satellite programme, together with contemporary declassified intelligence reports, were used to interpret Cold War sites in the former Soviet Union (Fowler 2008). A case study describes how, from 1954, fifty-six sites were deployed in a layered defence of two concentric rings around Moscow, with radii of c.45 km and 85 km from the centre, together with seven support facilities (Fig. 3.2). Each site comprised an area of sixty launch positions for the V-300 SAM, joined by a road network in a characteristic herringbone arrangement together with guidance area for the radar bunker, and a support area. Yet despite obvious similarities, these are not homogenous sites. Closer investigation of aerial photographs reveals diversity of form: some types are associated more with Moscow's inner ring for example, and others with the outer. Some variations in typology appear to be

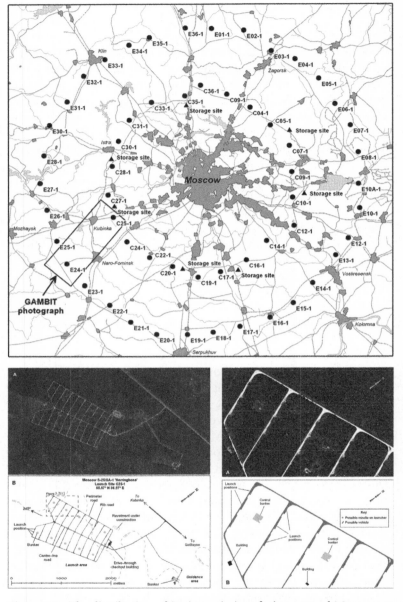

Figure 3.2. The distribution of Soviet anti-aircraft sites around Moscow, as revealed by satellite photography. The images show the overall distribution, a site plan with aerial photograph, and detail of missile launch areas. (This drawing, originally published in *Antiquity* (Fowler 2008), supplied by Martin Fowler.)

influenced by topography and terrain, but not all. It is in these more subtle questions of form and content where further archaeological investigation may prove beneficial. From analysis at this wider geographical scale, one can also assess the impact of the infrastructure associated with this missile system on the landscape, and its continuing influence today. The fact that two ring roads were constructed to serve the sites is an indication of the scale of the construction, as is the fact that the sites would together have accommodated 27,000 personnel.

Aerial photography is also used to record the changing landscape. Many of the images in English Heritage's (2007*a*) 'Modern Times' *Conservation Bulletin*, and in *Images of Change* (Penrose 2007), both key publications on the archaeology of the contemporary past in England, are predominantly aerial views. The popular BBC television series 'Britain from Above' (Harrison 2008) has succeeded in giving this perspective widespread and popular exposure reflecting a familiarity gained in the later twentieth and early twenty-first century in particular from the routine availability of cheap international flights. Delores Hayden's book *A Field Guide to Sprawl* (2004) uses aerial photographs to document the late modern landscapes of North American suburbia. Aerial photography provides a distinctive way of capturing the surface layer of an archaeological landscape at a particular point in time. Online resources such as LiveLocal and GoogleEarth provide additional possibilities, and provide access to high quality, high resolution imagery for anyone with fast online access. Although one must always be aware of the possibility of manipulation and 'masking', for example by conveniently placed low clouds, these images are mostly accurate, and do therefore provide potential for researching the contemporary landscape from afar. The development of widespread, free access to high quality aerial imagery has revolutionized the possibilities for undertaking archaeological studies of both late modern and earlier time periods. For example, researchers in Australia have used GoogleEarth alone to create fantastically detailed maps of ancient sites in war zones such as Afghanistan, where first-hand site inspections are currently impossible (David Thomas and Claudia Zipfel pers. comm.).

Field (including earthwork and building) survey is applied routinely now to modern sites and landscape (e.g. English Heritage

Figure 3.3. Survey of the Black Beacon on Orford Ness (Suffolk, UK), built in 1928 but continued in use under the Atomic Weapons Research Establishment. (Photo: English Heritage.)

2007*b*: 31–3) (Fig. 3.3). In the UK, English Heritage has surveyed a range of military and industrial places over the past decade, often interpreting physical remains within their technological and political contexts. English Heritage undertakes three levels of survey, depending on circumstances and the types of information required (English Heritage 2007*b*: 23). Level 1 is mainly a visual record, supplemented by the minimum of information needed to identify the site's location, date, and type, based largely if not exclusively on easily available information. A Level 2 survey involves field investigation to provide a basic and interpretative record of an archaeological monument or landscape. This will be metrically accurate and analytical. Level 3 is an enhanced and integrated multi-disciplinary record of a monument or landscape, resulting from field investigation, usually enhanced by specialist research such as geophysical or aerial survey. Level 3 surveys are often the most appropriate for archaeological sites and landscape of the contemporary past. The surveys conducted at the Cold War atomic testing establishments at Foulness, Essex and

Orford Ness, Suffolk (Cocroft and Alexander 2009) are examples. Both are two-phase sites where the intention was to identify, record, and explain the features for designation and public presentation. In identifying the buildings and structures the principal objective was to link building phases to known bomb projects and the high politics surrounding them (Wayne Cocroft pers. comm.). There is an argument that for sites with few phases and where very specific information is needed about their former use, traditional analytical survey may be the most appropriate interpretative technique. Here, we argue, the traditional archaeological methods of investigation form a valid approach to historical inquiry, comprising: plan-making, note-taking, description, and photography, in addition to the use of map regression and aerial photographs and the integration of historical and in some cases oral historical sources.

But what types of research question, specifically, might such traditional approaches address? At Spadeadam (Cumbria), another Cold War site in the UK, a key question addressed by archaeological field survey was whether or not the feasibility of a fully underground system had actually been tested through the construction of a silo or launch tube. As Cocroft (2006: 8) states, one of the uncertainties in the use of such a 'hot-launch' system was whether the acoustic shock produced by vibration from the engines would shake the missile to pieces before it left the silo. Interestingly there was a historical invisibility to the elements of the underground launch facility project destined for Spadeadam, compounded on the one hand by the abandonment of the system and the split responsibility between government organizations and a private company, and on the other, the fact that the scheme was virtually unknown to many of the former Rocket Establishment employees. What does exist provided context for the archaeological survey, or at least the expectation that some trace might be found as part of the wider Spadeadam project. One clue was a note in a Royal Aircraft Establishment Blue Streak monthly report for June 1958 describing the intended function of the 'U1' facility at Spadeadam, to 'investigate the conditions associated with firing a missile in an underground launching facility' (ibid. 9). Another clue was a letter from the Ministry of Supply to the Treasury which verified that plans were well advanced for the construction of an underground launching facility at Spadeadam by

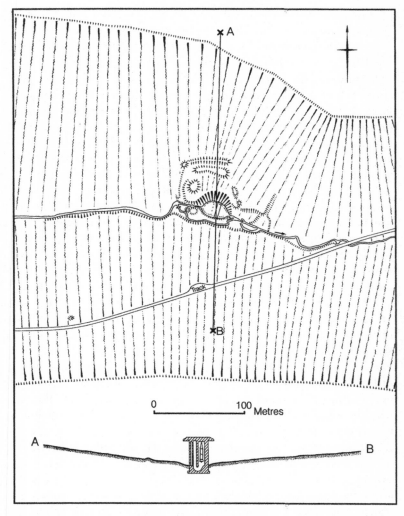

Figure 3.4. Site plan of the missile silo at Spadeadam, Cumbria, England. (Drawing: Allan Adams.)

September 1958 (ibid.). Finally, an aerial photograph of August 1961 showed evidence that work had begun on the silo, in the form of an excavation with disturbed ground to its north and traces of heavy vehicle tracks headed west. Survey in 2005 revealed the surviving traces of this important and unusual structure (Fig. 3.4).

Similar work has been conducted in the United States, where archaeological survey has been undertaken at the Nevada Test Site (e.g. Beck 2002). Here fieldwork commissioned by the Department of Energy generated a record of surviving archaeological traces in the Nevada Desert, ranging in date from prehistoric to late modern, and specifically the material legacy of its Cold War atomic weapons testing programme. Documentation involved inventory and surveys of structures built for testing and the testing support facilities. From work completed to date, three categories of historic structures and remains can be identified: first, those associated with atmospheric and near-surface underground tests; second, contained underground tests; and third, non-explosive experiments related to radiation effects and the application of nuclear energy. The support facilities are overarching: the town of Mercury for example, with sufficient facilities to support a full community of test site workers; and various camps that served workers' needs. The remains are extensive, diverse of character, and extraordinary in their appearance. They can also be problematic for survey, but not for what may appear obvious health and safety reasons. First, because as Beck (2002: 68) points out, nuclear testing consisted of experiments in which scientists were constantly pushing at the limits of knowledge and understanding. Thus, structures built for these purposes were often unique to nuclear testing and not common to Western culture. So, like earlier archaeological remains, they were unfamiliar. Second was the problem of how to describe these places: there are simply no terms in our language to describe accurately the architectural presentation of some constructions. This presents an interesting dilemma for popularizing this particular archaeological record: that the public focus will inevitably be on those structures that most closely resemble similar structures in everyday life, such as a train trestle, bank vault, or house. Yet while examples of these structures do survive, they are not the most common. This project has sought to document both the familiar and unfamiliar and to provide some understanding, primarily in this case for resource managers and users, but also—ultimately—for the wider public.

Measured surveys are not uncommon, therefore, in archaeological studies of the contemporary past. But why, some might argue, would one wish to create detailed survey drawings of sites that are so well documented, with original design and architects' drawings available for public consultation? The reason, simply, is that there is no foundation for supposing that documents alone necessarily do provide such an accurate representation of what exists on the ground, or of what was originally built, assuming of course that such documents exist at all. Design drawings will typically portray what was intended. Sometimes what was built was not quite the same, or subsequent additions or changes have introduced significant alterations to what is depicted. Further, many sites are not designed at all, but just 'appear'. Examples include sites of protest, such as the numerous peace camps at Greenham Common (Schofield and Anderton 2000; Schofield 2009a), and the protest camp at Nine Ladies Stone Circle, Derbyshire (Badcock and Johnston 2009). At Greenham, site visits with council employees who had been present during the protests, combined with a trawl of published literature, revealed the names and locations of numerous peace camps around the base perimeter. Subsequent field visits revealed conditions conducive to the survival of archaeological remains at several of these camps, while others would clearly not have survived road widening and other works that accompanied the closure and development of the base for private industry, and its return to common land. At those camps where remains were likely, rapid field investigations revealed their approximate extent and character; they included slight earthwork features, artefacts, and the remains of ephemeral campsite structures, such as washing lines suspended in trees, fire pits, and clearances in the scrubby undergrowth. A more detailed field survey was conducted at one camp—at what the women called Turquoise Gate—revealing the details of artefact distribution and topographic features (Schofield 2009a). Oral historical research led to the rediscovery of a further camp, previously unrecorded, at Emerald Gate: this was small, supporting only three women at any one time, and the remains were transient and occasional, the women packing everything away and hiding it in gorse on each departure. A return visit with one of our informants, a previous occupant of this camp, revealed a coffee pot, three mugs, and the rolled materials for temporary shelters, exactly where she had left them.

As is evident at Turquoise Gate, there is also value in archaeological survey for interpreting artefact distributions. Studies have investigated depositional phases and actions as well as post-depositional distortion in the back of a Ford Transit van (Bailey et al. 2009), the archaeology of Francis Bacon's studio (Cappock 2005; see further Ch. 4), and the evidence of occupation in an abandoned council flat (Buchli and Lucas 2001b). In this last case, already mentioned in Chapter 2, archaeologists gained two days' access to a recently abandoned council house with a view to exploring the theme of alienation from the dual perspective of the material culture of marginalized and socially disenfranchised people, and the alienation that we, as archaeologists, effect on the people we study. The project was conducted as though this was a more conventional archaeological site—planned room by room, and all the objects photographed, recorded, and interpreted.

As we saw earlier with field survey of archaeological sites and monuments, the level of detail and rigour appropriate to one's investigation is determined by the questions one is asking, and the motivations behind the inquiry. For some studies, precise details of artefact locations and alignments will be central to understanding the human behaviours behind them, and addressing questions of social interaction at micro-scale, for example. But in other cases a simple photographic record of a room or landscape might be sufficient to capture the essence or character of the place, perhaps to serve some management outcome, or simply as a record prior to removal (for further discussion of photography, see Ch. 4). The means will determine the ends, for archaeologies of the late modern just as for earlier periods.

MODERN RUINS: ARCHAEOLOGY AND
THE 'EXPERIENCE' OF PLACE

As archaeologists of the late modern period, our engagement is often with sites and buildings that either remain in use or have been recently abandoned, engagements that will inevitably set the archaeology of the contemporary past apart from those with earlier sites. Edensor's (2005) study of industrial ruins and of the close and diverse connections we often have with the familiar is significant here. Edensor (2005: 4) says this of engagements with former industrial buildings:

[H]owever mundane they may seem, ruins still contain... promise of the unexpected. Since the original uses of ruined buildings have passed, there are limitless possibilities for encounters with the weird, with inscrutable legends inscribed on notice boards and signs, and with peculiar things and curious spaces which allow wide scope for interpretation, unencumbered by the assumptions which weigh heavily on highly encoded, regulated space.... Ruins offer spaces in which the interpretation and practice of the city becomes liberated from the everyday constraints which determine what should be done and where, and which encode the city with meanings. Accordingly they offer the opportunities for challenging and deconstructing the imprint of power on the city.

It is hard to imagine many people making such intimate and ambiguous connections to medieval or earlier ruins. Connections are made, certainly, but the nature and intensity of that connection can be very different. But we also need to be mindful of the ways in which the appearance of ruins is 'read' and made meaningful within contemporary societies. While there is something romantic about certain ruins, others are read as representing social and moral decay. For example, the US photographer Phil Buehler notes in his photo-essay 'Modern Ruins' (2009): 'I photograph modern ruins because I find it disturbing to find familiar objects and technology to be abandoned. I'm reminded that nothing is permanent, that everything is always in a state of transition. And we see ourselves in our own transitions, sometimes too focused on where we're going to notice and appreciate where we are.' The archaeology of late modern societies exists as an intervention in this process, as something that simultaneously draws attention to the process of decay whilst also being implicated in its arrest (Pearson and Shanks 2001).

Contemporary ruins are also sometimes considered to represent the accelerated rate of change that is a feature of late modernity (see further Ch. 5). The abandoned Russian industrial town of Chernobyl, for instance, has a significant web presence, and routinely appears in television documentaries that assess the trajectory of change beyond human habitation: how fast things fall into disrepair and erode and collapse. As a site it is firmly locked in memories of post-industrial cultural decline. What is lacking of course in many such post-industrial situations, including arguably this one, is the human angle: the stories age, as the potential for networked disasters of modernity increase. Chernobyl is a place that is closely familiar to those of us of a certain age, not least from its frequent and periodic repetition in news coverage. It is a place we all know, and may even feel as though we have visited such is its familiarity.

What then can we do archaeologically in such situations? At Piramida, a Soviet mining town in the High Arctic has been recorded by archaeologists (Andreassen, Bjerck, and Olsen forthcoming). Abandoned in 1998 after fifty years of continuous activity, the town was left devoid of all humans but still with all the material culture constituting a modern city. As Andreassen, Bjerck, and Olsen (ibid.) have said: 'In its ruined state Piramida stubbornly carries the means to trigger the involuntary memories of its untimely past. As a site of remembrance—or rather unforgetting—the memories it holds become inseparable from its materiality and from things' unique ability to bring forth these memories.' The method adopted here, as with Edensor's survey, was a simple one, in this case involving two archaeologists and an artistic photographer, which at the time of the survey constituted the town's entire population. The fieldwork is described as preliminary and experimental: being there, trying to grasp and sense the place. The intervention was low tech, using notebooks and cameras as the main modes of documentation. But most important was 'the bodily experience of actually being present and to encounter the imposing materiality of the site' (ibid.). This seems to us an important means for archaeologists of the contemporary past to study their subject matter: simply by experiencing or encountering a place; by being there and thinking through a landscape, much as Davis (2008) has done for the Cold War landscape at Orford Ness and we describe for Nevada in Chapter 8. Following her day's visit to Orford Ness, Davis (ibid. 149) reflected on returning by boat to the mainland. As she says, one might think something along these lines: That,

[i]n an age where war has become invisible, above our heads, it is appropriate that a monument to older wars has such highly visible buildings. It could occur to you that your slow movement around Orford Ness was like a

tribute to the old wars of movement, where now there are only wars of communication and instantaneity. You could reflect on those moments when the site-in-use seemed to come alive in your eyes, as if you were there or it were here.

Thinking through and analysing the places we experience are normal processes that people go through often as a matter of course. And for us this seems to be the essence also of an archaeological approach. No digging required. Just observe, engage, and think. In her account Davis seems to suggest (citing English Heritage and the National Trust) that archaeological site surveys in the conventional sense fail to capture adequately the 'essence of a landscape', stating also that the defining and describing of sites' 'aesthetic qualities' is 'pitifully underdeveloped'. There may be an element of truth in this, though it should be stressed of course that such ambitions rarely form part of the brief for archaeological surveys. Similar observations have emerged from the work of the archaeologist Michael Shanks (1992; see also Pearson and Shanks 2001; Shanks 2004), who argues that much of what we experience as archaeologists working in the field is not conveyed in the conventional site descriptions and reports that are a feature of professional archaeological writing, and calls for a more embodied approach to archaeological practice. We agree, and suggest that description and literary prose, alongside photography, can contribute significantly to the understanding of late modern places and as such have an important role in doing the archaeology of the contemporary past. We explore these themes in Chapter 4.

EXCAVATION

No technique defines archaeology as a professional practice as much as excavation. However, given that many of the material remains that relate to the contemporary past linger above ground and indeed often remain in use, one might initially wonder what role excavation plays in contemporary archaeology. While there are a number of examples of controlled sub-surface excavations in the contemporary and recent periods (some of which we will discuss below), excavation and the meticulous and controlled removal and recording of context also have a place in a range of non-traditional archaeological contexts. For example, although it was not buried, the work undertaken on the Transit van (discussed more fully in Ch. 6) was approached as a form of excavation in the sense in which all contexts were recorded and removed as layers, the stratigraphy recorded, and finds bagged and labelled according to archaeological context. Similarly, Christine Finn's mantelpiece was treated as an archaeological site, its contents excavated as if layers of stratigraphy and meaning were systematically removed (Finn 2009).

A number of 'conventional' archaeological excavations relating to Second World War sites have been undertaken (see further Ch. 2), providing close comparison to any excavations of sites of the contemporary past. At Tottenham Hale in the north of London, for example, excavations have revealed the full extent of communal air-raid shelters, provided by factories for their employees during the Second World War. Excavations revealed not only their extent, but their content, condition, and—by virtue of public archaeology initiatives—their social significance too (John Lowe pers. comm.). Similarly, in Australia, excavations associated with depression era itinerant camps (Barker and Lamb 2009) and mid to late twentieth century Aboriginal worker's dwellings (Harrison 2002) have been carried out (Fig. 3.5). These excavations were undertaken within depositional environments where soil had rapidly built up and in which the remains themselves were ephemeral in the first instance. Indeed, much of the conventional excavation that has taken place on mid to late twentieth-century archaeological sites has tended to occur in contexts in which the sites themselves are characterized by ephemerality. This is true, for example, of excavations undertaken in Cape Town, South Africa in District Six (Hall 2001). In 1966, the government declared District Six a whites-only area under the Group Areas Act, after which 60,000 residents were forcibly relocated and the former settlement bulldozed. Excavation of one of the former houses in the 1990s revealed not only details of the life of residents of the area in the 1960s, but also served as the focus for a process of collective remembering within the context of a reimagining of the place of District Six within the history of post-colonial South Africa and widespread calls from former residents to allow for their return (see also Rassool 2007).

Figure 3.5. Detail of discrete hearth and associated artefact scatter from the Old Lamboo Aboriginal pastoral workers' fringe encampment site in south-east Kimberley, north-western Australia, excavated by Rodney Harrison in the late 1990s. Its main occupation occurred during the period 1901–67, with some ephemeral occupation after 1967 and reoccupation in the 1990s. (Photo: Rodney Harrison.)

One area of contemporary archaeology in which excavation is routinely employed is in human rights and disaster archaeology. In *Matériel Culture* (Schofield, Johnson, and Beck 2002), for example, three chapters explain the relevance of forensic investigations for mapping and investigating war crimes or conflict situations, either for justice or to ensure the repatriation of human remains. Helen Jarvis (2002) wrote about Cambodia's 'killing fields', in the context of attempting to bring the Khmer Rouge to justice. She spoke of the possibility of a trial and the significance of the plethora of documentation uncovered, catalogued, and summarized over five years by the Cambodian Genocide Program and the Documentation Centre of Cambodia, which reveals beyond doubt the scope of Khmer Rouge's human rights violations. This included documenting as well as mapping the physical traces of genocide. Jarvis noted how over five hundred genocide sites had been mapped in twenty-one of Cambodia's twenty-four provinces. Rebecca Saunders spoke of human rights abuses in Guatamala and the former Yugoslavia, where excavations were supported by the American Association for the Advancement of Science and the United Nations. Saunders (2002: 103) also summarizes the development of this particular aspect of historical archaeology in recent years, and the various justifications for this specifically archaeological approach:

1. to counter government or military denials of human rights abuses;

2. to provide evidence in litigation against high-ranking individuals under whose direction human rights abuses took place;

3. to confirm or correct survivors' accounts by detailing site taphonomic processes;

4. to excavate the remains of victims and to discover, through physical anthropology and associated artefacts, the cause and manner of death;

5. to identify the victims by comparing physical anthropological data to an ante-mortem database containing physical characteristics of known victims;

6. to notify families so that some closure can take place; and ultimately

7. to deter future human rights violations by demonstrating that the actions of the past are recoverable.

Finally, Zoe Crossland examined Argentina's 'disappeared', from the period of the military dictatorship of 1976–83. As she (2002: 125) states,

The excavations, in addition to providing evidence for the law courts, took a great deal of their symbolic force from the physical uncovering of the bodies, revealing the secret activities surrounding the disappearance and deaths of those buried there. This made the crimes of the juntas visible and contributed to maintaining public consciousness and memories of the years of the repression.

More detailed descriptions of archaeological field methods associated with Disaster Archaeology are provided by Gould (2007), while forensic and human rights archaeologies are discussed in a

range of additional sources (e.g. Cox 2001; Doretti and Fondeb-
rider 2001; Hunter and Cox 2005; Funari and Zarankin 2006;
Ferllini 2007; Cox et al. 2008; Sterenberg 2008; Zarankin and
Funari 2008).

It is worth pausing to reflect on the ethical arguments that
accompany interventions with the very recent or contemporary
past, and the circumstances under which excavation might not
be undertaken for ethical reasons. In studying the Greenham
Common peace camps, the research team presumed to think
excavation of the campsites would be acceptable, only to discover
that it was not. To their former occupants, the campsites were
sacred spaces, for which unnecessary intervention was inappro-
priate, not least perhaps with a team including men (Schofield
2009a). Work at Peace Camp (Nevada) created a degree of tension, with protests involving traditional owners, the Western Shoshone, in a prominent role (see Beck, Drollinger, and Schofield
2007). While the spiritual leader had given his support for the
archaeological project, others in the community disagreed, leading
to some angry confrontations on site, and begging the question of
whose view prevails in such situations. Further, to what extent
might a study of street homelessness amount to voyeurism, and
does the participation of a few street homeless volunteers make it
an acceptable study, or is voyeurism made worse through token-
ism? And in terms of recent conflict sites, too, do the dead have
rights as individuals (Moshenska 2008)? When is it acceptable to
recover the remains of soldiers, and to film it for television? The
archaeology of the contemporary past draws these ethical considerations into clear focus. Ethical issues and guidelines and regu-
lations on photographic and sound recording, for example, will
also be relevant where living individuals and private property are
concerned.

Palaeo-environmental studies have rarely been used in twentieth-
century contexts, though where this has been done the results
have provided some additional insight. In the case of the Transit
van (Bailey et al. 2009; Newland et al. 2007), Davis investigated
remains from a range of internal contexts, and commented that
the deposits were clearly recent as they contained modern intro-
ductions, though noting that the general conclusions might

equally refer to a timber-framed building! The presence of grain beetles indicated a storage function while little evidence existed for the 'site's' environs. Potential has also been demonstrated by police and other forensics work in this area (e.g. Morris 2006; Stauffer and Bonfanti 2006).

WHAT WE ARE TOLD: INTEGRATING ORAL ACCOUNTS

While obvious similarities exist with earlier periods, the archaeology of the twentieth and twenty-first centuries is also clearly different to that of earlier periods in some key respects—in the availability of oral historical sources, and the volume and diversity of documentary records for example. There is also the historiographic perspective—increasingly reflexive histories of our closely familiar past, telling us how events and attitudes were documented at different times. Oral historical sources have the clear benefit of giving colour to the often grey architecture of the modern period; they tell us what things were like, again adding detail and personal perspectives to the official records and instructions issued to staff and personnel. The internet has made the gathering and dissemination of oral historical information much easier than before. In the case of Greenham Common and other former military and industrial establishments, veterans, 'old boys', and social networking websites give easy access to large numbers of former personnel, and their own social networks. But with this increased access to communities comes a greater sense of responsibility in the ways in which their past and present are constructed by archaeologists. Wilkie (2001) writes of the challenges of a project excavating twentieth-century archaeological sites associated with the African-American community in Louisiana, working in consultation with former residents. She notes, 'as a white researcher, the discourse of the interviews forced me to acknowledge how structures of racial inequality, established in the early twentieth century, continue to shape and limit my effectiveness as a white researcher working with African-American populations today' (p. 116). Nonetheless, she concluded, ultimately, by maintaining a dialectic between the past and the present, we can only improve the nature of our archaeological research and interpretations (p. 117).

There is also the question of how people remember, and how they can misremember. Schiffer (2000), for example, refers to 'indigenous theories', in referring to how what people say or write can and often is contradicted by material facts. Graves-Brown (2007a) describes in his study of the AK-47 assault rifle, how it was often claimed that the weapon's design was based on that of the StG44, yet examination of the artefacts indicates only a superficial resemblance. Of course, there are tensions around issues of multivocality, but people do misremember.

Archaeologists have developed a number of techniques to record the observations of contemporary or past occupants of the places they study. Archaeologists often conduct their interviews *in situ*, in the buildings and spaces in which people formerly lived and worked. With the places open and accessible, and the people that occupied them willing to speak, particular insight can be gained from carefully chosen lines of inquiry. In social anthropological practices, some refer to 'bimbling', a methodology described by Jon Anderson (2004) as interviews conducted in and through a place, to generate a collage of collaborative knowledge and give people the opportunity to re-experience their connections with landscape and to reminisce, prompting 'other life-course memories associated with that individual's relationship with place' (p. 258). In Australia, Byrne and Nugent (2004) and Harrison (2004) describe the ways in which aerial photographs were used as the basis for recording oral accounts of the use of portions of the landscape that were subsequently transferred on to a GIS database, as a form of 'landscape biography' or 'geobiography'. Others have referred to similar methodologies as 'story-trekking' across the landscape (see Green, Green, and Neves 2003; Harrison 2005).

Bimbling formed the basis for Schofield and Morrissey's (2007) archaeological investigation of the hidden and 'shameful' places of Valletta, Malta (see further Ch. 8). Here a street in the World Heritage city (Strait Street, also known as The Gut) lies largely abandoned, its former bars, music halls, hotels, and guesthouses and (some say) its brothels empty, closed up as the allied navies left in the 1960s and 1970s. This was a street no one locally dared speak of, such was the stigma attached to the businesses that thrived here. Yet some of those employed in the bars and guest houses still occupy the flats above their former workplaces, living in poverty and largely forgotten by the authorities. These were people whose heritage was unimportant and unmentionable, and who have never been asked about life on the street or why these places mattered to them. But in asking those very questions, answers were forthcoming, especially where people were confronted with the places where they once worked: a space they had not visited for years, even a picture or some distinctive wallpaper unlocking memories and stories, that together revealed values and meanings attached to places on the street. As Andreassen, Bjerck, and Olsen (forthcoming) put it, there exists 'a thing's unique ability to bring forth these memories'. Former sailors, bar workers, and musicians all remember clearly the Egyptian Queen for example, a bar just off Strait Street, its personnel and its unique atmosphere. Being in and around that space and talking to people about it from a position of close proximity brings the potential to reveal more than any detached interview can ever achieve.

There is an argument, introduced earlier, that documents are in some way definitive, telling us all we need to know and removing the need for field investigation. Of course, documents *can* be definitive in terms of what was built at a certain time, and why structures were built in a certain way. Historic maps, drawings, and photographs may also reveal, in minute detail, structural alterations, and even the schemes of decoration: paint colours and so on. For the study of the Second World War in the UK, for example, documents held in the National Archives at Kew (formerly the Public Record Office) contain vast reserves of documentary sources detailing Britain's defence provision, revealing for all the major classes of monument, what was built, where, when, and why (Dobinson, Lake, and Schofield 1997). Similarly, much survives for the study of the Cold War period. Large industrial companies also have archives of documentary sources, many of which are as yet unexplored. These are useful (and generally useable, accessible) resources for research and investigation. However it would be a mistake to assume that documentary sources will always be definitive, that they will provide all we need, and thus render field investigation unnecessary. As for earlier historic periods, documentary sources and field investigation work best together, each testing and extending the other, drawing out comparisons as well as inconsistencies. It is worth noting also, that for many aspects of modern life, documentary sources are not available to us, or are in largely unusable format. Researching the Cold War has involved topics where documentary sources have played little or no part. Work on the Greenham Common and Nevada peace camps, for example, reveals a situation in which the closest the researchers came to documentation was the media reports of the time, and in the case of Greenham, council minutes where actions to remove the peace camps are described. Similarly, research on the Cold War experience in eastern Europe cannot rely on the use of documents, as even where they are suspected to exist, they are usually inaccessible. At the Soviet barracks of Forst Zinna (Boulton 2006), a conscript army comprising many ethnic and language groups was stationed in East Germany, far from home. The abandoned base, investigated after the end of the Cold War, revealed no abandoned documentation with the exception of a few posters, and no clue as to where documents regarding this site might have been deposited. Inertia for this subject amidst many eastern European countries means that historical and archaeological research there is unlikely to locate documentary archives relating to particular sites. It is this circumstance, and the frequent absence also of oral historical sources in these particular situations, that prompted comparison between archaeological research into the Cold War with studies of prehistory, where only the physical evidence remains (Schofield 2005).

DEALING WITH THE WIDER LANDSCAPE

So far in this chapter we have reviewed a range of different ways in which archaeologists approach the process of recording and documenting both artefacts and the remains of recent archaeological sites in the field. In most cases (excepting oral accounts and, to a large extent, archives—which feature in some of the examples of later chapters) approaches derived from the archaeology of more distant time periods have been found to be just as relevant for the recent as for the deeper past. The precise emphasis may be different but in essence the approaches are the same for archaeologies of all periods, and in all places. In Chapter 1, we suggested that one of the distinguishing features of an archaeology of the contemporary past is the way in which it approaches the present as a surface layer, working 'backwards' through time to explore the ways in which the past intervenes in the present, rather than forwards from a point of origin. This means that the archaeology of any time period might be implicated in field research (see also Lucas 2004).

Following that particular line of argument is the wider view of landscape, as seen already in applications of online aerial photographic mapping and investigation, and in Historic Landscape Characterization (HLC), a rapid GIS-based overview of the present landscape and of historic processes that have shaped what exists today (Fairclough 2008; Dingwall and Gaffney 2007). Over the past decade HLC has introduced a coarser-grained view of past human activity, taking the modern landscape as its starting point and identifying human traces and influences that have persisted within it, whether from points of origin in the Bronze Age, in medieval agricultural practices, or the Cold War. Historic Landscape Characterization comprises a holistic, symmetrical view, a view also that fails to recognize conventional distinctions, between 'old' and 'recent' for example, or between designated places and those that have no legal protection. In English Heritage's 'Modern Times' (2007*a*) and *Images of Change* (Penrose 2007), the ubiquitous 'big sheds' are described, a characteristic of later twentieth-century industrial expansion, alongside motorways and airfields, and post-war suburban development. These are ordinary, mundane sorts of places, but that is what gives them interest. These are people's familiar landscapes; the places often representing home, or the homely (after Read 1996). Paul Graves-Brown's (2007*b*) study of an out-of-town retail park at Trostre (south Wales) encapsulates this sense of social significance, as well as being a particularly good example of an archaeological study of a contemporary landscape. We return to this example in Chapter 7.

A consideration of recent work on the town of Milton Keynes, in the UK, illustrates how HLC and the benefits of a Geographical Information System (GIS) can enable the broader landscape view to then be 'excavated' into its various layers or phases, as in the physical act of excavating urban stratigraphy (Green and Kidd 2004). Milton Keynes was the last of several 'new towns' that were created to attempt to deal with housing shortages and to redistribute the population across the UK following the Second World War. Located approximately 70 km north-west of London, it was designated in January 1967, and is unusual for the UK in its design around a regular 1 km street grid (rather than a radial pattern like most of the UK's city centres). The site was chosen to be equidistant from the cities of London, Birmingham, Leicester, Oxford, and Cambridge, with the intention that it would ultimately become a large regional centre. The Milton Keynes Development Corporation who took responsibility for town planning was strongly influenced by Modernist planning principles. In 1967, the area designated for the new city was occupied by approximately 40,000 people spread across three existing towns (Bletchley, Wolverton, and Stony Stratford) and another dozen or so villages in the area. The population of the borough today is over 200,000 people.

Figure 3.6 highlights the twentieth-century landscape character of Milton Keynes. Surprising to some may be the extent of areas where twentieth-century character prevails; but equally surprising for those that know Milton Keynes may be those areas where it does not, where the prevailing character is more historic. Indeed in numerous places around Milton Keynes, and in particular in the built up areas, the well-preserved earthwork remains of medieval settlements and field systems survive, often by virtue of having been designated as scheduled monuments prior to the main building phase of the new town in the 1970s and 1980s. Of course these preserved medieval sites, surrounded by late twentieth-century houses and designed landscapes of retail and leisure, have also now become twentieth-century landscapes, of conservation and of the desire to protect and preserve for the future. The irony now is that the shopping centre at Milton Keynes has also been designated as a building of special historic interest.

A further obvious benefit of GIS and the wider landscape view is the ease with which we as archaeologists, alongside planners and anyone else that cares to look, can view and interpret change. Sheffield is an example of this (see <http://www.sytimescapes.org.uk/>): a major metropolitan area which has seen significant change since the 1970s when a declining steel industry affected change in the city's spatial geography, with retail replacing industry on the city limits for example. The maps in Fig. 3.7, from a project undertaken by Sheffield

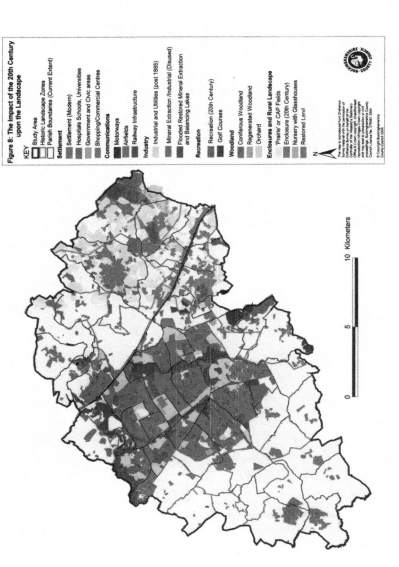

Figure 3.6. Historic Landscape Characterization map of Milton Keynes, England, showing the impact of the twentieth century on the region. (Image courtesy of Buckinghamshire County Council.)

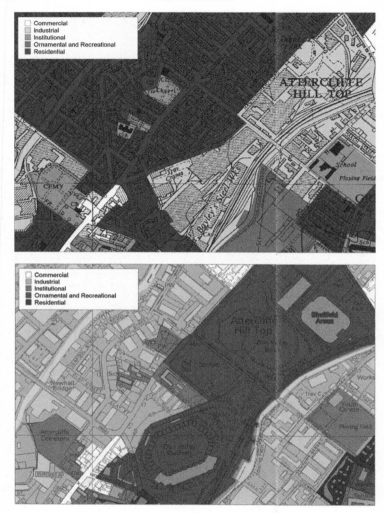

Figure 3.7. How cities have changed in the late modern period. The maps are of Attercliffe, an industrial suburb on the southern flank of the lower Don Valley, in 1958 and 2005. It is an example that captures the essence of much of the most dramatic changes to Sheffield's landscape during this period. (Maps copyright of the South Yorkshire Archaeology Service, 2009. The underlying maps are copyright Ordnance Survey and, for the historic map, Landmark Information Group.)

City Council funded by English Heritage, are of Attercliffe, an industrial suburb of Sheffield on the southern flank of the lower Don Valley in 1958 and 2005 respectively. It is an example that is representative of much of the most dramatic change to Sheffield's landscape during this period, to the industrial river valleys, the working-class housing areas, and the eastern side of the city in general.

We should place this narrow time-slice in a longer-term context of Sheffield's industrial past (after Dan Ratcliffe pers. comm.). Attercliffe was by the eighteenth century a linear settlement along the road now called 'Attercliffe Common'. Its historic core lies to the south-west of this area, which was mostly occupied by 'Attercliffe Common' itself, enclosed by act of parliament in the later eighteenth century. The surviving chapel near the centre of these map extracts is the historic core of the small ancillary hamlet of 'Attercliffe Hill Top' and dates to the late medieval period. The valley's industrial explosion began with the construction of the canal to the south-east in the late eighteenth century and the railway alongside it in the mid nineteenth century. The former common area was well suited to the development of heavy industry due to these transport links and the flat topography (rare in Sheffield) which allowed heavy castings to be moved around large sites. The Brown Bayley's Steel Works was developed for primary steel production and its processing by casting and forging in the late nineteenth century. Housing, much built speculatively and 'back to back', was constructed at much the same time around the earlier historic cores, which as elsewhere were retained as institutional and commercial hubs. As the industries of the valley became less labour intensive and less economically sustainable in the mid to late twentieth century the majority of the valley's housing was demolished, leaving the older historic cores, institutional buildings, pubs, and street patterns. As a result the present industrial areas, which are mostly of 'light industrial' characteristics, retain legibility of the nineteenth-century landscape. Brown Bayleys closed down in 1983, and its cleared site was landscaped and developed for the 1991 World Student Games. The railway track-bed was reused later in the 1990s for the Sheffield Supertram system, whilst the River Don to the north now features an industrial heritage trail.

Characterization is a method of assessing through archaeological and historical geographical principles, what distinctive qualities and characteristics define an area, the extent to which these characteristics are historic, and how one area differs from its immediate neighbours in terms of the historic processes and characteristics that define it. And as a method it can be applied and examined at broad and local scale. As with HLC, the intention with localized characterization studies also is to create a framework within which opportunities for change can be presented to planners, developers, and those charged with designing future landscape, going beyond merely offering the 'constraint' of designation. At RAF Scampton, Lincolnshire, changes to the RAF station could compromise the site's historic fabric and plan form, and thus impact on its historic significance as the base used by the Dam Busters in the Second World War and as a front-line Cold War airbase. It is, as Talbot and Bradley (2006: 43) have said, arguably the best known of all the RAF Bomber Command Airfields in the UK. We will use this example, and that of Bletchley Park, to illustrate the methods by which such site-based characterization studies are undertaken.

As we have seen, characterization studies are essentially straightforward, map-based analytical exercises, in which modern and earlier maps are compared, and the modern landscape 'characterized' according to older patterns of land use that have persisted and remain visible in the landscape today. Each character area has a set of characteristics that can thus be described and mapped (polygonized) in a GIS. For Scampton the study was no different, except that instead of only maps, other historic and archaeological sources were used: a buildings survey previously conducted at the site, and historic plans of airfield development. Groups of technical buildings, domestic areas and associated landscaping, and redundant and undeveloped areas with potential for earlier archaeological remains were identified, with analysis addressing broader and intangible issues that contribute to current perceptions: how far each area is associated with key historical and political events, for example, and whether military technologies are reflected in building design and fabric, and the legibility of the history of each area through architectural details or current use. All of this information is mapped, and included in associated database fields. In addition, phase plans are produced showing the broad physical development of the airfield.

Those with detailed prior knowledge of Scampton may find this approach oversimplifies the reality, and glosses over key points of detail. The benefits however lie in the speed with which these studies can be completed, and thus the number of sites that can be approached in this way, and the degree to which the product is welcomed by planners, owners, and developers. The results of these characterization studies are easy to use, by specialists as research tools and non-specialists for deciding how sites like Scampton can absorb change.

Characterization does not have a single uniform methodology however. The principles are widely held, but details vary. A very different approach was taken at Bletchley Park, Buckinghamshire, a site globally renowned for the achievements of its code-breakers and for their contribution to the outcome of the Second World War, the development of the modern computer, and associated achievements in a range of subjects from mathematics to linguistics (Lake, Monckton, and Morrison 2006: 49; Lake and Hutchings 2009). At Bletchley Park the principles of characterization were adopted but expanded to incorporate what became described as a 'values approach'. This was defined as being based upon a 'clear understanding of the site's character as a product of past change, filtered through an understanding of Bletchley Park's overall cultural values and context, and [identification of the] issues [on which] the perceptions of value held by the wider public and other professional groups converge and diverge. The next step was to determine the extent to which surviving fabric and landscape both informs and reflects these key values' (Lake, Monckton, and Morrison 2006: 50). The point about surviving fabric, and its relationship to the site's functionality, was key, and addressed through a combination of fabric analysis and documentary research. Block D was investigated in this way, and from a combination of these research methods, within the framework of a characterization study, it became possible to describe and analyse the wartime rooms and corridors, and their survival, in a building central to deciphering and analysing German Enigma traffic. This analysis fed into the values paper, and represents an example of how the methodology can inform heritage management decision-making, whether at a local authority (planning) level, or in national (e.g. designation) decisions. It was clear from this study that Block D exemplified through its scale and planning the fusion and integration of signals intelligence that had such an influence on the post-war development of GCHQ...and the US National Security Agency. This heightened the importance of those parts of the internal plan that most clearly exemplify the operations of signals intelligence, including the critical working hub of the Watch sections of Huts 3 and 6.   (ibid. 56)

DISCUSSION

A lesson from Bletchley Park is that, with archaeological research of the contemporary past, what is often needed is an analysis of the

buildings and [the] landscape around them, using the techniques of architectural and archaeological survey in combination with the documentary sources and available oral testimony. None of these techniques could work in isolation: they had to ask questions of themselves and of each other, and set out the basis for unlocking how the site's present character reflects not only wartime but also earlier and later phases in its history.   (ibid.)

Critical among the various considerations we have discussed here is scale, and the research questions one is asking of archaeological material. For determining information about the nature of earthwork or buried remains, all of the usual archaeological methods apply: geophysical survey, earthwork recording, and aerial photography in particular transcend all time periods and geographical areas. For standing buildings too conventional methods are useful, with a focus perhaps on documenting architectural and construction details, and the traces of change and adaptation evident in the fabric, and damage, especially in areas of conflict. A key difference between archaeology of the contemporary past and the record of human activity in earlier periods is the fact that so much survives, and it is here that different and often innovative archaeological approaches can be most helpful. Much of the contemporary past is characterized by a coincidence of place and memory. Mapping memory, and placing narrative in the context of cartographic depictions of place and landscape, create additional layers of meaning and significance. Such 'memory maps' also create a social context for the places that remain. Photography (as we will see in Ch. 4) has a particular part to play in documenting the world around us, and here geographers, artists, and anthropologists have had a prominent role, the results of their endeavours also amounting to an archaeological survey of sorts. A study of RAF Coltishall, involving buildings' recording and three separate but linked artistic representations (e.g. Dunlop 2008) is an example of how the process of change can be documented, as opposed to merely generating 'before' and 'after' photographs which record the process as key stages. Filmmaking is an extension of this, allowing other dimensions of place to be captured: sound for example. Finally, a broader landscape view of the world as we see it today, one that recognizes the historic dimension that still persists to influence present-day landscape character, and is dependent on the new technological capabilities of GIS, provides context and overview, above and beyond the more detailed site-specific work we have described. Landscape characterization may be rapid and coarse-grained, but it is simply and comparatively cheaply repeatable, providing a framework for identifying the predominant landscape character of 'everywhere', and for managing appropriate change in the future. It is these archaeological methods, developed in the context of archaeology of the contemporary past, but arguably with wider implications and applications, that make our subject both an innovative and exciting extension of the ways in which archaeology has been practised in (and on) the past.

CONCLUSIONS

This chapter has sought to review and summarize some of the more significant field methodologies employed by archaeologists working on the late modern period. Beginning with a brief consideration of the nature of the twentieth and twenty-first century archaeological record, we have considered artefact analyses, and then the role of aerial photography as a tool for prospection and site mapping, alongside approaches to field survey for contemporary and recent archaeological sites. We have reviewed traditional and non-traditional forms of excavation in so far as they have been applied to contemporary archaeological sites, noting that excavation as an archaeological method is not limited to buried contexts, but that the systematic recording of context can be applied to a wide range of sites, including mantelpieces and vehicles. We have considered the contribution of oral accounts to the archaeology of the contemporary past, and the role of documentary sources. Finally, we have considered techniques that allow archaeologists to take a landscape approach, recording the contemporary world as an archaeological layer composed of an amalgam of remains from both the deep and more recent past as well as the present.

Clearly, there is no one method for undertaking archaeological studies of the contemporary past, just as this panacea does not exist for archaeological inquiries of any period. As this chapter has shown, archaeologists have adapted existing methodologies developed to research the archaeology of earlier time periods to their work on the recent past. A key feature of the archaeology of the recent and contemporary past as it has developed over the past decade is the extent to which it has also drawn on the ideas and methods of other academic disciplines, a subject we look at in more detail in Chapter 4. Based on the experiences of archaeologists working on contemporary and recent time periods discussed here, in Part II of the book we further examine methods that will be of interest to practitioners embarking on their own research in the field. At this point in time there is an element of the experimental about this: for some topics the usefulness of research techniques is as yet unproven, and only further work will determine how productive some approaches really are. How far will excavation, as traditionally defined and executed, contribute to understanding military actions of the Cold War for example? Such questions remain to be answered by future archaeological research.

4

Working Across Disciplines

INTRODUCTION

In the previous chapter, we considered those methodologies that might be seen to characterize the archaeology of the contemporary past. One of the issues raised there was the extent to which an archaeology of the contemporary past is defined by, and is even reliant upon, working with and across a series of different academic disciplines and areas of subject specialisms. In this chapter, we will look in more detail at the relationship between the archaeology of the contemporary past and the various academic disciplines on which it draws and with which it overlaps. Rather than a field defined by a series of other academic disciplines, we argue that the archaeology of the contemporary past emerges from this review as a discipline characterized by a particular vision and approach to the material culture of the contemporary world. These issues are explored in relation to various examples which illustrate both the similarities and differences between an archaeology of the contemporary past, and those various specialisms with which it has close relations. This chapter will also explore the relationship between the archaeology of the contemporary past and contemporary art, both in terms of artistic engagements with the archaeology of the contemporary past and the idea of archaeology as a form of contemporary artistic practice.

ANTHROPOLOGY AS ARCHAEOLOGY

A number of authors have written in detail about the historical relationship between archaeology and anthropology (e.g. Gosden

1999), and we do not have space to cover the topic in the detail it deserves here. The relationship between archaeology and anthropology is, however, particularly relevant when we are considering the archaeology of the contemporary past, as in almost all instances we are considering the material remains of societies contemporary with us. Archaeology and anthropology, although closely related, have developed along divergent lines in the different countries of the world in which they are practised, so for this reason we will focus our discussion on the historical relationship between archaeology and anthropology in North America and Britain, and the role of an 'anthropological archaeology' in approaches to the archaeology of the contemporary past.

Anthropology is, in its broadest sense, the study of human societies. Within a North American intellectual tradition, it is common to distinguish between the 'four fields' of physical anthropology, cultural anthropology, archaeology, and linguistics (e.g. Keesing 1985). In Britain, it is more common to recognize a top-level division of the fields of physical and cultural anthropology, with cultural anthropology further subdivided into the fields of archaeology, technology studies, ethnology or social anthropology, and sociology (the comparative study of contemporary social phenomena) (Kuper 1996). As Gosden (1999: 119) notes, one of the great divisions within the history of anthropology as a discipline is between social and cultural anthropology. Social anthropology stresses the centrality of social relations to the study of human societies, and is closely associated historically with the work of Pitt-Rivers, Malinowski, and Radcliffe-Brown, who placed the study of kinship in the foreground of the anthropological endeavour (Leach 1982). Cultural anthropology, on the other hand, focuses on the concept of 'culture' and the ways in which relationships between people are reflected by, and maintained through, interrelationships between humans, objects, and the environment. Cultural anthropology is associated historically with the work of Boas and Levi-Strauss. The term 'sociocultural anthropology' is sometimes used to refer to both forms in unison. Contemporary archaeologists tend to be most strongly influenced by the field of cultural anthropology, with its emphasis on material culture and its interest in the historical dimensions of human culture.

Ethnography, or participant observation (the use of fieldwork to produce information for the study of particular human groups), is a core methodology for both social and cultural anthropology. We suggest that we might think of the archaeology of contemporary life as a form of 'archaeoethnography' in which the contemporary world of material and cultural relations forms the object of study. We use the term 'archaeoethnography' to distinguish such a pursuit from ethnoarchaeology, or the interpretation of the archaeological record based on the observation of contemporary relationships between human behaviours and material culture (e.g. David and Kramer 2001; see further Ch. 2). The archaeology of one's own society, then, is always going to be simultaneously archaeology *and* anthropology, because it involves an archaeological approach while also existing as a form of participant observation or ethnographic inquiry into contemporary life. While the concerns of archaeologists tend to overlap most with cultural anthropologists, within the archaeology of the contemporary past we also note that there is significantly greater scope for an archaeological approach to the more traditional interests of social anthropology due to the ability to focus on an 'ethnographic present' in their work.

Gosden (1999) and Trigger (1996) consider in detail the historical relationship between archaeology and sociocultural anthropology. The New Archaeology (see Ch. 2), which emerged first in North America in the late 1950s, was closely linked to the establishment of a connection between archaeology and anthropology (as it was practised in that country at the time) through the emphasis on archaeology as a functionalist anthropological inquiry based on the elucidation of general theories of human cultural behaviour and a broadly evolutionary perspective of human culture (Gosden 1999: 5–6). Nonetheless, as Gosden points out, archaeology and anthropology have grown apart over the past four or five decades in North America due to the divergent interest of anthropologists away from evolutionary frameworks (ibid. 6). In Britain, on the other hand, there has been a long tradition of separation between archaeology and anthropology. This largely persisted up until the 1980s, despite the influence of the New Archaeology. In recent years, British post-processual archaeologies have been involved in a much closer alignment of anthropological and archaeological interests, associated with a greater interest in historical perspectives within anthropology, combined with a shared interest in material culture, landscape and human bodily practices (ibid. 7–8). This contrasts with the situation throughout Europe, Asia, and South Africa and in many New World countries with a younger tradition of archaeology such as Australia and New Zealand, where there is generally a large disciplinary gulf between archaeology and anthropology as academic disciplines.

Much of the work that has emerged within the last twenty years or so on how to approach doing anthropology within one's own society would seem extremely relevant to the archaeology of the contemporary past as a form of archaeoethnography or autoarchaeology (Harrison and Schofield 2009). 'Autoethnography' is a term that has come to denote the anthropological investigation of the self using ethnographic methodologies (e.g. Reed-Danahay 1997; Ellis 2004; Chang 2008). It differs from traditional anthropological research in the sense in which it takes for its focus the author's subjective experience rather than the beliefs and practices of others, and relates to a broader movement within sociocultural anthropology that is increasingly concerned with the relationship between the self and fieldwork (e.g. Coffey 1999; Young and Goulet 1998) and the dialectical relationship between anthropological subjects and anthropologists themselves (e.g. Clifford 1988, 1997).

Autoethnography shares with the archaeology of the contemporary past a broad interest in the relationship between researcher and subject, and the subjective experience of research. We use the term 'autoarchaeology', after autoethnography, to refer specifically to investigations into the archaeology of the self. Some examples of autoarchaeology are discussed further in Chapter 6. Other examples include Schofield's (2009c) investigation of the archaeology of the former English Heritage office in Savile Row in London where he had worked.

ARCHAEOLOGY AND MODERN MATERIAL CULTURE STUDIES

We have already mentioned the influence of the field of 'material culture studies' on the archaeology of the contemporary past (Ch. 2).

In this section we will trace the influences and divergent interests of several distinct fields of study that are concerned with contemporary material culture—anthropological material culture studies, Science and Technology Studies (STS), Social Construction of Technology (SCOT) studies, and cultural studies—and their relationship to an archaeology of contemporary life.

Material Culture Studies

As Buchli (2002: 2) notes, the field of research now known as material culture studies emerged from the study of collections held in the great Euro-American museums of the nineteenth century. These collections, which were the creation of a series of ideas about the relationships between human cultures and the material world (e.g. Bennett 1995; Russell 2001), informed the development of the field of anthropology throughout the nineteenth and early twentieth centuries, and were intimately linked to various linear evolutionary views of progress and human culture. The field declined with a lessening of emphasis on these ideas themselves and the rise of a new field of social anthropology which was less focused on the material world and more interested in the social (Gosden 1999: 33ff.). Nonetheless, a material thread in anthropological thought continued throughout the mid twentieth century, which Buchli (2002) associates particularly with the work of the British Marxist archaeologist Gordon Childe. The contemporary field of material culture studies emerged in Britain during the 1970s and 1980s amongst a group of archaeologists inspired by a Marxist approach at University College London and the University of Cambridge, and in the work of Peter Ucko (e.g. 1969) and Mary Douglas (e.g. Douglas and Isherwood 1979) and others at the Department of Anthropology at University College London at the same time. This emergence was associated with the ascendant interest in semiotics (e.g. Baudrillard 1968) and structuralism within archaeology and anthropology in the US and UK (e.g. see Stocking 1985; Kopytoff 1986; Appadurai 1986; Miller 1987; Gell 1988; Tilley 1990). The term 'material culture studies' has come to be particularly associated with the work of scholars such as Daniel Miller (e.g. 1987, 1995, 1998*a, b,*

2005*a*, *b*), Alfred Gell (1988, 1992, 1996, 1998), Christopher Tilley (1990, 1999; see also Tilley et al. 2006) and others.

Miller (2005*a*: 1) describes the aim of material culture studies as the integration of specialized approaches to the study of individual items of material culture themselves, such as materials conservation or typological analyses, with more anthropological or sociological frames of reference which utilize semiological or symbolic analyses of material culture. It is possible to argue, following Buchli and Lucas (2001*a*), that the line between material culture studies and the archaeology of the contemporary past is blurred, at best (if not entirely non-existent). Others have sought to make a clear distinction between the two approaches. For example, Shanks and Tilley ([1987] 1992: 172) characterized the difference between material culture studies and the archaeology of the contemporary past as being one in which material culture studies consider the discourses around material things, whereas archaeology looks at the things themselves. Similarly, Graves-Brown (2000*a*: 1) sees a deficiency in material culture studies in their lack of attention to 'artefacts in themselves—essentially the triumph of surfaces of things over what they can do'. A similar critique of the focus on discourse and 'the social' in social archaeology has been levelled by Webmoor and Witmore (2008). However, many contemporary material culture studies are interested as much in the materiality of objects as in the discourses that surround them (e.g. Attfield 2000; Hallam and Hockey 2001; Küchler 2002; Tilley 2004).

There are many important insights for contemporary archaeologists in the field of material culture studies. Material culture studies apply an explicitly comparative perspective (Miller 2005*a*: 2–3), and in this sense, help to foreground the relationship between the local and the global. Material culture studies also consider the field of 'material culture' as an invention of a particular mode of thinking within social and cultural anthropology (Buchli 2002). As Buchli notes, no one sets out to 'create' material culture; instead, people make objects that are useful and meaningful within their own cultural milieu and are transformed into 'material culture' once removed from that context and studied by anthropologists. This mirrors contemporary archaeologists' interests in archaeology as a social and political practice. As Lucas (2004: 117) has suggested, prehistoric stone tools should be considered contemporary objects as much as mobile phones and cars are, as they are a creation of the archaeological imagination and forms of archaeological categorization in the present (cf. Piccini and Holtorf 2009: 14). Nonetheless, material culture studies remain primarily anthropological in their approach, and do not necessarily directly intervene in the material world in the same way that archaeology does. We have already argued that there are particular methodologies that define an archaeology of the contemporary past (see Ch. 3), including the use of excavation and the principles of stratigraphy and seriation, and this continues to be a useful way of defining the differences between the archaeology of the contemporary past and other forms of modern material culture studies.

Science and Technology Studies (STS) and Actor Network Theory (ANT)

We have already mentioned the influence of Science and Technology Studies (STS) (e.g. Latour and Woolgar 1979; Latour 1987; 1993, 1996, 1999, 2005; Bijker, Hughes, and Pinch 1989; Callon 1989; Callon, Law, and Rip 1986; Woolgar 1991; Law 1992, 1993, 2002, 2004; Law and Bijker 1992; Bijker 1995; Law and Hassard 1999) on the archaeology of the contemporary past in Chapter 2. One of the most relevant areas of STS to archaeology is Actor Network Theory (ANT). ANT was developed by French STS scholars Bruno Latour and Michael Callon and British sociologist John Law as an approach to address the ways in which the material and cultural simultaneously work together. Latour (2005) notes that the term 'social' has come to mean both a process of assembling groups of people and a type of material, arguing that the social sciences should not be concerned with establishing the correct frame of reference for understanding social relations, but should be concerned with tracing networks of connection. He terms this approach the 'sociology of associations'.

It should be the simplest thing in the world. We are all bound by social interactions; we all live in society; and we are all cultural animals. Why do these ties remain so elusive? ... [O]ne reason has been offered up as an explanation. The adjective 'social' designates two entirely different phenomena: it's at once a *substance*, a kind of stuff, and also a *movement* between non-social elements. In both cases, the social vanishes . . . it's traceable only when it's being modified.   (ibid. 159)

Latour maps out a series of strategies for making the social traceable, including a focus on the local sites where the global is in the process of being assembled (and the actors involved in the production of social processes or movements), to look at the ways in which the local itself is generated, and to study the connections between these sites.

[T]he question of the social emerges when the ties in which one is entangled begin to unravel; the social is further detected through the surprising movements from one association to the next; those movements can either be suspended or resumed; when they are prematurely suspended, the social as normally construed is bound together with already accepted participants called 'social actors' who are members of a 'society'; when the movement toward collection is resumed, it traces the social as associations through many non-social entities which might become participants later; if pursued systematically, this tracking may end up in a shared definition of a common world, what I have called a collective; but if there are no procedures to render it common, it may fail to be assembled.   (ibid. 247)

An important aspect of ANT is the contention that objects have agency and can be thought of as 'actors' in tracing these networks of association. This contention calls to mind the important work of anthropologist Alfred Gell (1992, 1996, 1998), whose work has been cited widely within the field of material culture studies to argue the active role that objects can play in social relations between humans. Latour differs from Gell in seeing objects as having agency that exists independently of human actors (or in Gell's terms, 'the artist') because ANT defines 'the social' in a unique way. The term does not define a field or a quality of a particular thing, but instead refers to

a movement, a transformation . . . an association between entities which are in no way recognizable as being social in the ordinary manner except during the brief moment when they are reshuffled together. To pursue the metaphor of a supermarket, we would call 'social' not any specific shelf or aisle, but the multiple modifications made throughout the whole place in the organization of all the goods—their packaging, their pricing, their labelling—because those minute shifts reveal to the observer which new combinations are explored and which paths will be taken (what later will be defined as a 'network'). Thus, social, for ANT, is the name of a momentary association which is characterized by the way it gathers together into new shapes. (Latour 2005: 65)

Latour uses the term 'actor' or 'actant' to stand for anything that modifies any particular state of affairs. Thinking this way shifts the emphasis from what objects 'symbolize' (as if the social field were somehow closed, or a 'done deal') to the ways in which material objects are involved in particular forms of interactions that create social 'features' such as inequalities in power or networks of social connection. We can trace the creation of these social features by looking to the shifts or movements in which the social becomes visible (or traceable) and new combinations of associations are made available to social groups by looking at the associations they choose to explore. Such an approach would allow archaeologists of the contemporary past to overcome the criticism of some anthropological material culture studies that has been raised by Graves-Brown (2000*a*), for example, of a focus on objects as texts, instead allowing them to trace transformations that occur in widely spaced networks and imagined landscapes.

But perhaps more importantly, the seriousness with which 'things' are treated within ANT raises the possibility of a consideration of the fundamental ontological indivisibility of objects and humans (Webmoor and Witmore 2008: 59) and the ways in which human and non-human agents are mixed together as part of a process by which the present is continually recreated through the networks of association that constitute everyday life. This way of thinking provides fertile ground for archaeologists of the contemporary past to refocus attention on the important role of materiality and non-human agency in the late modern period. Some of the implications of a theoretical approach that considers the symmetrical relationships of agency that exist between humans and the realm of material culture are discussed further in the case studies in Chapters 6 and 9. Approaches that consider the agency of non-human actors, including material objects (e.g. Graves-Brown 2007*a*) and animals (e.g. May

2009), are becoming increasingly common within the emerging field of the archaeology of the contemporary past.

Another important contribution of ANT to the archaeology of the contemporary past is the way it seeks to deal with the complex, fluid, elusive, and 'messy' nature of the contemporary world. The archaeology of the contemporary past is characterized on the one hand by an excess of material and information, and on the other by often vague, ephemeral, marginal, and hidden aspects of the material world. The work of sociologist John Law (e.g. 2004) is concerned not with minimizing complexity and 'mess', but with reconceptualizing research methods to enable them to deal with vague, ephemeral, and multiple realities. Indeed, Law (2004: 141–54) argues that research methods in the social sciences have been responsible for the creation of their own orderly results; they are performative and blinkered, and constitute a particular (modernist) way of framing the object of research. Law argues that we might begin to conceptualize alternative forms of research method—that emphasize process over product, that aim for symmetry and acknowledge multiplicity, that are reflexive and imaginary, that accept a degree of indefiniteness and which might undermine the dualities of 'good' and 'bad', 'natural' and 'cultural', 'active' and 'passive', and 'us' and 'Other' that have underpinned much research in the social sciences. We attempt to respond to this challenge in some of the case studies that form Part II of this book.

Social Construction of Technology (SCOT) Studies

Social construction of technology (SCOT) studies refers to a field of sociology closely related to STS that is concerned with explaining processes of technological change and the relationships between technology and society. SCOT holds that the relative 'success' of technologies cannot be understood through a consideration of technology alone, but resides as much in the social and political context of the reception and perpetuation of technology as it does in the function of technological objects themselves (Bijker, Hughes, and Pinch 1989). This research field is also commonly referred to as 'constructivist studies of technology' and is based in a historical and sociological approach to the material world of technology (Bijker 1995: 6). 'Constructivist studies of technology strive not to consider the fact that a machine "works" as an explanation, but to address it as a subject requiring explanation. In this approach, machines "work" because they have been accepted by relevant social groups' (ibid. 270).

SCOT is associated with a particular set of methods that structures its approach to the study of material culture. In the SCOT model, the development process of a particular artefact is seen as a process of variation and selection (Pinch and Bijker 1989). Central to these methods is the view that it is not only inventors, but all groups within society that contribute to the development of new technologies. Instead of mapping the development of a technology as a linear process in which the outcome is a result of scientific experimentation and the failure of less successful variants, SCOT studies analyse technological developments from a multidirectional model that does not assume a particular outcome as taken for granted or technologically determined. By identifying the relevant social groups who are users of a particular artefact, it is possible to model a series of problems raised for each group. The study of the asymmetrical relationships of power and economics help us to understand the ability of these groups to influence technological adaptations that are made to solve these problems. A phase of closure or stabilization of technology follows an experimental phase, in which the relevant social groups come to understand any controversy over the function of a piece of technology to be solved (rhetorical closure) or during which the problem the technology originally sought to address is redefined. At this stage, the form of technology becomes relatively stable, and it is accepted as a 'successful' invention.

Pinch and Bijker (1989; see also Bijker 1995) discuss the case of the development of the bicycle and apply a SCOT methodology to its development. They note that by identifying different 'relevant social groups' (defined as groups of individuals who share the same set of meanings that are attached to a particular technology or artefact) we can identify different problems for each of these groups, and the various solutions to these problems. These solutions and problems might not always be technical, but could also be economic, judicial, or moral. In the case of the bicycle, we see a history of the emergence of a bicycle with a small front-wheel diameter only after an initial increase and subsequent decrease in front wheel size. Prior to the 1860s, two-wheeled 'running machines' were popular, in which the wheels turned freely and the 'bike' was propelled by the feet making contact with the ground. In the 1860s, the velocipede was invented, in which the (larger) front wheel was powered directly by the circular rotation of the feet on pedals. For various social reasons, bicycling became associated with athletic, sporting display, and the size of the front wheel of the bicycle increased to reflect its status as a difficult, skilful sport (as in the 'penny farthing'). These early bikes presented several problems to users—middle-aged and older users found them difficult to mount and ride, women with long skirts found them impossible to ride without exposing their legs, and others found the vibrations caused by the contact of the metal wheels with small rocks and other obstacles unbearable. A wide range of solutions to these problems were sought, giving rise to a series of different bike forms and mechanical innovations. A series of new designs existed in competition for the approval of the various users. The eventual acceptance of the low front-wheeled safety bicycle relied on the acceptance of the air tyre, not for the original problem it was invented to address (vibration) but through the creation of a new bicycle form. Through the mounting of the air tyre on a racing bicycle, this new technology became associated not with anti-vibration, but with enhanced speed. The adoption of the air tyre favoured the acceptance of the low-wheeled variety of bicycle, leading to the phasing out of high-wheeled penny farthings and ultimately to the shape and design of bicycle with which we are familiar today.

SCOT methods hold various insights that might be useful for an archaeology of contemporary material culture. SCOT studies remind us of the importance of the social context of technology, and the ways in which decisions about the adoption of material culture are often structured around social and economic factors as much as technological ones. Indeed, such an approach can be seen to underpin contemporary archaeological practices (e.g. papers in Graves-Brown 2000*b*; Buchli and Lucas 2001*d*; and Piccini and Holtorf 2009). In addition, we might also consider the potential overlap with the work of various historians of technology, especially Langdon Winner, a political scientist whose 'Do Artifacts Have Politics' (1980) is widely cited, and Brian Pfaffenberger's work on the social anthropological aspects of technology (e.g. 1992, 1998, 2001).

Cultural Studies

While STS, ANT, and SCOT represent one set of approaches to contemporary material culture that have emerged from sociology, it is also possible to distinguish an alternative approach to material culture that is concerned with the ways in which the cultural practices of institutions and individuals are mediated with reference to material objects. 'Cultural studies' is an interdisciplinary academic field of research that emerged in Britain in the 1960s and is closely associated with the work of scholars such as Raymond Williams (e.g. 1966), Richard Hoggart (e.g. 1969) and Stuart Hall (e.g. 1997). It takes for its subject the social and political context of 'culture' and the relationship between cultural practices and power (or authority) in society.

The cultural studies approach to contemporary material culture is perhaps best illustrated by the work of Stuart Hall and colleagues in their study of the Sony Walkman (Du Gay et al. 1997). In attempting to chart the influence of the Sony Walkman on contemporary culture, they identify a series of five linked cultural processes that can be used to structure the study of any contemporary text or artefact. These cultural processes—representation, identity, production, consumption, and regulation—are said to belong to a 'cultural circuit', suggesting that it is impossible to understand the cultural role of contemporary artefacts or texts unless the relationship between the object and all five cultural processes is examined. In the case of the Sony Walkman, the authors argue that to study it culturally, 'one should at least explore how it is represented, what social identities are associated with it, how it is produced and consumed, and what mechanisms regulate its distribution and use' (p. 3).

Du Gay et al. (pp. 4–5) suggest that the 'meaning' of the Sony Walkman does not arise from the object itself, but from the ways in which it is *represented* in oral and visual language. The meaning of the Sony Walkman is initially fluid but is made permanent through its representation in the media and advertising, but also through its particular associations with individuals in society as a result of these representations. A consideration of the way in which the Sony Walkman is produced culturally (as opposed to physically) demonstrates how material objects are encoded with particular meanings as a part of both their physical and cultural production process, and their relationship with individual *identity*. In addition to the production of individual and group identity, representations of the Sony Walkman are also used in the production of a corporate identity for Sony as a company. The authors then consider the ways in which the processes of *production* and *consumption* are articulated through the design process in which an identification between the objects and a particular set of consumers is established. The articulation of production and consumption is also noted as a strategy by Sony to develop a 'cultural package' of combined software and hardware that relates to their efforts to become a global entertainment corporation. They chart the ways in which meanings continue to be made by consumers independently of those encoded by producers, and the ways in which consumers produce new meanings for objects through the uses to which they are put in everyday life. Finally, they explore the influence of the Sony Walkman on the *regulation* of cultural life, suggesting that it challenges the distinction between public and private space and leads to the development of new institutions to regulate its usage, which have subsequently influenced the design and production of the Walkman by Sony (p. 5).

In relation to the work of sociologists Hoggart and Hall, we should also mention another Birmingham University Centre for Contemporary Cultural Studies researcher, the British sociologist Dick Hebdige, whose book *Subculture: The Meaning of Style* ([1979] 1988), was influential in the development of a field of subculture studies and focused attention on the material aspects of black and white youth cultures in Britain in the 1970s. Hebdige's work has been widely cited within archaeology (e.g. Schofield 2000). Occupying a more literary area of cultural studies is the 'Thing theory' of Bill Brown (2001), Professor of English at the University of Chicago, which explores the ways in which particular objects become 'things' through a process by which they are set apart from their context and the fascination for particular 'things' in literature and culture.

It is worth reflecting briefly here on the extent to which similar approaches to the study of contemporary material culture appear to have arisen independently within the field of the archaeology of the contemporary past itself. There are a number of points of similarity, for example, between SCOT methodologies and the approach of archaeologist Michael Schiffer in his study of the portable radio (1991). In this study, Schiffer explores the history of the portable radio in America and the ways in which its technology has responded to consumer preference, how its spread might be understood to relate to that of linked forms of technology, and how what he terms inaccurate corporate 'cryptohistory' is responsible for the widespread belief that the portable radio was invented in Japan. While his approach to the radio's adoption as a technology is similar to SCOT studies, his discussion of cryptohistory and the role of the consumer might be seen to employ similar methods to the cultural studies discussed above in relation to the Sony Walkman. We think it fair to say that many of these methods that have subsequently become associated with different disciplines were developed or explored independently in the work of early contemporary archaeologists such as Schiffer, albeit with slightly different emphases. In this sense, we argue that the archaeology of the contemporary past as a field should not be seen as defined by the methodologies of other disciplines, but as an arena for interdisciplinary experimentation with method that is characterized by a particular vision and approach to the material culture of the contemporary world.

PSYCHOLOGY AND CONTEMPORARY MATERIAL CULTURE STUDIES

Another area of scholarly research in which the study of contemporary material culture has formed an important focus and that has informed aspects of the archaeology of the contemporary past is the study of cognitive and behavioural psychology. Psychological theories on material culture use were introduced explicitly to archaeologists of the contemporary past in a chapter (Williams and Costall 2000) that appeared in Graves-Brown's (2000*b*) *Matter, Materiality and Modern Culture*. In the chapter, the authors considered the issue of 'materiality' within social psychology through a case study of the ways in which psychologists have theorized autism and autistic people's relationships with material culture. The chapter considers the wider background of ecological psychology, an area concerned with the ways in which humans come to understand the preferred functions and meanings of material things through the mediation of other humans. For example, children are taught preferred functions of objects through the encouragement and sanction of parents. They cite psychologist James J. Gibson's theory of affordance (1979), which describes the qualities of an object that allow particular actions to be performed by individuals using or within proximity of it. Gibson's work on affordance has been influential in archaeology and has been cited by anthropologists who are interested in human perception of the environment such as Tim Ingold (e.g. 2000), but is potentially useful in exploring the possibilities inherent in contemporary material culture and in shifting our attention away from the mediation of material culture by way of signs and symbols to focus instead on the 'material' capabilities of technology. This is particularly the case for the more 'socialized' model of affordance advocated by Williams and Costall (2000: 106ff.; Costall 1995) in which consideration is also given to the sociocultural context of learning object use, in addition to the affordances of objects themselves. You will recall that a shift away from individual structures of meaning towards a focus on the external agency of material objects themselves also forms a central part of the writing around ANT discussed earlier in this chapter.

Other work in psychology that has relevance to the study of contemporary material culture includes the work of Soviet psychologists Lev Vygotsky and Aleksei N. Leontiev, whose writing was rediscovered in the 1960s and has been applied to the study of early tool use, language, and human behaviour (and forms the basis for Ecological Systems Theory), but would be equally relevant to the study of modern material culture use, as would be other linked work on skilled practice and situated learning by social anthropologist Jean Lave.

Vygotsky was concerned with the ways in which children learned how to undertake particular tasks, observing the ways in which tasks involving material culture are culturally mediated and learned through guided participation. Vygotsky's work has influenced studies in cognitive anthropology (e.g. Dougherty 1985; Keller and Keller 1996) in the relationship between culture and human thought. Similarly, Blandine Bril who collaborates with French ethnoarchaeologist Valentine Roux (previously introduced in Ch. 2) is a psychologist, and her work has in turn had an influence on the field of ethnoarchaeology in relation to cognition and tool use (e.g. see Roux, Bril, and Dietrich 1995; Bril and Roux 2002; Roux and Bril 2005).

We might also consider the potential for engaging the theories of Hungarian psychologist Mihaly Csikszentmihalyi on 'flow' (1990, 1996), described as the optimal state of activity when people are so focused on a task at hand that they become absorbed by it, a state that some might describe as being 'in the groove' or 'in the flow'. Csikszentmihalyi suggests that such a state is reached when a balance is struck between the challenge of a task and the skill of the person performing it. Flow theory has been used to explore processes of creativity and innovation, but would be equally applicable to understanding engagements between humans and complex, multifaceted contemporary technologies. We suggest that, in general, the potential for using psychological theory within archaeological studies of the contemporary past has been under-realized, but see this as a situation that will change as the work of behavioural and cognitive psychologists on learning and material culture use becomes more widely known in archaeological circles.

ARCHAEOLOGY AS ART, ART AS ARCHAEOLOGY

We have been arguing throughout the last two chapters that it is the application of what we would recognize as 'archaeological' method and the 'archaeological gaze' to the remains of the contemporary past that defines the subject above all else. What is interesting about the archaeology of the contemporary past is the way in which the application of an archaeological recording method to particular sorts of surprisingly prosaic modern site draws attention to the ways in which archaeology could be thought of as 'performance', and politicizes the archaeology of the contemporary past and its objects of study in very specific ways (see also Ch. 5). The shock of seeing an archaeologist recording or excavating an object or building that we think of as 'modern' using the same techniques that might be applied to a prehistoric site draws the nature of the past and the way that we engage with it into sharp relief.

As we have argued above, because the archaeology of the contemporary past takes for its subject the material legacy of the recent past, it must necessarily be cross-disciplinary. Some of the most fruitful collaborations in the archaeology of the contemporary past are emerging from the engagement of archaeology with art as a way of documenting and representing the recent past (e.g. Pearson and Shanks 2001; Jameson, Ehrenhard, and Finn 2003; Finn 2004; see further discussion in Edmonds and Evans 1991; Renfrew 2003; Schofield 2006, 2009*b*: 185ff.; Piccini and Holtorf 2009). Colin Renfrew (2003) has argued that the aims of archaeologists (of both the deep and recent past) can be understood to converge with the aims of visual artists in that they both seek to answer questions that are fundamental to an understanding of who we are as humans through a consideration of the past, present, and future. He compares and contrasts the way in which contemporary artists seek to understand the world by acting on it, and the way archaeologists seek to understand the world through the material traces of such actions.

Renfrew (2003: 8) suggests that while archaeologists have invested time and energy in the technical aspects of excavating and documenting the remains of the human past, our understanding of the past is actually very limited, restricted as it is to what we know about human societies in the present. He proposes that contemporary art offers archaeologists fresh insights into the relationship between people and the world that might help them to understand and analyse human relationships with each other and the material world in the past in new and innovative ways. Renfrew considers the ways in which a certain school of post-war contemporary art, which he terms 'process art', has been as interested in the engagement between artist and material world through the process of creating an artwork as with the end product itself.

He suggests that this parallels the process by which archaeologists are enmeshed in engagements with the material world as a result of their own fieldwork, and seeks to draw greater attention to the sensual and material processes by which they work as an integral part of the process of archaeological knowledge formation (Renfrew 2003: 103–6; see also Shanks 1992, 2004; Pearson and Shanks 2001; Lucas 2004).

We argue here that the archaeology of the contemporary past has a special relationship to contemporary artistic practice. Indeed, the earliest appearance of the phrase in the sense in which we use it here belongs to the establishment in 1966 of an Institute of Contemporary Archaeology by a group of artists based in London (Schofield 2006, 2009*b*: 185; Piccini and Holtorf 2009: 15–16), reflecting the close relationship between contemporary artistic practice and archaeologies of the contemporary past. Boyle Family, a group of collaborative artists, established the Institute to give context and identity to their work 'Dig', albeit as a 'light-hearted institution with no particular membership' (Elliott 2003: 15–16). As Sebastian Boyle has recounted: 'it fitted in with our approach of trying to be objective, to see the world as it is, accepting reality and not trying to embellish it for the sake of art' (Schofield 2009*b*: 185). He recently explained further how each one of their Earth Pieces is the product of an attempt to reproduce a single 'quadrat' of the Earth's surface, sampled randomly as in an archaeological survey (Sebastian Boyle pers. comm. 7 June 2009). Chris Townsend (2008) describes the intellectual project of the Institute of Contemporary Archaeology in ways eerily reminiscent of the new agenda that emerged for the archaeology of the contemporary past at the turn of the millennium (see also Fig. 4.1).

In the mid-1960s, one of the titles under which the group of artists we now know as Boyle Family worked was the Institute of Contemporary Archaeology. As Mark Boyle has often remarked, 'the billing was not really an issue for us, our primary objective was to make work, our second was to survive.' Nonetheless in the concept of a group of artists working as 'archaeologists', isolating fragments of the past and returning it to public attention, we begin to have an understanding of the Boyle's project. Boyle Family—Mark, Joan, Sebastian, Georgia—is who they are, but Archaeology, of a sort, is what they do. But unlike academic archaeologists, or indeed those artists from Paul

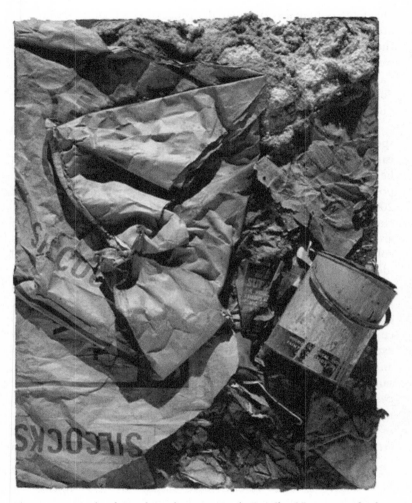

Figure 4.1. Norland Road Study 1964, Boyle Family. (Courtesy of Sebastian Boyle.)

Nash to Richard Long working in that well-defined if minor British tradition that uses the excavated past in representing the landscape, Boyle Family operates through a paradox. What they expose for re-evaluation, for re-placing in the value structures of contemporary culture, is not the salvage of the past, but fragments recovered from the detritus of the present. When I see these frighteningly exact, one might say, in the manner in which they are conceptualised, photographic, reproductions of tiny fragments of our built environment, or of the natural world, I'm reminded especially of the fragments of Roman mosaic which we so often exhibited in our museums in this way... The archaeology which the Boyles undertake is to reach into that pile of debris, the wreckage which modernity leaves in its wake, and yet which, in its aggregate it incessantly contemplates, and *restore to our attention that which has been discarded or neglected, that which, even if we have not thrown it away, is so familiar that it is outside our gaze*, so quotidian that we tread on it unthinking, because we have better things to think about.

(emphasis ours)

We have already seen in Chapter 2 the ways in which Buchli and Lucas (2001*a*) emphasized the role of the archaeology of the contemporary past in bringing to light that which had been forgotten or neglected, and Graves-Brown's (2000*a*) suggestion that the archaeology of the contemporary past made the familiar 'unfamiliar'.

This early articulation of a need for an archaeological approach to the present from within the discipline of artistic practice, as exemplified by the work of Boyle Family, suggests that we might fruitfully explore the relationship between the archaeology of the contemporary past and contemporary art in more detail here. One of us (Schofield 2009*b*: 185ff.) has recently defined three areas where the interface of archaeology and art might be explored:

- art as an archaeological record (i.e. an archaeology of art),
- archaeological investigation as performance (i.e. archaeology as art), and
- art as interpretation, narrative, and characterization (i.e. art as archaeology).

In the paragraphs below, we will explore in more detail these three areas where archaeology and contemporary art overlap.

Art as an Archaeological Record

In thinking of art as an archaeological record, we consider the ways in which archaeological methods could be used in the investigation of contemporary art as a social and physical phenomenon of the contemporary world. For example, we could look at the painting by Anselm Kiefer titled *Nigredo*, held in the collection of the Philadelphia Museum of Art, which performs a sort of reverse archaeology by building up complex layers of straw and paint on the canvas to represent a German landscape. Like an archaeological representation of this landscape, it is not reportage (but see further discussion later in this chapter), as it is separated by time, but it seeks to represent a historical space in ways that allow the viewer to read or understand intention, and stresses the distance in time and space between the viewer and the historic landscape. Indeed, what is interesting in Kiefer's work from an archaeological perspective is that it encourages what we might consider to be an archaeological approach to art criticism, being constructed as it is with a complex stratigraphy that could reveal obscured aspects of the image. This raises another potential collaboration between archaeology and art criticism, in presenting new readings of artwork using archaeological methods— the idea of actually 'excavating' a painting like this as an archaeological 'site', and documenting the resulting excavation in order to understand better the way in which it was put together. Of course, art historians often use non-destructive methods such as x-ray imaging to look beneath the surface of paintings such as this—and this itself mirrors the use of archaeological prospection methods such as ground penetrating radar and aerial photography—but the idea of 'excavating' a piece of contemporary art such as *Nigredo* serves as a symbol for a potential collaboration between archaeologists and artists in which art objects are considered to be simply another part of the archaeological record of contemporary life.

A recent collaboration of this kind saw the excavation, recording, and reconstruction of the artist Francis Bacon's studio, which was excavated and disassembled in its original location in 7 Reece Mews, South Kensington, London, before being transported and reassembled in the Drury Lane Gallery in Dublin (Campbell 2000; Bradley 2005; Cappock 2005; see Figs. 4.2 and 4.3). Francis Bacon is considered to be one of the most important post-war painters, and is perhaps best known for his painting *Triptych, May–June 1973*, which documents his lover George Dyer's suicide by drug overdose on the eve of Bacon's retrospective at the Grand Palais in Paris in October 1971.

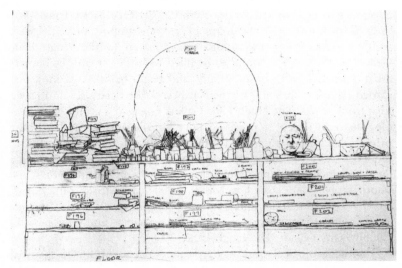

Figure 4.2. Archaeological elevation showing the interior wall of Francis Bacon's studio prior to excavation, drawn by Edmond O'Donovan. (Collection: Dublin City Gallery The Hugh Lane. Copyright: Dublin City Gallery The Hugh Lane.)

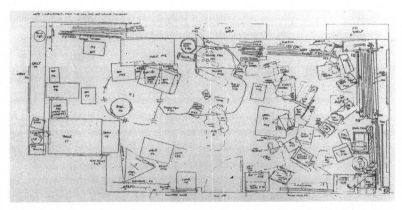

Figure 4.3. Archaeological site plan of the excavation of Francis Bacon's studio, drawn by Edmond O'Donovan. (Collection: Dublin City Gallery The Hugh Lane. Copyright: Dublin City Gallery The Hugh Lane.)

Bacon lived and worked in the studio at 7 Reece Mews from 1961 until his death in 1992, and many of his most important works were painted there. When the studio was donated to the Hugh Lane Gallery in 1998, it was found to be filled with the remains of Bacon's artistic practice—torn photographs and pages from magazines, discarded paint brushes and pigment tubes, slashed canvases and leaves torn from books. The Hugh Lane Gallery engaged a group of archaeologists to document in precise detail all of the remains in the studio, prior to excavating them and removing them for reconstruction in Dublin. Over 7,000 items were documented, mapped, and logged in a database, including 'approximately 570 books and catalogues, 1,500 photographs, 100 slashed canvases, 1,300 leaves torn from books, 2,000 artist's materials and 70 drawings. Other categories include the artist's correspondence, magazines, newspapers and vinyl records' (Dublin City Gallery The Hugh Lane, 2008).

The archaeological work at the Francis Bacon studio has allowed archaeologists and art historians to explore spatial and chronological relationships between pigments through the study of discarded paint tubes and paints, and Bacon's 'creative process' through the study of the juxtaposition of items within the studio. For example, Cappock (2005) notes that there was no artist's palette found in the studio, but that various materials, including the walls themselves, were clearly used for mixing paints. Examples of materials used in place of paintbrushes, such as pieces of corduroy fabric and old socks, as well as various shapes (including cut-out images of George Dyer's head) used as stencils were also recovered. Such finds provide a tangible insight into Bacon's artistic practice. The archaeologists were also able to establish, amidst what initially appeared to be a chaotic jumble of paint, brushes, and canvases, the existence of distinct 'activity areas' where the artist 'painted, stored his paint brushes and canvases, where he kept and analysed source material, such as his collection of books, photos, sketches and even where he discarded empty champagne bottles' (Dawson and Cappock 2001: 20 cited in Bradley 2005: 8). Associations between particular images known to be the sources of inspiration for particular paintings have been made with other, unknown sources, allowing a better picture to emerge of the history and inspiration for particular paintings as a result of stratigraphic and contextual analysis of the archaeological remains (Bradley 2005: 9).

Blaze O'Connor (2008; following Cappock 2005) suggests that Bacon's studio was intentionally created to be the artistic equivalent of an archaeological 'midden' as it allowed Bacon constantly to encounter 'traces' that formed a source of inspiration as part of his artistic practice (see also Bradley 2005: 5). Such an interpretation may not have been possible without the archaeological focus on the material remains of Bacon's studio. Another point raised by O'Connor is the way in which the apparently 'scientific' exploration of the studio attributes value to the remains, which are seen to be worthy of attention. In this way, she draws attention to the way in which the archaeology of the contemporary past is a form of performance (a theme already pre-empted in our discussion of Renfrew's work above and explored further below).

Another application of archaeology to the field of art is found in the archaeological study of graffiti. For example, Cassidy Curtis (<www.grafarc.org>) has produced an interactive compilation of photographs of popular graffiti spots in San Francisco, New York, and Los Angeles that represents a time-lapse collage of the ways in which these particular walls have changed over time. The 'grafarc explorer', which is linked to a timeline representing the time at which a particular photograph was taken, allows the user to 'excavate' the surfaces to see what lies beneath (Fig. 4.4). Other archaeological studies of graffiti include Cocroft et al.'s (2006) study of military wall murals and Blake's (1981) study of contemporary graffiti and racism in Hawaii. In a study of post-war Aboriginal stockman's graffiti at the former East Kunderang pastoral station in north-eastern New South Wales, Harrison (2004: 107ff.) interprets graffiti as a form of resistance to the exclusion of Aboriginal stockmen from official histories of sheep ranching in Australia. This idea of indigenous graffiti art as a form of resistance also finds expression in archaeological research by David and Wilson (2002). Frederick (2009) draws on insights from rock art research to investigate contemporary graffiti art in two cities in Australia. She reflects on the images not only as representations in the present, but also in terms of the circulation of references to the past, and the deployment of key political messages and tactics in their spatial placement, both in terms of the messages they convey as 'writing', and the meanings of the imagery that graffiti art can embody.

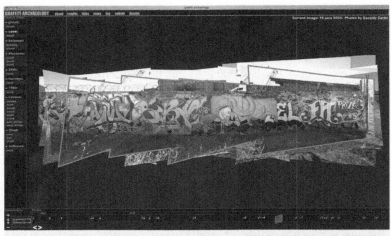

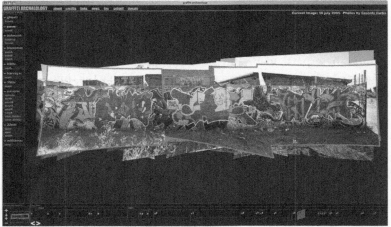

Figure 4.4. Screenshot showing Cassidy Curtis's 'grafarc explorer'. Both screens show the east wall of 'The Cove' in San Francisco. The records for this wall extend back in time approximately 18 months from mid-2004 to 2005, however, records for other walls date back as far as the late 1990s. The top image shows a photomontage dated 19 June 2005, while the bottom shows the same site on 18 July 2005. Note that the layers are 'excavated' using the timeline at the bottom of the screen. (Image courtesy of Cassidy Curtis/Graffiti Archaeology.)

Archaeological Investigation as Performance

In considering archaeology as a form of performance, we move on to a consideration of archaeology *as* art. We have already noted that a major concern within archaeology since the 1980s has been a 'critical archaeology' which considers archaeology as a contemporary engagement with the past and as part of a process of creating the past-in-the-present (Ch. 2). Pearson and Shanks (2001; see also Shanks 1992) have developed an extended argument in which they consider the connection between archaeology and performance. They note the ways in which contemporary performance theory can be used to illuminate aspects of archaeological practice in terms of the ways in which archaeology involves an engagement with the material world through the senses and the human body. They argue that the activities and meanings that are generated around the process of 'doing' archaeology—during an excavation in a public place, for example—can be studied in terms of the 'political economy' of archaeology, the things that hold the archaeological process together socially in the world (Pearson and Shanks 2001: 44; see also Edgeworth 2006).

It is an ecology of mobilising resources, managing, organising, persuading, of practices like collecting, walking and intervening in the land . . . archaeology is a process in which archaeologists, like many others, take up and make something of what is left of the past. Archaeology may be seen as a mode of cultural production . . . moving from source materials or resources to the consumption of an end product such as a book, excavation report or museum exhibition.   (Pearson and Shanks 2001: 50)

Both artistic performance and archaeology can be thought of as social practices, to be processes of cultural production, to constitute embodied practices that work on, and negotiate, cultural identities, and that work with fragments and traces (ibid. 54–5). Both artistic performance and archaeology focus on particular details, attending to the particular cultural and historical context of material things, and both are concerned with the documentation of events and their aftermath (ibid. 55–9; Lucas 2004).

Pearson and Shanks's (2001) *Theatre/Archaeology* helps us to begin to understand the peculiar ways in which the process of 'doing' the archaeology of the contemporary past is perceived as a form of performance.

We have already noted the ways in which the attention of the public can be turned to reflect on the practice of archaeology itself through a 'performance' of the archaeology of the shockingly quotidian. This process was used effectively in the work of the artist Mark Dion, whose *Tate Thames Dig* was commissioned by the Tate Gallery in London and carried out in 1999 (Dion 1999; Renfrew 2003: 84). The artist and his team undertook an archaeological surface collection on the banks of the Thames River in London at several sites associated with the Tate Britain and Tate Modern galleries, leading to a display of the material that was held for a number of years in the Tate Modern gallery. The team of 'excavators' set up tents on the front lawn of the Tate in August 1999, where volunteers cleaned and sorted the collections, which were then classified by Dion and conserved for display. Dion is interested in drawing attention to the processes by which different forms of scientific knowledge are formed. His work is surprising because it is carried out in very visible spaces within the public eye, and focuses on spaces that we might consider to be too 'modern' or 'disturbed' to be interesting (although clearly archaeologists are interested in the Thames, and a number of important finds have been recovered from the Thames and its immediate environs). The excavation, classification, and display of modern credit and phone cards as archaeological objects (see Renfrew 2003: 187), for example, takes an ordinary object with which we are all familiar and presents it in the same way as an ancient find. In doing so, Dion draws our attention to the process of archaeology as a particular sort of intervention and knowledge-making practice in a way normally hidden from view. This calling into question of archaeology as a practice through the 'performance' of an archaeology of the contemporary past is an important feature of the work of many archaeologists who focus on the contemporary period.

An example of archaeology staged as a performance can be found in Holtorf's (2004*b*) 'incavation' (a term that denotes a sort of archaeology in reverse, or the burial of artefacts, as opposed to their 'excavation') in 2001. During this incavation, eight contemporary and mundane domestic assemblages were buried in the garden of a Berlin townhouse. In undertaking this 'incavation', Holtorf made a powerful statement about archaeology as a performance and a particular form of material engagement with the past. As he explains, whether one incavates or excavates, archaeologists...construct the past and its remains like artisans create their craft. It takes desire, creativity, skill and persistence.... Incavating is not however about faking archaeological evidence, about making archaeology appear a futile exercise or about drastically diminishing the cultural impact of what is being hidden in the ground. Instead, what is incavated is archaeological evidence in itself. (2004*b*: 47–8)

Such performances, whether staged by artists or undertaken by archaeologists, force us to think about archaeology and its relationship to the present. They also force us to 'shine a light' on particular aspects of the past that may have been hidden from public view. We will discuss the political dimension of the archaeology of the contemporary past further in Chapter 5, but for now, it is worth thinking about what it might mean, for example, to undertake an archaeology of homelessness (e.g. Zimmerman and Welch 2006) or of an abandoned council flat (e.g. Buchli and Lucas 2001*c*). How might this process force both us as archaeologists and the public who view our work to perceive homelessness differently? In undertaking an archaeology of the contemporary past, we can draw attention to the lives and histories of people and places that would otherwise remain hidden and clandestine. In doing so, we bring them to public attention in potentially powerful and poignant ways.

Art as Interpretation, Narrative, and Characterization

Finally, we consider contemporary art as a form of archaeology. We are concerned here principally with the use of archaeology as a form of interpretation of the past, and the engagement of artists with archaeological sites as a form of public interpretation. Of course, the use of creative reconstruction of archaeological sites has a long history in archaeology. Papers in Jameson, Ehrenhard, and Finn (2003) document the broadening of artistic practice to interpret the results of archaeological research in a wide range of public interpretation projects, through the use of plays, opera, stories, poetry, the visual arts, sculpture, and performance. Recently, authors have begun to argue that art can go beyond feeding an archaeologist's vision to the public to provide a significant new dimension to the understanding and interpretation of place (e.g. Schofield 2008: 192). As Feversham and Schmidt (1999: 166) have said, 'There is an argument that contemporary art has a vital, if largely unsung part to play... acting as an agent provocateur in re-energizing spaces which by virtue of their very historicity are in danger of being perceived as sacrosanct.' In this sense, we can see the aims of archaeology and art converge, as artistic practice becomes a competitor with archaeology as another way of representing and engaging with the past. Renfrew (2003) suggests that artistic practice and archaeology converge in the consideration of three main areas—what it means to be human, the nature of the world as a landscape and human inter-actions with it, and the role of material culture in society. Here we give some brief examples of artistic works that seek to answer what might have previously been considered to be archaeological questions.

Lucy Orta's work (Pinto, Bourriaud, and Damianovic 2003) is often a critical response to sensitive areas of society, reflecting on themes such as social inclusion and community, dwellings and mobility, and recycling; making the invisible visible. *All In One Basket* and *Hortirecycling* (1997–9) grew from Orta's shock at witnessing food wasted in markets. Her response was to organize the collection of leftover food and ask a celebrity chef to cook it, resulting in a buffet for passers-by, uniting rich and poor in a demonstration of gastronomic recycling. Her work can be seen to engage with some of the same questions raised by Rathje's Garbage Project (described in Ch. 2). Rathje (2001: 63) notes:

From the outset, the primary goal of Garbage Project research was to demonstrate the utility of archaeological methods and theories for achieving a better understanding of issues of current public concern—including assessments of resource waste and proposed methods of waste minimaliza-tion, measures of diet and nutrition, evaluations of household participation in recycling programs... and... base data for the design of new 'environ-mentally friendly' packages.

While Orta's work is not archaeological in the same material sense as Rathje's, we can see them both as alternative interpretations of the contemporary world, of the material objects that characterize it, and of people's interaction with both.

Increasingly, artistic engagements with the contemporary world are finding a place alongside archaeological ones in writing about the archaeology of the contemporary past. For example, Angela Piccini's

(2009) 'micro road movie' video and live spoken word performance *Guttersnipe* explore the similarities between documentary photography and contemporary archaeological practice through a consideration of different ways of reading and interpreting a particular 'surface'. Similarly, Louise K. Wilson (2009) has documented her artistic (audio and video) engagements with former Cold War sites in England alongside the work of archaeologists, some of whom she recorded as part of her artistic practice. John Schofield (2007) has written, as an 'archaeologist', about the artist Angus Boulton, whose film *Cood Bay Forst Zinna* (2001) documents the character of an abandoned camp in the former East Germany. According to Schofield, Boulton captures the essence of this place, as an abandoned site, and documents it in ways that bear close comparison to more conventional archaeological and buildings recording methodologies. But Boulton's study has a further dimension, in giving the viewer the illusion of having actually been there. One feels as though one knows the site intimately—not so much its layout and plan-form, but the character of the place, its aura, and the ghosts of place that inhabit the decrepit rooms and open spaces (after Bell 1997; Edensor 2005).

We have defined three areas where archaeological and artistic practice meet—art as an archaeological record (or the archaeology of art), archaeological investigation as performance (or archaeology as art), and art as interpretation, narrative, and characterization (or art as archaeology). In doing so, we have explored not only the areas where artistic and archaeological practices overlap, but also the ways in which contemporary artistic practices might inform an archaeology of the contemporary past. These areas will be investigated in more detail in the second part of the book, where we look at archaeological approaches to understanding contemporary societies at various different scales of analysis.

ARCHAEOLOGY AS REPORTAGE AND EXPERT WITNESS

Another area of cross-disciplinary engagement in archaeology concerns documentary photography and reportage. We would like to suggest here that the origin of commercial archaeology as a form of 'rescue archaeology' leads us to consider the overlap between archaeology and reportage, and particularly, the documentary or 'record' tradition of photography. 'Rescue archaeology' or 'salvage archaeology' refers to archaeological documentation carried out in conjunction with the development process to record archaeological features that are to be destroyed or covered over by construction work or other commercial development. The aim of rescue archaeology is to excavate and/or make an accurate record of the remains to be destroyed so as to mitigate the loss of the remains to scientific research on the archaeological record. Rescue archaeology is an important part of the professional process of heritage archaeology known as Cultural Heritage Management or Cultural Resource Management.

The record tradition in photography has its roots in a belief in the objectivity of photography and the desire to capture an objective picture of contemporary society (see Harrison and Linkman 2010). Indeed, during the late nineteenth century photographers in the record tradition turned their attention to aspects of architecture, street scenes, and 'everyday life' because 'the commonplace of to-day is frequently only the memory of to-morrow' (Gower, Jast, and Topley, 1916: 186–7, cited in Harrison and Linkman 2010: 62). In the early twentieth century, documentary photography became intimately associated with the preservation of heritage and the development of an archive of culture through its formalization in schemes such as the Historic American Buildings Survey (HABS) in the US. Grand documentary photographic surveys undertaken in the 1930s by Italy, Russia, Germany, and the US (Badger 2007: 72) might profitably be compared to archaeological projects undertaken by the same governments at this time (e.g. see papers in Kohl and Fawcett 1995) as propaganda exercises to foster a sense of nationhood.

Similarly, both archaeology (see Ch. 2) and photography have come to be implicated in the legal system as tools for the production of an 'objective' record of past events. As Susan Sontag (1977: 5) notes, 'Photographs furnish evidence. Something we hear about, but doubt, seems proven when we're shown a photograph of it... a photograph passes for incontrovertible proof that a given thing happened. The picture may distort; but there is always a presumption that something exists, or did exist, which is like what's in the picture.' We might compare Sontag's statements with those of Gould (2007:

193) regarding the goals of 'Disaster Archaeology', already cited in this volume: 'the archaeological facts can speak for themselves if we let them ... disaster archaeologists must be guided by the evidence'. Both archaeology and documentary photography deal with modes of representation that are evidentiary. However, both modes of representation are equally open to manipulation. What makes them so persuasive is the way in which they purport to document the physical and material 'facts' as a documentary record or archive.

We can see the interests of documentary photography and the archaeology of the contemporary past converge in a consideration of Harrison's research project on the archaeology of the welfare state in Britain (Harrison 2009*b*), the work of Buchli and Lucas (2001*c*) on an abandoned council flat and the work of the London College of Communication (LCC) project to document the regeneration of the Elephant and Castle council estates in South London (Sutherland 2008*a*, *b*). In this latter example, each year LCC students from the MA Photojournalism and Documentary Photography course are set a project to document the area, which was developed as an experiment in modernist urban planning and housing in the 1960s and is currently undergoing a major regeneration. One aspect of this regeneration project has been the closure and the relocation of residents of the Heyworth Estate, a large public housing project that was built to house over a thousand residents between 1970 and 1974, and the Aylesbury Estate, one of the biggest public housing projects in Europe, built between 1967 and 1977 to house over ten thousand residents. As part of the process of relocating the residents of these estates and prior to demolition, LCC students have responded in different ways to the task of completing a documentary record of a community and its housing. Matteo Borzone's work *(Garage) × 350* is a set of photographs of each of the 350 garage doors from a series of five blocks on the Heygate Estate (Sutherland 2008*a*: 48–53; see Fig. 4.5). This work can be compared with the series of photographs of front doors which were made by Harrison on estates in Southwark to demonstrate varied modifications to council flats made by owner-occupiers (see Harrison 2009*b*). Another approach was taken by Maximiliano Braun, whose *Cast Off* is a series of photographs representing an inventory of objects found left behind in flats on the Heygate Estate prior to

Figure 4.5. Matteo Borzone, *Garage Doors*. (Images courtesy of Matteo Borzone.)

them being locked and sealed off (Sutherland 2008*a*: 76–83; see Fig. 4.6). This calls to mind Buchli and Lucas' (2001*c*) 'excavation' and inventory of material left behind in a council flat that had been abandoned by the family that had inhabited it (see further Ch. 2).

Figure 4.6. Maximiliano Braun, *Cast Off.* (Images courtesy of Maximiliano Braun.)

Both the archaeological and photographic approaches have produced similar records, although with less interest in context on behalf of the photographers. Nonetheless, we think it is helpful to consider the ways in which such processes of documentary recording might help inform an archaeology of the contemporary past. One of the interesting aspects of the LCC documentary project is its concern not only for the 'left behind', but also in photographing places in use by a community, and the people who inhabit these places. Thus, for example, Shehani Fernando has photographed the last remaining residents of the Aylesbury Estate who have occupied their flats since it was constructed, and has done so inside their flats, as a documentary record of life on the estate. This approach to recording places whilst they are still 'in use' could be thought of as a sort of anthropological archaeology, a way of recording and responding to the material and physical dimensions of a place prior to its ruination. Earlier in the chapter we looked at anthropological approaches to recording one's own society and the use of autoethnography as a research method. This approach to documentary photography can be seen to be another tool to be used in conjunction with these anthropological approaches to record the archaeology of societies that are contemporary with us.

ARCHAEOLOGY AND FORENSIC SCIENCE

We have already mentioned the ways in which one subfield of the archaeology of the contemporary past involves the application of archaeology to investigate questions of interest to the legal system, in particular criminal or civil law. The discussion of forensic archaeology and its role in the investigation of mass graves and the sites of mass executions resulting from genocide and political 'disappearances' necessarily forces us to consider the role of archaeology in remembering, or paying tribute to the events of the past as an 'expert witness' (see Buchli and Lucas 2001a; Buchli 2007; Gould 2007; González-Ruibal 2008; Zarankin and Funari 2008). However, we should note here that forensic archaeology is different to much of what we define as the archaeology of the contemporary past in the sense in which it is only really concerned with evidence which relates to a specific event—be it a disaster, massacre, or murder. In this sense, forensic archaeology is very narrow, in a way in which we have argued that the archaeology of the contemporary past must be explicitly broad, taking into account all evidence from the past where it intervenes in the present.

Although we do not have space to cover it in detail here, there is nevertheless a clear overlap between archaeology and the specific field of forensic science. We have already seen in Chapters 2 and 3 that forensic archaeology has developed into an important field of endeavour through the use of archaeology in disaster recovery, crime investigation, and war crime and human rights abuse trials. The specialized techniques of forensic archaeology are set out in technical publications such as Cox et al. (2008) and Hunter and Cox (2005). However, it is not only in the field of forensic archaeology that such specialized techniques can make a contribution. For example, we have already discussed the specialized palaeo-environmental study of the deposits from the Transit van excavations using techniques similar to those used in forensic studies in Chapter 3 (see further discussion in Bailey et al. 2009; Newland et al. 2007).

CONCLUSIONS

In this chapter we have argued that to be effective and socially relevant, the archaeology of the contemporary past must *necessarily* be interdisciplinary. This is not least due to the nature of its subject matter, which forces archaeologists to draw on the methodologies and insights of a series of different academic disciplines. However, that is not to say that the archaeology of the contemporary past is defined by these other disciplines. Indeed, what emerged from our review of the archaeology of the contemporary past in Chapter 2, and a discussion of its methods in Chapter 3, was a sense in which an archaeological approach to the contemporary past involved a distinct set of methods, research strategies, and ways of 'seeing' that distinguish archaeology from these other approaches. But it is important to understand not only the place of other disciplines with regard to the archaeology of the contemporary past, but also their potential contribution to 'doing' the archaeology of contemporary or late modern societies. In the following chapter we will consider a series of theoretical approaches to understanding what characterizes the contemporary world with a view to developing a framework for the second half of the book, where we consider practical approaches to the archaeology of late modern societies at different scales of analysis.

5

Theory and Politics

WHEN WE WERE MODERN: ON THE NATURE OF LATE MODERNITY

If we are to undertake an archaeology of the contemporary past, we need first to be able to characterize it—to understand both those quotidian aspects of contemporary life as well as what makes this period distinct from other periods that preceded it. Although we have already suggested in Chapter 1 that the archaeology of the contemporary past should not be considered a period study, it is nonetheless important to understand both the continuities and discontinuities in contemporary life that might form the object of an archaeology of the present. This chapter will introduce a theoretical framework on which to build an archaeology of the contemporary past through a consideration of what various cultural theorists have written about the nature of the subject and its relevance to the study of contemporary places and material culture. There is a large literature on the nature of modernity and late modernity (a term we use to describe both 'postmodernity' and 'supermodernity' in a historical sense, see further discussion below), from which we have drawn a selection that we consider helpful in understanding the topic of contemporary archaeology, and that provides a theoretical background to the work of archaeologists who study the contemporary past. This chapter will also explore the ways in which archaeology as a form of documentation becomes a political and social intervention when its gaze is turned towards the contemporary past. We argue that this political dimension is one of the defining characteristics of the archaeology of the contemporary past.

Although we noted in Chapter 1 that this is not a book about heritage, the issue of heritage is in many ways integral to understanding the role of contemporary archaeology, as it relates to the ways in which we engage with, and understand, the past in the present. Indeed, in this chapter we argue that the rise of a heritage industry is itself a tangible artefact of the same impulse that led to the rise of contemporary archaeology as a distinct field of study (see also Ferguson, Harrison, and Weinbren 2010). At the same time, understanding these impulses that have given rise to heritage and the archaeology of the recent past helps us to understand what makes the period unique, and lays the foundation for a thematic framework for undertaking an archaeology of the contemporary past. For this reason, heritage, as an illustration of the ways in which the past is perceived and consumed in contemporary society, will be referred to in some detail in this chapter. We point to a series of interlinked themes in understanding the nature of late modernity and the contribution archaeology might make to understanding it—the idea of a present 'haunted' by the past; the production of 'non-places' and the disassociative spatial elements of a postmodernity that simultaneously shrinks space and produces a sense of isolation, solitude, melancholy (cf. Buchli 2007) and nostalgia; generic objects and spaces and their association with mass production and mass customization; speed, experienced as the acceleration of time; the idea of archaeology as a form of exorcism and its redemptive potential; the role of archaeology in presencing absence; and the idea of archaeology as a form of material witness.

CHARACTERIZING LATE MODERNITY: NOTES ON A PRESENT HAUNTED BY THE PAST

Why should we study the contemporary past when it is so close to us? What can the archaeology of the contemporary past contribute to an understanding of a time through which we have ourselves lived and which we have shaped in our everyday lives and practices? The idea that people in the contemporary world have become increasingly disconnected from their past as well as their present environment emerges as a strong theme in writing about the nature of modernity and postmodernity. Indeed, it has been argued that this 'sensory disconnection' is directly linked to the rise of the heritage industry during the 1970s in the West. The later part of the twentieth century saw an incredible proliferation and diversification of both official and unofficial practices of heritage around collecting both the 'modern' and deeper past. We need only think of the rise of vintage clothes as fashion rather than thrift, the proliferation of amateur collectors of twentieth-century technology and design, and the increased popularity of oral and family history to get a feeling for the range of unofficial practices around heritage that relate to the growth of nostalgia for the contemporary past in the late twentieth century. These unofficial practices were mirrored by a series of official heritage practices around recognizing, collecting, and conserving the heritage of the twentieth century, as discussed in Chapter 2.

Many authors have pointed to the changes in developed societies that have come about during the mid to late twentieth century as heralding a new and distinct period of history. In the same way that we are used to thinking of the modern age, or 'modernity', as relating to the outcomes of the Enlightenment and the Industrial Revolution, some authors have suggested we use the terms 'postmodernity' and/or 'supermodernity' to define distinct historical periods that can be seen as separate to modernity. They point to a series of phenomena that seem to mark the late twentieth century as separate to that which came before it, including

- the growth of new communicative technologies and electronic media;
- the globalization of technology, and its association with altered patterns of production and consumption;
- the widespread experience of mass migration and the associated rise of transnationalism (in terms of capital, technology, labour, and corporations);
- new modes of capitalism involving more flexible forms of capital accumulation and distribution; and
- increased time available for leisure activities.

In *The Postmodern Condition,* French philosopher and literary theorist Jean-François Lyotard ([1979] 1984) suggested that *modernity* should be seen as a cultural condition characterized by constant change and the pursuit of progress, while *postmodernity* is the logical end product of this process, where constant change has become the status quo. Under such circumstances the notion of progress fails to have any meaning, as everything is constantly in flux. We might think here of the expectation that we have when we purchase a laptop or personal computer that it will become instantly outdated, or the idea that as soon as we drive our brand new car out of the showroom, it immediately loses value. Paul Virilio (1994, 2000; see also Tomlinson 2007) comments on the ways in which the late twentieth century has experienced an acceleration of time, or a sense of speed, which leads to a situation in which humans are so overwhelmed by the reversal, acceleration, and simultaneous nature of time that space itself becomes an element of time. This produces a sense of 'time-in-flux' that comes to be experienced as a fundamental part of the postmodern landscape.

Postmodernity Defined

One of the major theorists of postmodernity, American literary critic and Marxist political theorist Fredric Jameson (1991), turned to Adorno and Horkheimer's analysis of the culture industry to suggest that postmodernity could be defined as the period in which the cultural sphere became entirely dominated by a newly organized corporate capitalism. He pointed to the frequent occurrence of *pastiche,* the imitation and mixture of styles or borrowing of aspects of other creative works in postmodern cultural forms such as art, architecture, film, and literature, and suggested that the merging of all discourse into an undifferentiated whole was a result of this process by which the cultural sphere had become entirely colonized by the culture industry. He saw the widespread adoption of pastiche in postmodern creative arts as a reflection of a crisis in historicity. In contrast with pastiche, parody in the creative arts requires a grounding or comparison with moral or societal norms. Jameson sees pastiche as a form of juxtaposition without a normative foundation. The crisis in historicity relates to the inability to reconcile an understanding of history as presented (through history books, heritage sites, museums, and the media) with the lived experience of everyday life.

Geographer David Harvey (1990) took a slightly different approach to postmodernity. For Harvey, postmodernity does not represent a radical break with modernity, as the basic rules of the accumulation of capital remain the same. Nonetheless, the changes in technology and society that occurred during the later part of the twentieth century have given rise to a distinct way of experiencing time and place.

> There has been a sea-change in cultural as well as in political-economic practices since around 1972. This sea-change is bound up with the emergence of new dominant ways in which we experience space and time . . . there is some kind of . . . relation between the rise of postmodernist cultural forms, the emergence of more flexible modes of capital accumulation, and a new round of 'time–space compression' in the organisation of capitalism.
>
> (Harvey 1990: p. vii)

This 'time–space compression' appears in a slightly different form in Jameson's analysis using terms derived from psychoanalysis to describe a breakdown in the chain of signification or the fragmentation and schizophrenic de-centring of the self. 'I take such spatial peculiarities as symptoms and expressions of a new and historically original dilemma, one that involves our insertion as individual subjects into a multidimensional set of radical discontinuous realities, whose frames range from the still surviving spaces of bourgeois private life all the way to the unimaginable decentring of global capital itself' (ibid. 413). Harvey, like Jameson, associates postmodernity with a phase of 'late capitalism' when more flexible forms of capital accumulation and distribution develop, which is characterized by more flexible labour processes and markets, increased spatial mobility, rapid shifts in patterns of consumption, and a revival of entrepreneurialism and neo-conservatism (p. 124). These shifts in material and economic conditions are understood to have produced fundamental changes in the ways in which people experience time and space in the period after about 1970. Harvey differs from Jameson in arguing that the resulting experience of a compression in time and space also characterized other periods that experienced times of change or flux in the capitalist mode of production.

Postmodernity and Heritage

We should reflect on the possible effects of this experience of time–space compression and the associated experience of flux in modes of production in terms of institutionalized structures of memory and nostalgia that find their expression in heritage. Some authors would suggest that what Jameson and Harvey describe as the postmodern condition should be seen as the setting for the rise of official forms of heritage as a formal phenomenon. As Harvey himself notes, Robert Hewison (1987) saw a link between the heritage industry and post-modernism in his book *The Heritage Industry*. 'Both conspire to create a shallow screen that intervenes between our present lives, our history. We have no understanding of history in depth, but instead are offered a contemporary creation, more costume drama and re-enactment than critical discourse' (Hewison 1987 cited in Harvey 1990: 87). Hewison (1987) coined the phrase 'heritage industry' to describe what he considered to be the sanitization and commercialization of the version of the past produced as heritage in the United Kingdom under the British Prime Minister Margaret Thatcher. He suggested that heritage was a structure largely imposed from above to capture a middle-class nostalgia for the past as a golden age in the context of a climate of decline.

Like Adorno and Horkheimer in their critique of the culture industry, Hewison believed that the rise of heritage as a form of popular entertainment distracted its patrons from developing an interest in contemporary art and critical culture, providing them instead with a view of culture that was finished and complete (and firmly in the past). He pointed to the widespread perception of cultural and economic decline that became a feature of Britain's perception of itself as a nation in the decades following the Second World War.

In the face of apparent decline and disintegration, it is not surprising that the past seems a better place. Yet it is irrecoverable, for we are condemned to live perpetually in the present. What matters is not the past, but our relationship with it. As individuals, our security and identity depend largely on the knowledge we have of our personal and family history; the language and customs which govern our social lives rely for their meaning on a continuity between past and present. Yet at times the pace of change, and its consequences, are so radical that not only is change perceived as decline, but there is the threat of rupture with our past lives. (ibid. 43–5)

What we see in the rising interest in heritage can be argued to relate, then, to the changes that occurred in Western economies associated with post-1970s economic liberalism/conservatism and free market economics. This was associated with the decline of major industries and a series of historical patterns of life that were begun during the Industrial Revolution. The passing of this old way of life created not only new ways of engaging with the world, but a nostalgia for the industrial and modern past that helped to fuel the heritage boom and the museumification of the West which took off in the 1970s and which is perhaps best symbolized by the development of the UNESCO World Heritage Convention in 1972. This could be compared to the same rush of nostalgia evoked by the rise of industrialization in the nineteenth century which was associated with a different sort of cult of the pre-industrial ruin, linked both with the roots of modern archaeology and particular ways of imagining the 'picturesque' and the Gothic in the Romantic movement in art and literature (see also Edensor 2005: 11). What we are suggesting here, following Hewison, is that we see the rise of the heritage industry in the West as a response to large-scale deindustrialization that occurred as a result of changes in the global economy in the 1970s, and an associated change in ways of relating to the world linked to changes in communicative technologies and society (see also Ferguson, Harrison, and Weinbren 2010).

If we are to acknowledge that it is this postmodern condition that provides the contemporary setting for the increased interest in heritage and the past in post-industrialized Western countries in the late twentieth century, what about the *heritage* of this recent past? It might be argued that if increased interest in heritage is a product of postmodernity precisely because it offers escape from the conditions of postmodernity, then it would seem perverse to use heritage to seek to establish a memory of that postmodernity itself. However, we have already discussed in Chapter 2 the rise in the public interest in, and demands for the conservation of, the heritage of the past of living memory. In addition to the growth in popular forms of nostalgia and heritage (both the very old, and the modern) throughout the twentieth century, we have also seen the development of a process whereby the present is made almost immediately past through the creation and conservation of what we might term *postmodern* heritage, in which certain aspects of everyday life that relate to the present are almost immediately conceived of in heritage terms, sometimes even before they move outside the realm of everyday contemporary life. It is this phenomenon, by which the past is perceived as imminent in the present, that both frames the apparently tautological 'contemporary past' and makes necessary an archaeological intervention in the present. With the pace of change in many societies so rapid, technologies and aspects of material culture become almost instantly redundant. This notion of immediate technological redundancy has saturated our interactions with the material world to such an extent that the idea of instant obsolescence, that material objects will immediately become museum pieces, is now widely held within contemporary post-industrial societies.

HERITAGE AND THE CONTEMPORARY ARCHAEOLOGY OF THE EXPERIENCE ECONOMY

In *The Experience Economy*, Pine and Gilmore (1999) argue for a late modern shift from a service-based economy to an experience-based one, in which goods and services come to be valued not so much for their function, but in terms of their engagement of the senses and the experiences that surround their purchase and use. They see the origins of the experience economy in the opening of Disneyland by Walt Disney in 1955, and urge their readers in business to consider the experiences they create as an integral part of the goods and services they provide. They discuss the ways in which modularization has allowed the development of schemes of mass customization, the prerequisite for the provision of individualized entertainment. Similarly, Jensen (1999) has argued that the late twentieth century saw the emergence of a 'Dream Society' characterized by the commercialization of emotion and the opening of new markets with which to exploit the commercial potential of human emotions. This helps us to understand the convergence of shopping and heritage (and indeed, shopping and virtually any other experience in the modern world). Indeed, the virtual indistinguishability of the airport and the shopping mall, for example, is an issue that will be explored in more detail in Chapter 9.

The manifestations of the experience economy—casinos, museums, entertainment spaces—have formed a major theme for archaeologists of the contemporary past, particularly in terms of the ways in which such places evoke the past and utilize reconstructions of archaeological sites and other historic places. For example, archaeologist Martin Hall and social anthropologist Pia Bombardella have written on the entertainment spaces of the new South Africa (Hall 2001, 2005, 2006; Hall and Bombardella 2005, 2007), while Cornelius Holtorf (2005*b*, 2007, 2009) has explored the relationship between archaeology and contemporary entertainment spaces such as archaeological theme parks and resorts in the US, UK, continental Europe, and South Africa. He argues for the importance of ideas surrounding the experience economy not only in terms of understanding the contemporary manifestations of heritage, but also in imagining what he terms 'a new archaeology for a new society' (2009: 58). This points us towards the unlikely spaces that must form the subject of archaeological research if we are to make sense of the contemporary world and its relationship to the past (see further discussion of theme parks and the archaeology of the experience economy in Ch. 9).

Supermodernity and the Contemporary Past

In his book *Non-Places: Introduction to an Anthropology of Supermodernity*, Marc Augé (1995) posits that the experience of 'non-places', those non-symbolized spaces within which one finds oneself in transit from one place to the next, is the fundamental experience of late modernity and defines what is critically different about the geographies of the late twentieth century compared to those that came before them. His description of the non-place will be dealt with in more detail below. However, here we want to focus on his discussion of supermodernity (or hypermodernity) and contrast it with that of the postmodern. Augé argues that supermodernity is a characteristic of societies in which the presence of the past in the present is so abundant as to overwhelm and clutter it. In such circumstances, the past and its traces are constantly recycled and people are unable to distinguish between its original and subsequent manifestations.

The presence of a past in a present that supersedes it but still lays claim to it: it is in this reconciliation that Jean Strabonski sees the essence of modernity... the hypothesis advanced here is that supermodernity produces nonplaces, meaning spaces which... do not integrate the earlier places: instead these are listed, classified, promoted to the status of a 'place of memory', and assigned to a circumscribed and specific position. (ibid. 75–8)

Augé suggests that supermodernity is characterized by three accelerations or excesses: time, space, and the individualization of the point of reference. By the excess of time, Augé refers not only to our accelerated experience of time (as noted above in the discussion of Lyotard, Jameson, Virilio, and Harvey; see further discussion in Tomlinson 2007 and González-Ruibal 2008) but also the ways in which we perceive and utilize time and a sense of the past. History 'is on our heels, following us like shadows' (Augé 1995: 26). The excess of space is 'complicated by the spatial abundance of the present. This... is expressed in changes of scale, in the proliferation of imagined and imaginary references, and in the spectacular acceleration of means of transport' (p. 34). The excess of the individual refers to shifts in the postmodern anthropological object of study, from the field to those texts produced about it, and finally from those texts to the author him- or herself. Augé sees this shift from the global to the local (and ultimately to the individual) as a reflection of the ultimate abstraction of reference that derives from the postmodern condition. As Tom Conley notes in his introduction to Augé's *In the Metro* (2002: p. xvii), for Augé, 'solitude accrues as the world accelerates'.

Supermodernity is the experience of modernity *made excessive*. It differs from postmodernity in the sense in which it is not concerned with deconstruction, but instead produces a situation in which 'the components pile up without destroying one another' (Augé 1995: 41). Indeed, postmodernity and supermodernity are integrally linked—like faces of the same coin, Augé suggests. Supermodernity is not concerned with the deconstruction of meaning, but selects from the abundance of information to produce new meanings that simply add to, but do not overwrite, existing ones. There is a suggestion in the work of many contemporary archaeologists of a present which is haunted by the past (e.g. Buchli 2007). This sense of haunting describes the supermodern experience par excellence.

Arjun Appadurai (1996) writes of a sense of unprecedented 'rupture' of the past from the present that characterizes late modernity. He relates this experience of rupture to the fundamental ways in which the electronic mediation of new media and communicative technologies transformed existing forms of communication and social relations. The electronic mediation of communication, coupled with mass migration and transnationalism, work on the imagination in peculiar—new—ways, as viewers and images circulate simultaneously. The work of the imagination takes on a new role in a post-electronic society, in which the individual imagination can be linked with what Appadurai terms a 'community of sentiment', which allows the individual imagination to become operationalized in a way which was not possible throughout history.

The work of Gilles Lipovetsky (2005) connects Augé's discussion of the spaces of consumption with the idea of an experience economy. Lipovetsky suggests that supermodernity is characterized by a form of 'hyperconsumerism' in which consumption is increasingly directed towards the individual experience of pleasure and away from the potential for consumption to enhance social status. This creates a sense of tension and anxiety within the individual that derives from their experience of a society devoid of tradition in which the future is uncertain and without direction. This sense of anxiety or tension can be seen to underlie the accelerated sense of nostalgia and interest in tradition in contemporary society.

What is seen by the spectator of modernity is the interweaving of the old and the new. Supermodernity, though, makes the old (history) into a specific spectacle, as it does with all exoticism and all local peculiarity. History and exoticism play the same role as in the 'quotations' in a written text . . . but they play no part in any synthesis, they are not integrated with anything; they simply bear witness, during a journey, to the coexistence of distinct individualities, perceived as equivalent and unconnected.   (Augé 1995: 110–11)

What we experience in the late twentieth and early twenty-first century is the interplay of both postmodernity and supermodernity. On the one hand, we exist within a present in which the past is both excessive and seemingly inaccessible. We shift constantly from a reification of the past to a deconstruction of it. These extreme polar responses explain this contemporary experience of a present *haunted* by the past. This not only helps us understand why contemporary archaeology has arisen as a popular field of academic inquiry in the late twentieth and early twenty-first century, but also helps us to clarify one of its most important themes—the nature of the past in the present. As we noted in Chapter 3, the role of the contemporary archaeologist is not to ignore those traces which remain of the more distant past, but to treat the surface remnants of both contemporary and deep past as a single layer, to analyse their relationships with one another and their uses in the present (a point also made by Piccini and Holtorf 2009). This is one of the defining characteristics of contemporary archaeology as an academic subdiscipline—it is not able to ignore any trace, but must treat them all as part of a single horizon in the present. As we have already seen, González-Ruibal (2008: 262) notes that 'there is no archaeology of the twenty-first century but only an archaeology of the twenty-first and all its pasts, mixed and entangled' (see also Olivier 2000: 400).

'NON-PLACES': THE LANDSCAPES OF SUPERMODERNITY

A new anthropological literature on diaspora and mass migration, clearly itself related to the contemporary global politics of refugee-ism and place (Deleuze and Guattari 1981; Clifford 1997), has concerned itself with the landscape as it is experienced by people on-the-move (after Bender 2001*a*, *b*). We return here to the concept of the 'non-place'. Augé (1995) uses this term to describe a whole series of types of space in contemporary society—airport lounges, shopping malls, motorways—which he suggests are to be distinguished from 'places' in the sense in which these spaces are not relational, historic, or concerned with the establishment of a sense of identity (all those things that characterize the traditional social anthropological interest in 'place'). For Augé, these 'non-places' are primarily associated with the experience of travel or transit, and are characterized by a feeling of solitude and the emptying of the consciousness in response to their generic or formulaic nature. 'The space of supermodernity is inhabited by this contradiction: it only deals with individuals (customers, passengers, users, listeners), but they are identified (name, occupation, place of birth, address) only on entering or leaving ... it seems the social game is being played elsewhere' (p. 111).

There is something that resonates deeply in Augé's work. The preface to the volume is an imaginary piece of partial autoethnography in which Augé describes his fictional character's movement through an airport lounge and onto an aeroplane that strikes a chord of familiarity with many readers and seems to describe quite succinctly something that is characteristically different about the late modern period—the experience of spaces of transit produced in such a way so as to be intentionally generic that serve to isolate individuals and internalize their experience. While his work has been criticized for overstating the non-relational and homogenous aspects of spaces such as airport lounges and motorways (e.g. Merriman 2004), the term 'non-place' remains a useful term for describing spaces of transit, consumerism, and movement which proliferate in the late twentieth and early twenty-first century. We also need to be careful not to see these as the only forms of landscape that are worthy of study in the contemporary past (see further Ch. 8), but we do see these landscapes of supermodernity as worth highlighting as new landscapes that require new archaeological techniques to study them (see further discussion in Ch. 9). Another aspect of non-place is the increasing supermodern trend towards modularization and mass customization. We will consider the archaeology of IKEA as an example of this phenomenon in Chapter 6. The physical experience of landscapes of sprawl (cf. Hayden 2004) is clearly of critical interest in understanding the landscapes of late modernity.

It is worth reflecting on the relationship between the production of generic space and what we have already noted as a contemporary sense of alienation and isolation that not only characterizes postmodernity and hypermodernity, but also helps to explain the rise of contemporary archaeology as a subdiscipline. The increased focus on the individual in supermodernity is made possible through the application of what we might think of as a series of 'technologies of isolation'. The headphones of the in-flight entertainment system one wears in the aeroplane, the iPod in the ears while working out at the gym or walking along ignoring others (beggars refer to these as ABDs or Anti-Begging Devices), the isolation of the car's cabin as we drive along the motorway, and the e-readers and mobile entertainment devices carried on public transport that deter others from making conversation or eye contact. All these material things might be thought of as the artefacts that both produce and are produced by this sense of supermodern alienation and the peculiar internalization of experience caused by a sense of solitude and isolation. '[T]hese shifts of gaze and plays of imagery, this emptying of the consciousness, can be caused ... by the characteristic features of what I have proposed to call "supermodernity". These subject the individual consciousness to entirely new experiences and ordeals of solitude, directly linked with the appearance and proliferation of non-places' (Augé 1995: 93).

Appadurai's work on (super)modernity and globalization is also important here. Appadurai (1996) suggests that the last few decades have seen a rupture from the past that relates to the twin forces of electronic media (including new communicative technologies) and mass migration in producing the imagination as a new form of social practice. This could be roughly equated with Augé's discussion of the isolation of supermodernity through its non-places.

The image, the imagined, the imaginary—these are all terms that direct us to something critical and new in global cultural processes: the imagination as a social practice. No longer mere fantasy (opium for the masses whose real work is elsewhere), no longer simple escape (from a world defined principally by more concrete purposes and structures), no longer elite pastime (thus not relevant to the lives of ordinary people), and no longer mere contemplation (irrelevant for new forms of desire and subjectivity), the imagination has become an organized field of social practices, a form of work (in the sense of both labor and culturally organized practice), and a form of negotiation between sites of agency (individuals) and globally defined fields of possibility... the imagination is now central to all forms of agency, itself a social fact, and is the key component of the new global order. (Appadurai 1996: 31)

These forces of internalization of experience and the externalization of imagination represent a key area of research for contemporary archaeology and material culture studies. Graves-Brown (2009a) has drawn attention to the trend of the increasing privatization of experience that characterizes late modernity. He notes that this trend towards privat-ization of experience, coupled with the increasingly mobile nature of contemporary life (e.g. mobile phones, car ownership, transnational-ism) creates a problem for contemporary archaeologists in the sense in which supermodern forms of privacy tend to be internalized, i.e. they are inherent, rather than physically documented in material things. He gives the example of the virtual privacy of mobile phone use which is not documented within the objects themselves.

If we are to agree that the imagination has emerged as a social practice, how are we to study the new imagined landscapes of supermodernity? Appadurai (1996: 33ff.) identifies a series of 'imagi-ned worlds' of late modernity. The *ethnoscape* refers to the shifting landscape of people in transit—tourists, refugees, business travellers, immigrants—those people who occupy a shifting space between the more traditional 'settled' communities and who appear, in aggregate, to exist in a constant state of movement. The *technoscape* refers to the global spread and organization of technology and its ability to move fluidly between state boundaries. The *financescape* describes the global configuration of capital. *Mediascapes* are the organization of electronic media and the networks and technologies that allow for the distribution of information, as well as the images produced by those media. Finally, *ideoscapes* are images and ideas that represent state ideologies and the resistance of state ideologies, the global flow of images and words relating to the political realm. The relationship between these various imagined worlds represents the new landscape of late modernity.

We could think of these new landscapes as landscapes of connec-tion and disconnection, radically discrete yet simultaneously present in the supermodern world. We might consider part of the role of an archaeology of the contemporary past as making these discontinuous landscapes more discernible, freezing them in time and space so that they might be studied and appreciated. Another role of the contemporary archaeologist is in the untangling of 'things' and 'symbols' (cf. Taussig 1992) that characterize such landscapes. Clearly these new imaginary landscapes of supermodernity, with all their complex patterns and networks of connection and disconnection, call on new archaeological approaches. We might look towards the raft of current approaches to the study of organizations and society gathered under the label 'Actor-Network Theory' (ANT), as discussed in Chapter 4, to help us develop new approaches to these materials (see further Chs. 6 and 9).

CONTEMPORARY ARCHAEOLOGY AS THE ARCHAEOLOGY OF POSTMODERNITY?

What is the relevance of this work for charting an agenda for the archaeology of the contemporary past? We would like to suggest that the development of an interest in the archaeology of the contemporary past that occurred in the years leading up to the new millennium and has expanded exponentially in the last decade relates to a recognition of these new social, economic, and technological conditions of postmodernity, and is simultaneously a response to the sort of time–space compression that Harvey suggests characterizes it. As we have seen in Chapter 2, archaeologies of the contemporary past have tended to focus on those aspects of the twentieth century that are seen to represent a radical break from the past—supermodern forms of conflict and warfare, totalitarianism, the relationship between globalization and technology, production/consumption and the free market economy, and the outcomes of post-colonialism. At the same time, we are forced to consider the archaeology of the contemporary past as a social phenomenon in a particular historical context. Lyotard's postmodernity as flux and Harvey's notion of the time–space compression explain the desire to control both the immediate and the more distant past by instantly objectifying it through archaeology. If we consider archaeology to be a way of creating the past in the present, we can see the archaeology of the contemporary past as a way of recreating a present made immediately past by postmodernity.

All this begs the question—is it possible to see historical archaeology as the archaeology of *modernity* and the archaeology of the contemporary past as the archaeology of *postmodernity* and *supermodernity?* While such a separation may indeed be tempting, it might have the effect of shifting our focus away from the longer-term processes that have been in operation since the Industrial Revolution. While postmodernity is seen as distinct from modernity, supermodernity must be seen as continuing various historical trajectories of modernity in the sense in which it refers to modernity made excessive. This means that an archaeology of the contemporary past must not only focus on those things that are unique in the late twentieth and early twenty-first centuries, but also consider the continuity with longer-term social, technological, and economic processes. Clearly there are continuities and connections between the archaeology of the contemporary past and historical archaeology, particularly when we are thinking about the First World War and other increasingly distant periods outside of the realms of living memory. Similarly a specific focus on late modern urbanized or suburban life would neglect to take into account the lives of people still living in small-scale societies and as hunter-gatherers in the contemporary world. We have already noted that such communities are no less part of late modernity, being caught up in globalized webs and networks of trade, communication, consumption, and imagery, which means that they are equally important to our understanding of post-industrial societies and the late modern world.

Indeed, both Latour's *We Have Never Been Modern* (1993) and Edgerton's *The Shock of the Old* (2007) point out the extent to which modernity and postmodernity still include so much that is old within their systems. For example, as Winfried Wolf (1996) explains, the motor car, an archetype of late modernity, is in fact still a piece of Victorian mechanical technology. The internal combustion engine has never been superseded by late modern technology such as turbines or the rotary engine (we thank Paul Graves-Brown for suggesting this example). So it is important to recognize that an archaeology of late modernity is an archaeology not only of the recent past, but also of the way in which the more distant past intervenes in the present.

ON THE POLITICS OF CONTEMPORARY ARCHAEOLOGY

As González-Ruibal (2008: 259) notes, 'the archaeology of the contemporary past *has* to be political' (our emphasis; see also Buchli and Lucas 2001*d* and Buchli 2007: 116). While it has become common to recognize that *all* archaeology is political in that it involves relations of power and contemporary interventions in the production of the past (see discussion in Ch. 2), the politics of an archaeology of the contemporary past seems particularly explicit, in terms not only of the subjects of study (e.g. war, concentration camps, protest) but also of how it involves turning an archaeological lens on ourselves. We return here to the themes outlined by Buchli and Lucas (2001*a*) as characterizing the archaeology of the contemporary past: of production/consumption, remembering/forgetting, disappearance/disclosure, and presence/absence. With the exception of production and consumption, all these themes engage more or less specifically with the materialization of memory, with the idea of archaeology both as material witness and as a politically positioned intervention in the production of both the past and the present. In this part of the chapter we will consider further some of the implications of an archaeology of the contemporary past in terms of the politics of the present.

Archaeology as Material Witness

When we speak of archaeology as a material witness, we refer to the potential for the archaeology of the contemporary to uncover that which is hidden, abject, obscured, clandestine, or forgotten. There are many reasons why individuals, groups, practices, and their material memories might become hidden. The archaeology of the contemporary past acknowledges a clear role in bringing to light those aspects of history and contemporary experience that are explicitly hidden from public view by governments, or are obscured by the absence of political power of individuals and groups within the public arena (Buchli and Lucas 2001*a*; González-Ruibal 2008; Zarankin and Funari 2008). Buchli and Lucas referred to this as the act of 'presencing absence'.

But what sort of material witness is archaeology? Clearly, one that is as much a result of its subject position as the absence that it seeks to address. For this reason, the role of archaeology in the production of memory seems to be emerging as a contentious issue within the archaeology of the contemporary past. It has been argued by some that within the growing field of forensic archaeology, which treats archaeology as evidence or witness, archaeological evidence must be divorced from theory and from the explicitly subjective and positioned nature of much contemporary archaeological practice owing to its use of archaeology in legal procedings. For example, Gould (2007: 193) notes that both processual and post-processual archaeologies (see Ch. 2) have been based on 'the assertion that the evidence does not speak for itself but must be structured and controlled by theory. So it may seem heretical to propose here that *the archaeological facts can speak for themselves if we let them*. Perhaps more than with any other kind of archaeology, disaster archaeologists must be guided by the evidence' (original emphasis). However, other forensic archaeologists such as Steele (2008; see also Zarankin and Funari 2008) would question this viewpoint. She suggests that forensic archaeology is a form of activism, although she does acknowledge 'inherent tensions between a belief in forensic investigation as the objective pursuit of physical facts, the pursuit of justice as a force to advance social goals, and the complexity of human emotions' (p. 426). A split seems to be developing between those archaeologies of the contemporary past explicitly concerned with representing varied perspectives on the past, and the more clearly scientific, evidence-based approach of forensic archaeologies. Indeed, both González-Ruibal and Meskell (in González-Ruibal 2008) have argued that forensic excavation of mass graves, for example, should not necessarily be considered archaeology for this reason, even though it uses archaeological techniques. While we remain concerned about the way in which the use of archaeology in forensic excavations seems to be heralding a return to the idea of archaeology as an objective science, the therapeutic (González-Ruibal 2008; Gould 2007) role of a forensic archaeology in terms of making manifest the forgotten or repressed (Buchli and Lucas 2001*a*, *c*) seems beyond question. As Gould (2007: 12) notes:

Disaster archaeology, in short, is an instrument of closure. It does everything it can to ensure that the fate of a victim of a mass-fatality disaster is not forgotten but is made known to families and friends as well as to history. Disaster archaeologists (and I include forensic anthropologists as well) speak for the victims of major, mass-fatality events in a way that no-one else can.

However, we believe that we must continue to question where power is manifest in the varied social and political relations surrounding the forensic archaeological act. Contemporary archaeology should also force us to question the narratives of the heritage industry and its focus on remembering, as this cloaks a more important process of forgetting (Holtorf 2005*a*; Appadurai 2001; Buchli and Lucas 2001*a*).

Archaeology as Exorcism and Therapeutics

Earlier in the chapter, we spoke of late modernity as haunted by its relationship with the past. We would like to suggest the potential for archaeology to exorcize late modernity of its ghosts. An archaeology of the contemporary past has a redemptive role in reconciling the present with its past. It does this, much as we outlined above, through the explicit acknowledgement of archaeology as a creative act *in the present*. González-Ruibal (2008: 262) speaks of the simultaneous therapeutic and critical power of an archaeology of the recent past not only in reconciling the past with the present, but also in acts of disclosure that can 'bring healing to those who have suffered supermodernity's violence'—whether that be the families of murder victims who are buried in mass graves or who were 'disappeared' (Crossland 2000, 2002; Funari and Zarankin 2006; Ferrándiz 2006; González-Ruibal 2008), the homeless and the poor who are brushed to the margins (Zimmerman and Welch 2006), or those who are subjected to the controls of the welfare state (Buchli and Lucas 2001*c*; Harrison 2009*b*). As Buchli (2007: 116) notes, 'To do the archaeology of the contemporary past is to engage directly with its raw and extremely painful nerves—such as homelessness, social exclusion, war crimes or reconciliation—to name just a few. These are, in effect, profoundly melancholic contexts that are unresolved and in which archaeology materialises these troubling absences and serves as a therapeutic device.' We have seen how this sense of melancholy might be related to the conditions of late modernity—the sense of speed, flux, and disengagement from a past that is ironically ever present. The potential for a contemporary archaeology to materialize absence, bring to light hidden histories, and heal the rift between past and present means we must consider its role in exorcizing the contemporary sense of haunting by the past, and its ability to act as a powerful therapeutic device in contemporary society. Indeed, Augé (2004) has argued that supermodern societies must undertake a complex balancing act of remembering and *forgetting* to combat the effects of acceleration, isolation, and the shrinkage and warping of space that occurs as a result of our contemporary engagement with non-places.

Archaeology as Political Commentary on the Present

An archaeology of the contemporary past has an important role to play as a form of political comment on the present. In her book on the geographies of urban and suburban sprawl, Dolores Hayden (2004: 9) notes that 'naming' contemporary suburban phenomena involved in the production of sprawl is essential to identifying the problem. We suggest there is a role for an archaeology of the contemporary to record and develop a typology of urban and suburban problems, and in doing so, help identify solutions to these problems. For example, Rathje's work on garbage has not only shown differences between historically documented patterns of consumption, but has also allowed him to develop a significant critique of patterns of consumerism and to suggest new ways of managing waste in contemporary society (e.g. see Rathje and Murphy [1992] 2001). Similarly, Zimmerman and Welch's (2006) work on homelessness has the potential not only to highlight the experience of homelessness itself but also to develop an understanding of homelessness that can help authorities and charities develop policies to address it. An archaeology of the contemporary past must always be a critical intervention in the present in the way in which it turns the archaeological lens on our own society. But in addition to this role, the archaeology of the contemporary past can also produce significant social commentary and suggest solutions to social problems that are based in the material record itself.

ARCHAEOLOGY AND THE STUDY OF EVERYDAY LIFE

We have argued that the archaeology of the contemporary past has an important role to play in making the familiar 'unfamiliar' (after Graves-Brown 2000*a*). In this sense, the archaeology of late modernity must focus not only on those aspects of contemporary life that are hidden and obscured, thus exposing the supermodern forms of violence and conflict that remain hidden by governments and political regimes, but also on the everyday. We will briefly review some of the writing on everyday life that has the potential to inform an inquiry into the archaeology of late modernity prior to our exploration of the case studies in Part II.

The emergence of a sociology of everyday life is itself an artefact of late modernity. As Bennett and Watson (2002: p. xiii) point out, the sociology of everyday life did not really develop as a field of study until after the Second World War, as part of the overall democratization of public life and in response to the emergence of new forms of social discipline. Approaches to everyday life have been heavily influenced by Michel de Certeau's *The Practice of Everyday Life* (1984), itself strongly influenced by the work of Michel Foucault, Pierre Bourdieu, and Jean-François Augoyard ([1979] 2007). For de Certeau, everyday life remains largely unconscious, and outside the realm of investigation for those who live it (see Highmore 2002*b*: 12–13). As he notes in the general introduction to the book:

The point is not so much to discuss this elusive yet fundamental subject as to make such a discussion possible... This goal will be achieved if everyday practices, 'ways of operating' or doing things, no longer appear as merely the obscure background of social activity, and if a body of theoretical questions, methods, categories, and perspectives, by penetrating this obscurity, make it possible to articulate them.   (de Certeau 1984: p. xi)

As a result of the silence of everyday life, the experience of the majority becomes marginalized through an emphasis on elite groups who are seen to be those who produce 'culture'. Thus, part of the rationale for a study of everyday life is to combat this process whereby the majority become marginalized.

De Certeau suggests an approach to everyday life that prioritizes the study of consumption on the one hand, and 'the tactics of practice' on the other. He defines tactics as ways of 'getting along' in the world, 'clever tricks' (1984: p. xix). These tactics are to be found in the analysis of everyday practices—walking, speaking, reading, dwelling. Most radically, de Certeau suggests that these practices are spatialized, and can be understood through a study of their geography, which (following Augoyard) he likens to patterns of speech.

As Highmore (2002*a*) notes, the study of the everyday brings together the study of the global and the local, the national and the cross-cultural. Its goal is to rescue the everyday from a sense of homogeneity to express the heterogeneity of everyday experience across the globe. 'It is precisely by bringing together the global generality of modernization with the specificity of regional and historical continuities and discontinuities, that the everyday is seen as a particularly appropriate perspective for cross cultural studies of modernity...a focus on everyday life would insist on the uneven experiences of modernity on an international and intranational scale' (2002*a*: 177). For archaeologists, everyday life has long been a topic of interest. However, in the late modern period, its study takes on a new sense of urgency as the globalized media and culture industry overlook the heterogeneity of everyday experience while also marginalizing it. While it may seem somewhat contradictory, the focus on the marginal and abject in the archaeology of the recent and contemporary past is also a focus on the everyday. It is this marginalization of everyday life that makes critical a focus on the quotidian in an exploration of the archaeology of late modern societies.

CONCLUSIONS

This chapter has drawn on a number of writings on the nature of late modernity, to explore not only the stimulus for the development of an archaeology of the contemporary past, but also some of those themes that distinguish it from what came before. We have focused most closely on those issues that might be able to be approached archaeologically—those aspects that engage with the materiality of social life, the new landscapes of postmodernity and supermodernity, and new ways of relating to time and the past. In particular we considered the idea of a supermodern present 'haunted' by the past; the production of 'non-places', and the disassociative spatial elements of postmodernity that produce a sense of melancholy and nostalgia; generic objects and spaces and their association with mass production and mass customization; and speed, experienced as the acceleration of time. What emerged clearly from this review is the need to see archaeology of the contemporary past in historical context—to consider the role of new communicative technologies and economic and social change associated with the late modern period as giving rise to a series of social conditions that have made it desirable not only to historicize the contemporary past but also to analyse and comment on it, whether this is motivated by a desire to control it or to bring it into question.

In the final part of the chapter we explored the political nature of the archaeology of the contemporary past and how the archaeological act itself becomes a political gesture when it 'excavates' hidden or unacknowledged aspects of recent time periods. In doing so, we considered the politics of an archaeology of the contemporary past, highlighting the idea of archaeology as material witness in presencing absence and bringing to light the histories of the abject and forgotten; the retributive potential of archaeology as a form of therapeutic exorcism; and the potential for archaeology to form a political commentary on the present. We also saw how a focus on everyday life is an urgent requirement for the archaeology of late modern societies, to overcome the tendency to homogenize and marginalize the experience of everyday life within the globalized electronic media.

This chapter concludes the first part of the book, which has explored methodological and theoretical issues in the archaeology of the contemporary past, and surveyed both the subdiscipline itself and various aspects of the writing that informs it. In Part II, we take a closer look at different approaches to the archaeology of the contemporary, exploring this theme from various, increasing spatial scales—from the artefact, to sites, landscape, non-places, and finally the virtual world.

Part II

Archaeological Approaches to Late Modern Societies

6

Artefacts

Stop reading this! In fact, read to the end of this paragraph and then put the book down and look around you. You may be in a sitting room, in bed, on the beach, in the bath, or in your study or office. It doesn't much matter where you are. Look around you, and think about what you see. If you are at home, think about how things are distributed and why: are they tidily stored or all over the place? Are you a tidy person? If you are on the beach we'd question your choice of reading material! But nevertheless look around you. What do you see? How do people occupy their surroundings and mark out their territory? Is there litter, and stuff either deliberately left for others or forgotten and presumably now lost? And if you are in a workplace, can you decipher specific traces and types of depositions, particular patterns of use, and attribute them to particular people? Is there someone who always leaves something at the photocopier? Now think about all this stuff as an archaeologist, if you haven't been doing so already. By freezing the house, room, beach, or study in time, and examining it as you would an old land surface, or a house submerged in ash (Pompeii) or encroached upon by the sea (arguably Skara Brae), what would you learn? How, first of all, would you begin to characterize and analyse the artefacts you encounter? What would be the categories, and the types? How accurately would you record their locations? How many subtypes of artefact would it be useful to distinguish before the level of detail becomes unnecessary, absurd even? And what would you learn about human actions and behaviours that caused these particular patterns? What would you learn about colleagues, housemates, or fellow travellers? What would you learn about yourself? OK, now put the book down. This is a time to pause and think....

INTRODUCTION

In the first part of the book we considered a number of influences on the emergence of an archaeology of the contemporary past, from the interests in contemporary small-scale societies that developed as part of the New Archaeology in the 1960s and 1970s, to the use of contemporary case studies to address particular archaeological debates about the relationship between material culture and social behaviour posed by post-processual archaeologists in the 1980s and 1990s. We have seen how the archaeology of the recent past began with a focus on the First and Second World Wars, and then the Cold War, eventually to encompass a field that is concerned with the archaeology of a much wider range of events that have only just passed or are still occurring today (e.g. Penrose 2007). In Chapter 3 we looked in detail at the sorts of field methodologies that are being applied by archaeologists of the recent and contemporary past, considering whether their field methods might be understood to be distinct from other forms of archaeology. In Chapter 4 we looked at the relationship between archaeology and other disciplines that focus on contemporary materiality, in particular anthropology, material culture studies, art, and documentary photography. And in Chapter 5 we explored some reasons why archaeologists might have developed an interest in the contemporary world, and the period of late modernity in particular, through an exploration of some of the conditions of late modernity that make it distinct from the periods that precede it.

In the second part of the book, we look in more detail at how we might approach the archaeology of the contemporary world, with reference to a series of case studies. As you read through this second part, you will notice that one of its distinguishing features is its dual perspective. We consider on the one hand places and material practices that are essentially extinct or have ceased to function, and on the other those places and practices that are still functioning, or, in Tim Cresswell's (2004: 37) words, are 'still becoming'. We have argued in Chapter 1 that it is this dual perspective that is one of the characteristic features of an archaeology of the recent and contemporary past. While in the first part of the book we were reasonably flexible in the time periods we considered to be 'recent', reflecting the broadest interests of the field as it has emerged over the decade since the Millennium, in this part of the book we focus particularly on the period after *c*.1970, encompassing as it does the period of 'late modernity', which we discussed as exhibiting distinct features relating to the growth of new communicative technologies and electronic media, the globalization of technology, and the rise of new modes of capitalism associated with a sense of alienation and 'haunting' by the past. This period encompasses the end of the Cold War and the beginning of the 'internet age'. While there will be many people who have living memory before this time, we focus on this period as a way of exploring in detail how archaeologists might approach the study of what is literally for us, the contemporary past. Although in places we will make reference to the archaeology of earlier time periods as part of a consideration of the surface layer that is an amalgam of all historical phases, the focus on the contemporary and very recent past of late modernity is what makes this book distinctive amongst others on the topic. While this book is not intended to cover all aspects of the archaeology of late modern societies, we have chosen topics that we feel reflect the breadth of the area of study and demonstrate the potential for an archaeology of the recent and contemporary past. The case studies also more or less closely map onto the themes identified as characterizing the archaeology of the contemporary past in Chapter 1, and developed in more detail in relation to the distinct features of late modern societies in Chapter 5. We hope these studies will stimulate interest in exploring the archaeology of readers' own contemporary worlds.

We begin this section of the book with a brief exploration of the importance of artefacts in archaeological research. Archaeologists study artefacts for the information they can provide about the human behaviours that created, shaped, or transformed them, and led to them being found where they have finally come to rest. Now of course this sentence alone contains a whole series of assumptions that we should disentangle and investigate. But really that is another book, or several other books. Here we focus attention on some more specific issues that apply to the archaeology of the contemporary past, the types of material culture that characterize late modernity, and the types of information we can expect to glean from them. This chapter explores a number of kinds of artefact and problems relating to their study that we might consider to be unique to, or characteristic of, the archaeology of late modernity. In particular, we consider the archaeology of mass-produced artefacts, IKEA and the archaeology of mass customization, and the archaeology of the home, before concluding with some observations regarding the problems inherent in the study of late modern artefacts for archaeology.

We have chosen in this chapter to focus our attention on very particular types of quotidian and ephemeral artefacts. Given the range of modern artefacts—from the tiniest manufactured objects such as micro-computer components to enormous mega-artefacts such as off-shore deep sea drilling oil rigs—we might have chosen to focus this chapter on more remarkable objects. However, we have already argued that a major role for the archaeology of the contemporary past is to bring to light those aspects of contemporary life that are hidden, obscured, forgotten, or subaltern. This is not to say that some of the mega-artefacts of late modernity—enormous mobile strip mining machines or the Large Hadron Collider at CERN, for example—are not worthwhile objects of archaeological study. We simply note that there is perhaps nothing more obscure or taken-for-granted than the everyday. Similarly, there is nothing more abject or hidden than the ephemeral. For this reason, we use this chapter to consider archaeology's distinctive contributions to the study of contemporary material culture by way of a consideration of these particular ephemeral and everyday artefact forms. In the discussion that concludes, we return to some of these 'mega-artefacts' to consider further some problems inherent in studying the archaeology of contemporary material culture in all of its forms.

MASS PRODUCTION: THE ARCHAEOLOGY OF A FORD TRANSIT VAN

Much traditional archaeological research has concerned itself with artefacts made by hand. Archaeology developed as a discipline through the study of such things as stone artefacts and pottery, and might be seen to have focused on these objects specifically at a time when the production of material culture was becoming increasingly industrialized and mechanized during the Industrial Revolution. We argue, following Thomas (2004, 2009), that it is no coincidence that this was the case. In many ways, archaeology developed as an inquiry into the nature of premodern lifeways only at a time when those lifeways had become distant enough to be viewed as obscure and requiring 'excavation' to recover. An emphasis on handmade 'craft' objects rather than mass-produced ones in archaeology is one of its enduring and most important character traits.

One area in which research into mass-produced artefacts has flourished is historical archaeology. Here the interest in mass-produced goods has been not so much the objects themselves but the analysis of changes in manufacturing techniques that might be used as dating tools and for understanding the 'meaning' of certain assemblages in wider explorations of, for example, the analysis of gender, ethnicity, and class. The fundamental ubiquity of mass-produced artefacts in the late modern period would suggest at first glance that there is little that might interest an archaeologist in their study. We argue instead that the study of mass-produced goods in contemporary society has the potential to go beyond these traditional concerns to give us an insight into the nature of contemporary societies and their relationship with the material world.

We will focus in this discussion on the study of artefacts recovered from the excavation in 2006 in Bristol, UK, of a late-1980s Ford Transit van (Bailey et al. 2009). Conducted as a formative and at the time experimental archaeology of an iconic site type characteristic of the contemporary past, this was also an intimate and reflexive archaeology, examining the actions and activities of archaeologists and of the works and maintenance teams that inhabited the site afterwards. The purpose was to question the justification for doing contemporary archaeology, and what one might learn from it, either from the finds and information recovered or from the process of undertaking the work. Indeed the question soon came up as to whether the process was more important than the outcome, a view some artists take of their own activities (Bourriaud 2002: p. x). Here we will focus on the finds arising from the excavation. In fact this site (or is it an artefact, or a micro-landscape?) yielded a very ordinary workaday assemblage highlighting what simple artefact research combined with meticulous archaeological recovery can reveal about recently past actions and activities. Two categories of artefacts were recovered from the van: those related to its archaeological use by the Ironbridge Institute (1989–95), and those associated with works and maintenance (1995–9), the latter being later subdivided into more specific categories. The analysis of artefacts from the Transit van, including both small finds from within the van and its component parts, was undertaken by Adrian Myers (2009). Let us consider specifically here the 'maintenance' assemblage.

In all, 255 (72%) of the 352 artefacts from the van were associated with the daily work of the maintenance crews. Of these, 110 (43%) cannot be associated with a specific maintenance activity (and are thus labelled 'indeterminate maintenance'), 78 (31%) are associated with electrical work, 50 (20%) with woodworking, 12 (5%) with metalwork, four (1%) with plastering, and one (0.3%) with plumbing. The large number and wide variety of screws in this assemblage allowed a detailed screw typology to be developed through internet searching using the Google search engine. Every screw in the assemblage, of which there are 111, was found to have one of four head types (pan, round, flat, or bugle), one of three drive types (slotted, Phillips, or hex), and one of three tip types (machine, wood, self-tapping). The various combinations of these simple screw characteristics allow for 36 different screw types (a number that does not take into account the different metals used for screws). Though the 111 screws represent the gamut of screw types and materials, one type of screw stands out as the most common: a small, brass, slotted-drive, flat-head screw. This is a screw characteristically used in the finishing and decorative aspects of woodworking. Brass is often used for finishing because it is slower to tarnish, and the 'flat' head type allows for the screw to be countersunk (the top of the screw ends up flush with the material around it). In all, 36 of these were found, all from a single context, and all in perfect condition. It seems likely that these 36 identical screws represent a single depositional event: the tipping over of a box of screws.

That no effort was then taken to recuperate these screws is representative of broader trends within this maintenance assemblage. Of the 255 maintenance-related artefacts, 156 are in usable condition (61%). Of the 50 woodworking artefacts, 41 (83%) are usable (36 of these are from the single depositional event mentioned above), compared to 22 of the 78 (28%) artefacts associated with electrical work, 11 of the 12 metalworking artefacts (92%), all 4 plastering artefacts, and 75 of the 110 artefacts categorized as 'indeterminate maintenance' (68%). These percentages seem to demonstrate maintenance practices almost characterized by careless waste. That these usable maintenance artefacts were spread throughout the two strata of the back of the van suggest that the practices were habitual and longer term. This carelessness says something about the nature of late modern life—that many artefacts are considered so cheap, so quotidian, that they are not routinely curated, and even often simply discarded and immediately forgotten if they are misplaced. These observations can be compared with those that have emerged from the work of the Garbage Project (discussed in Ch. 2) to suggest certain patterns of behaviour that relate to discard and the value of quotidian objects in the late twentieth and early twenty-first centuries.

There is another lesson from studying artefacts from the van, and one that relates closely not only to the motor car, but to many mass-produced objects of the late modern era. The fact that most pieces of technical equipment, and their complex range of component parts, have part numbers can bring particular benefits to any archaeological study, benefits that invariably involve research amongst part directories, templates, and manufacturers' and other websites. We can illustrate this through Adrian Myers's study of part numbers from the Ford Transit van (Myers 2009).

Following the conventions of twentieth-century assembly-line mass production, the components of the Transit van were produced in exact replication by the tens of thousands. And as with so many late modern mass-produced artefacts, at the moment of their manufacture, many of the components that made up the vehicle were embossed with a part number and a date stamp. The part number is unique, referring to one particular part, though many thousands of identical parts are produced. Part numbers can be decoded to yield information about the history of design and production. Date stamps appear less frequently than part numbers, and the precision of the date varies. Though neither part numbers nor date stamps offer singular identifying information, every vehicle is assigned a unique sequence of letters and numbers known as the Vehicle Identification Number (VIN).

The Vehicle Identification Number

The VIN (in this case BDVLMJ83619), broken down into its constituent signs, gives a minimalist outline of the history of the vehicle up to this point. The 'B' indicates the vehicle was made in Britain; 'D' that it was made at the Southampton Assembly Plant; 'V' stands for 'van'; 'L' signifies the style of van (Mk 3 Transit); 'M' stands for 'September', the month the engine joined the chassis on the assembly line; 'J' signifies the year, in this case 1991; and finally, '83619' is the unique number of the engine and was assigned from a string of rising sequential numbers.

We can therefore tell this story. It was at Ford's Southampton assembly plant in southern England in late 1991, at the stage on the production line when the engine joined the chassis, that this Transit van received its VIN. It is at this precise moment of the union between frame and power plant that Ford recognizes what was formerly just 'parts' as a distinctive vehicle. The code from the chassis (BDVLMJ) was added to the code from the engine (83619) and vehicle BDVLMJ83619 thus became a unique entity. The string of letters and numbers not only identifies this from every other Transit, but this vehicle from every other vehicle in the world. In this way, the VIN makes the van simultaneously unique but also connected through a complex series of global networks to all other vehicles on the planet. This complex relationship of uniqueness and interconnection could be said to characterize many late modern mass-produced artefacts.

Ford Part Numbers and Date Stamps

As with the VIN, the identifying numbers on original Ford parts can be deciphered (Fig. 6.1). Unlike the VIN, however, this system of letters and numbers is proprietary. It is created and overseen by Ford, and aspects of the system are officially classified as 'confidential' by the company. It is a partially hidden, almost secret symbology. For the benefit of this and any future projects, the decoding of the van's parts was taken as far as possible, while staying within the scope of information freely shared by Ford. The simplest Ford part numbers in the United Kingdom are a string of eleven numbers and letters, for

Figure 6.1. Examples of date stamps and part numbers from the Transit van. (Photos: John Schofield.)

example: '91BB-12345-AA'. This format of three sets of letters and numbers separated by dashes is nearly ubiquitous amongst Fords. However the composition of letters and numbers and the length of the sets vary considerably.

According to Ford, the final set (which is usually two letters early in the alphabet, most commonly 'A' and 'B') represents two things. First, it distinguishes between 'left' (nearside) and 'right' (offside) versions of parts. This applies to components that are mirror images of each other—for example, the left and right headlights on every car. Second, the two letters also indicate revisions to a component. For example, if a part initially ending in 'AA' was subsequently altered, the letters might be changed to 'AB' to reflect the revision. Instructions on how specifically to decipher these two-letter combinations could not be obtained from Ford. Even less is known about the logic behind the middle set, except that it is the essential identifying component of the part number; it is the string that ultimately distinguishes one part from the next.

The meaning of the first set, again, is only partially known. Nevertheless it is the most useful. The first set of the invented part number is '91BB'. While nothing can be said about the two letters, the two numbers indicate the year the part was first designed. Thus '91' stands for '1991', '00' for '2000', and so on. A Ford part number provides one method of estimating the age of a car part. If found in a conventional archaeological context, a car part with its part number will contribute precise information towards establishing a *terminus post quem* (TPQ). While encounters between archaeologists, automobiles, and automobile parts do already occur (see e.g. Rathje and Murphy [1992] 2001: 6; Smith 2002; Holtorf 2005*b*: 28; Forsyth 2007: 21; Burström 2009) it is likely that the phenomenon will only become more common.

Many Ford automobile parts are not only stamped with unique identifying numbers, but often also with the date of actual manufacture of the part (Fig. 6.1). The markings usually display the month and date, but are sometimes precise to a specific day of the month. A date stamp can contribute to more accurate dating as it will inevitably push forward a TPQ established using a part number, as the date of manufacture must come after the design.

What then can be learnt from this intensive archaeological study of an everyday, mass-produced artefact and its constitutive parts and associated archaeological assemblage? We have already suggested (after Myers 2009) that patterning in the artefacts recovered from the vehicle indicates that certain types of artefact, such as the screws recovered from the rear of the vehicle, are not well valued in contemporary society, and are discarded rather than recycled or reused. We also looked at the ways in which, although mass-produced, the van might be thought to be simultaneously unique through the inclusion of a unique VIN, and connected to a global network of other vehicles through this system of unique identifiers. We can also examine here the globalized economy from a material cultural perspective. The van components were examined both in terms of their reported point of origin, prior to being assembled in Southampton, and—from the facility that shredded the van and then shipped the metals and other materials out from Avonmouth Docks, Bristol—information on their destination (see Fig. 3.1). The point here is one of recycling on a global scale, and with parity of function and form. Of the components derived from the van, many were returned to points of origin where they were used once more in vehicle manufacture, once again for export to the UK.

While we are perhaps comfortable with this idea of mass production, we highlighted another theme from late modern Western societies in Chapter 5, relating to objects produced with the capacity for modularization and 'mass customization'. We suggested that this phenomenon was connected to the ideas of Jensen (1999) and Pine and Gilmore (1999) relating to the existence of a dream or experience society. In the case study that follows, we will consider the IKEA 'Billy' bookcase as an example of such an artefact, and reflect on the ways in which such artefacts might inform an archaeological exploration of contemporary life.

MASS PRODUCTION, MASS CUSTOMIZATION AND THE AGENCY OF OBJECTS: THE ARCHAEOLOGY OF IKEA'S BILLY BOOKCASE

IKEA is one of the world's most successful global brands. As of August 2008 there were 253 IKEA stores in twenty-four countries. Counting IKEA suppliers raises this number to 1,380 distribution points in fifty-four countries. In 2008, over 565 million people visited an IKEA store (IKEA Group 2008: 2–3).

IKEA was founded by the Swedish designer Ingvar Kamprad (Lewis 2008). Having developed the concept of designing 'flat-pack' furniture in the mid-1950s, IKEA opened its first store in Älmhult in southern Sweden in 1958. By 1964, its business booming, it had opened stores in Stockholm and Oslo (Norway) which would form the template for all later IKEA stores, incorporating large parking spaces and a 'cash and carry' style combined showroom and warehouse (ibid. 56). Between 1965 and 1973, a further seven stores opened across a series of Scandinavian countries. But the global success of IKEA came in its ability to sell low-cost, modular, mass-customizable flat-pack furniture through selling Scandinavian 'style'. Throughout the late 1970s and early 1980s, IKEA stores spread across

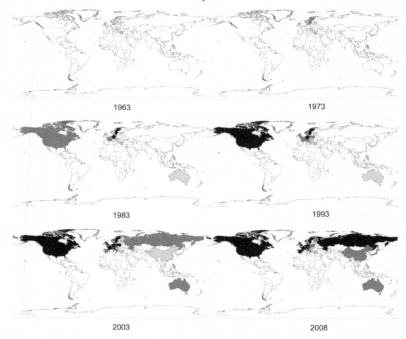

Figure 6.2. The IKEA tide: map showing the spread of IKEA stores since 1963 in 10-year increments. Light grey shading = 1 store, dark grey = 2–7 stores, black = more than 7 stores. (Drawing: Rodney Harrison.)

Europe, North America, and Australia. IKEA had become a truly global brand. In recent years, IKEA stores have opened in Russia, China, Japan, and a host of Eastern European countries. For the purposes of this case study, we might think of this global spread as the 'IKEA tide'. Figure 6.2 illustrates the global spread of IKEA stores across the world after 1963 in ten-year time-slices to arrive at the situation in 2008 in which IKEA is present throughout Europe, North America, Russia, China, Japan, and Australia, with only the poles, parts of south-east Asia, and the continents of Africa and South America left untouched by its influence.

One of the most emblematic and ubiquitous items from the IKEA catalogue is the Billy bookcase. The Billy bookcase is a simple modular shelving unit which is available in two different heights (106 and 202 cm) and widths (80 and 40 cm) and a number of finishes and colours (at the time of writing, these included beech veneer, birch veneer, black, black patterned, blue, medium brown, oak veneer, red, silver, and white), with a fixed depth of 28 cm. Shelving is adjustable and fixed to the inside frame of the bookcase using small bolts placed into pre-drilled holes. Various accessories, including height extension units, extra shelves, dividers, and other associated modular units that can be fitted to the Billy are also available. The bookcase is made of coated particleboard, so it is light, and is flat-packaged, so it is easily transported. Designed and launched in 1978, over the thirty-year period to 2008, over 28 million such bookcases had been sold by IKEA worldwide (Lewis 2008: 11).

The Billy Bookcase as an Archaeological Dating Aid

As we noted earlier in this chapter, one of the traditional aspects of the study of mass-produced goods in historical archaeology relates to their ability to act as guides to dating the use of particular archaeological sites. Objects found in association with archaeological sites that we know to be bracketed by particular date ranges in their manufacture can be used, in isolation or combination, to help obtain an estimate of the period in which an archaeological site was in use. We could think of the IKEA tide as one such dating aid. IKEA flat-pack materials and furniture is unlikely to appear in any volume in rubbish or landfill predating the period in which the company began trading in the country under consideration. In the United States, for example, it would be very unusual to find IKEA items or packaging in contexts dating to before 1985, as IKEA did not open its first store (in Philadelphia) until then. However, the possibility of using individual items of IKEA furniture for dating during the late modern period is potentially even more fruitful. The Billy bookcase, for example, has undergone a number of slight modifications since it was introduced in 1978. Countersunk holes for the fixings that form 'brackets' on which the shelves sit were added, and the back board, which was originally a single piece, has become a tri-fold piece, which allows the bookcase to be shipped in a smaller box (Pearman 2007)

Figure 6.3. White IKEA Billy bookcase showing 80 × 202 cm unit with 35 cm height extension paired with 40 × 202 cm unit with 35 cm height extension. (Photo: Rodney Harrison.)

(Fig. 6.3). New colours have been added to the range, and old versions of current colour schemes have also changed. This becomes obvious when comparing a beech veneer Billy bookcase manufactured before 2005 with one manufactured after 2005, for example. Similarly, the packaging itself has changed, and is now made entirely of card, instead of card and polystyrene. Indeed, despite the fact that IKEA is a global company, its components are locally manufactured by thousands of different companies. This means that changes have not necessarily been introduced simultaneously, nor is every Billy bookcase identical to the others.

As discussed above, such variations can be charted and used as dating aids in the manner conventional for historical archaeologists. But perhaps more importantly, these physical variations point us towards something more profound about understanding mass-produced goods—that they are not, in fact, identical. In the same way in which handmade artefacts preserve aspects of their individual manufacturing histories, so do mass-produced objects. This suggests that a study of these variations might yield the same insights as an investigation of small-scale craft production. Tim Ingold (2000: 372) draws a comparison between the ways in which artefacts are produced and the ways in which organisms are reproduced. He writes that 'every artefact, formed as it is within the process of production, is an original, not a replica. And whatever variation may be introduced in the process lies in the dynamics of making.' Variation becomes the key to understanding the complex dynamics of making which do not relate to reproduction, but to human influence or 'interference' (see Harrison 2010c) in the process of manufacture. Such variation holds the answer to understanding the role of human agency within the process of mass production.

Mass-Produced Artefacts and Material Meaning

In addition to being mass produced, Billy bookcases represent a modular and generic artefact flexible enough to allow it to be used in many different circumstances. We argue that such modular artefacts form the basis for an archaeology of the non-place (a theme explored in more detail in Ch. 9). As modular artefacts, Billy bookcases are produced in a range of colours and sizes that allow for adaptive or cosmetic mass customization, where goods are produced to a standard model and either modified by the end-user or marketed to different groups in different ways (Pine 1992). But what is the importance of IKEA in understanding everyday life? IKEA represents the concentration of a series of ideas about home, class, wealth, and modernity. Despite their ubiquity, Billy bookcases have a range of different meanings within different societies. For example, in the book *Fight Club*, written by Chuck Palahnuik (1996) and the film of the same name (released in 1999 and directed by David Fincher), the Billy bookcase (and IKEA in general) is a symbol of slavery to a consumer economy. It is emblematic of the consumer artefact par excellence. For many, the ability to own IKEA furniture represents a form of class equality owing to the low prices of IKEA goods, and the accompanying cultural capital that is acquired through purchasing good, 'modern' Swedish design. But as DeFazio (2002) notes:

The superfluidity of commodities...is itself an index of the class basis of production. There is such an excess to begin with because of the small amount of time it takes workers to reproduce their daily needs with today's technology compared to the bulk of the time they spend producing value for the capitalist in the form of commodities. More and more workers cannot afford to buy what they themselves produce because of the cheapening of labor due to the competitive use of technology for profit. By fetishizing the effects these conditions have on the form of commodities the changes in 'style' are themselves trivialized as matters of pure taste above and beyond the social contradictions of class, which is, of course, not a neutral position but precisely the cultural view of those few whose needs are sure to be met because they live off the surplus labor of the other.

For some, IKEA represents cheap furniture associated with the lower and working classes, thus emphasizing the distance between classes; whereas in other circumstances, it is associated with widening access to consumer goods and the dissolution of class boundaries. Cross-culturally, its meanings are even more diverse. The popularity of IKEA in Sweden resides more in its ubiquity and price, whereas outside northern Europe, its marketing has focused on the exoticism of 'Swedish design'. Thus the 'meaning' of the Billy bookcase can be read in many different ways. This problem of multiple meanings in modern material culture will be dealt with further towards the end of this chapter. In the meantime, as we have argued in Chapter 4, we should turn away from the Billy bookcase as a 'discourse' and focus on its material qualities and involvement in networks of agency that link together humans and non-human actors across time and space.

The Distributed Agency of Mass-Produced Artefacts

The Billy bookcase raises the issue of the relationship between individual items of modern material culture and agency, which has become one of the central concerns of historical archaeology (e.g. Cochran and Beaudry 2006: 198; Hall and Silliman 2006: 9–10; Hicks and Horning 2006: 287–91). Can mass-produced artefacts exhibit agency in their interactions with humans? In Chapter 4 we introduced Latour's (2005) use of the term 'actor' or 'actant' to stand for anything that modifies any particular state of affairs.

We noted that this accent shifts the emphasis from what objects 'symbolize' to the ways in which material objects are involved in particular forms of interactions which create social 'features' such as inequalities in power or networks of social connection. The anthropological perspectives on material culture developed by the late Alfred Gell (1998; see further discussion in relation to material culture studies in Harrison 2006 and 2010c) provide a useful way of thinking through the social efficacy of artefacts. Gell presents a model in which material objects can mediate the social agency of humans, acting as the 'indexes' of this agency, as 'material entities which motivate inferences, responses, or interpretations' (Thomas 1998: p. ix). Gell's theory of the 'art nexus' describes the mediation of agency by way of a series of 'agent–patient' relationships that are described according to four main referents that are said to exist in the vicinity of objects: artists, indexes, prototypes, and recipients. For Gell (1998: 26) the social relations that surround artefacts can exist only when they are made manifest in the form of actions. Those people or things that perform social actions are agents with reference to those things on which they perform them, which are known as patients. Drawing on Marilyn Strathern's (1988) concept of the distributed person in Melanesian anthropology, Gell explains the way in which objects become part of the distributed personhood of the 'artist'—the person who is considered to be responsible in the first instance for the existence of the index, or art object (cf. Wagner 1992). Thus for Gell (1998: 222–3), humans are not confined to a spatial or temporal framework particular to their physical body, 'but consist of a spread of biographical events and memories of events, and a dispersed category of material objects, traces and leavings, which can be attributed to a person and which, in aggregate, testify to agency and patienthood during a biographical career which may, indeed, prolong itself long after biological death'. Gell distinguishes between the primary agency of intentioned and conscious actors, and the secondary agency of objects. Leach (2007) significantly extends Gell's discussion of the agency of material objects. He suggests that Gell's anthropological theory of art should be seen as essentially flawed, as it places primary agency only in the hands of human actors (or 'artists' in Gell's words) who are seen as the ultimate starting point in the chain of agent–patient relationships he describes. It is only when we effectively admit that an artefact or art object might have primary agency of its own that we can use the distinctive life histories of material objects to generate innovative critical positions and alternative models of the efficacy or agency of individual items of material culture.

We can apply these ideas to the analysis of the Billy bookcase by thinking of each of the 28 million bookcases that have been sold over the globe as interconnected. Each bookcase is an extension of the distributed agency of IKEA, and each bookcase has the ability to exert its own agency independently of the agency of the company. Indeed, the common parlance that attributes modern companies with per-sonalities of their own, and which sees them as an 'entity' with agency is a useful frame for considering the ways in which their artefacts come to produce a set of values and have their own forms of agency in their relationship with humans and non-humans in this process. Lewis (2008: 147) discusses a company philosophy referred to as 'the IKEA way'. The company encourages a corporate culture in which managers are able to ask themselves, 'is this an IKEA kind of thing to do?' and formulate an answer. In this way, the philosophies of the company are not abstract, but are manifested throughout the multinational network of individuals that makes up the corporation. If we start to think of multinational companies as the conglomeration not only of their management but of the things they produce, and the physical effects of the things they produce on the people who use them and society as a whole, this provides us with a framework within which to analyse the material agency of mass-produced objects.

So what sort of agency do Billy bookcases exhibit? Cheap modular storage like Billy has been associated with pushing the 'flat-pack philosophy' which authors such as Ritzer ([1995] 2004: 17) associate specifically with the 'McDonaldization' of society (see further Ch. 9). Due to the great simplicity of the home construction methods of the Billy bookcase and its dominance in the market of bookcase sales, it has helped familiarize people with the idea of flat-pack shipping and home assembly, which in turn has assisted IKEA to promote more of its products to a broader market segment and to develop a dominance in the market. Through their ubiquity in the West, and their ability to be customized by the user, they have also been involved in a broader process of allowing the storage of larger quantities of consumer goods within the home and the increased isolation of the individual within the space of the home. The increased ownership of devices such as computers, video game consoles, and individual ownership of television sets, which requires individuals to have their own isolated space within the household (Mason 2009), has gone hand in hand with the development of modular storage facilities and the overall requirements for more, rather than less, living space. Ironically, given that the Billy bookcase is marketed as a storage solution for small spaces, it has in fact been involved in a series of developments that have contributed to the overall growth in the average domestic floorspace (ibid.). Some of these issues surrounding the isolation of the individual through technology and design in the late modern period will be revisited in Chapter 9.

Edgerton (2007) makes the point that it is not the great technological inventions, but the most quotidian technologies that have the greatest influence on people's lives. This is certainly true of widespread, mass-produced modular items of material culture such as the Billy bookcase. We have seen how shifting our frame of reference to consider the Billy bookcase as an extension of the distributed agency of IKEA helps us to understand the connection between people, abstract notions such as 'corporations' and 'things', and the agency of late modern mass-produced, modular, and mass-customizable goods. In the next case study, we will turn to consider briefly another aspect of everyday material culture, the home, and the role that the archaeological study of artefacts might play in helping us understand ourselves through an analysis of its material culture.

OUR FAMILIAR OBJECTS: AN AUTOARCHAEOLOGY OF THE HOME

In Chapter 4 we discussed the potential for an archaeology of the contemporary world to be written as a form of autoethnography. One aspect of archaeology of the contemporary past to emerge in the twenty-first century that underpins its critical and self-reflexive aims is the investigation of our own personal lives and those of close family members, often through the objects and artefacts we encounter at home. How many of us, as archaeologists, have rummaged through our parents' or grandparents' stuff and questioned their propensity to collect or hoard, or their value judgements, or even taste? And how many of us, equally, do this to ourselves, sorting materials in advance of (or following) a house move: 'why did we keep this for so long?' or 'why did we throw such-and-such away?' Christine Finn is a British-based archaeologist who has thought about this more than most, not least in dealing with the death of her parents and inheriting the family home in Kent in 2006. A commentary, recorded for BBC Radio on visiting her home following the death of her remaining parent (entitled *Leaving Home*), describes the experience as a kind of memory walk. At one point she finds a record on top of a wardrobe, listening to which recalls particular memories and trains of thought. And the hall carpet she had always hated: no time was lost in tearing that up. The commentary of *Leaving Home* (and the follow-up *Leave–Home–Stay*) describes the mantelpiece too, and how each object on it released not one narrative but generations of them (Fig. 6.4). A specific dimension of this exercise has been Finn's treatment of

Figure 6.4. 'Last Mantle, Installation I', from *Leave–Home–Stay* 2007, by Christine Finn, for   RIBA South-East Architecture Week/Arts Council England. (Image copyright: the artist.)

the mantelpiece as archaeological site. Likened to Roman *lares* and *penates*, the household gods at the hearth, 'we have an equivalent in the mantel as a fixed place and focal point, even if the "votives" are secular and come in a bag from IKEA' (Finn 2009: 1). As Finn says, 'every object in a home tells a story, but the mantel is a place to perform, a paradise for people-watching, where the gilt-edged "stiffy" and the Mother's Day card can be fighting for space with the spare set of car keys and the TV remote' (ibid.). Following Finn, we might see the mantelpiece as an archaeological site, clearing the mantel as excavation, and remembering and transforming it as a process of change in microcosm.

A similar approach to the autoarchaeology of family was undertaken by Jonna Ulin (2009), who excavated the remains of her grandmother's childhood home in northern Sweden. She describes this as a piece of 'post-memory' work, an investigation into her own past that was simultaneously a work of biography and a creative act of memory. Archaeologically, investigating perceptions and constructions of home through memory and materiality is something which is almost exclusive to the recent and contemporary past. It is something clearly evident in Finn's archaeological approach to her former home, and in the work of the Australian historian Peter Read. In his *Returning to Nothing* (1996) Read explores definitions of home, and how it can operate and have definition at a variety of scales: a region, city, suburb, house, a room within a house, or a plant in the garden. But as well as the space, people conceptualize home for the functions it performs: an enclosed space, or an area formed of particular social relations. Home is something people value, to the extent that its loss can be traumatic. Here we describe home as raising a particular set of questions and responses that, as the work of Finn and Ulin has shown, can benefit from archaeological inquiry.

These two brief examples demonstrate the significant potential for contemporary archaeology as a form of autoethnography, or an investigation into ourselves. The process of autoarchaeology (see also Harrison and Schofield 2009), perhaps more than any other, forces us to consider archaeology as a contemporary act, and one that is intimately connected with broader processes of remembering and forgetting. It also forces us to reflect on the broader role of archaeology within society in excavating memory and memorializing particular forms of material culture. Archaeology is not a mute witness, but a process by which meaning is produced by assembling different forms of material as part of a series of knowledge-making practices in the present. The role of an autoarchaeology is to draw attention to the ways in which these processes operate behind the scenes within contemporary society, and to focus on the role of archaeology as a particular form of knowledge-making process.

ISSUES IN THE STUDY OF CONTEMPORARY MATERIAL CULTURE

In this final part of the chapter, we briefly raise a series of issues that inform the archaeological study of late modern and contemporary material culture. There have been a number of recent publications from within the field of material culture studies that outline a broad agenda for material culture studies in the new millennium (e.g. Buchli 2002; Tilley 2006; Tilley et al. 2006; Hicks and Beaudry 2010), and rather than oversimplifying their arguments in the limited space available here we will instead draw out a number of issues relevant to the studies we explore in later parts of the book, and to the archaeology of the contemporary past in particular. We highlight the postmodern tendency for artefacts to embody multiple or reversed meanings; the ways in which recycling and retro fashion modify the relationship between artefact use and discard; problems of physical scale and the speed of technological change; and the nature of late twentieth and early twenty-first century conflict in the study of contemporary material culture. While this list is by no means exhaustive, we hope this part of the chapter will raise a number of questions that will stimulate future research in modern material culture studies and archaeologies of the contemporary past.

Reversed Meanings

In December 1976 in Britain, four young men swore openly on prime-time TV, shocking the nation to its core. *The Daily Telegraph* headline described how '4-Letter Words Rock TV'; *Daily Express*: 'Fury at Filthy TV Chat'. Punk had arrived on an unsuspecting but, arguably, deserving nation. Their legacy is a fascinating one, in that it reversed meanings and levels of acceptability, in music, for example, and fashion. For punks there was a desire constantly to display the division they felt between 'us' and 'them', expressed largely through a form of self-presentation, often quite literally as walking rubbish sculptures. Things that most people would discard were used or worn, and items often placed out of context: safety pins as ear-rings for example, and zips in trousers where they served no useful purpose. In that summer in the mid 1970s, the world changed, and as archaeologists this is a point at which our reading of material culture through the analogy of contemporary usage takes a completely new and unforeseen direction. Dick Hebdige ([1979] 1988: 106–7) pro-vides a graphic illustration of the materiality of punk, one worth repeating at length (also after Schofield 2000: 150):

Like Duchamp's 'ready mades'—manufactured objects which qualified as art because he chose to call them such—the most remarkable and inappro-priate items—a pin, a plastic clothes peg, a television component, a razor blade, a tampon—could be brought within the province of punk (un) fashion. Anything within or without reason could be turned into part of what Vivienne Westwood called 'confrontation dressing' so long as the rupture between 'natural' and constructed context was clearly visible. Objects borrowed from the most sordid of contexts found a place in the punk ensembles: lavatory chains were draped in graceful arcs across chests encased in plastic bin liners. Safety pins were taken out of their domestic 'utility' context and worn as gruesome ornaments through the cheek, ear, or lip. 'Cheap' trashy fabrics (PVC, plastic, lurex etc.) in vulgar designs (e.g. mock leopard skin) and 'nasty' colours, long discarded by the quality end of the fashion industry as obsolete kitsch, were salvaged by the punks and turned into garments...which offered self-conscious commentaries on the notions of modernity and taste. Conventional ideas of prettiness were jet-tisoned along with the traditional feminine lure of cosmetics...Hair was obviously dyed, and T-shirts and trousers told the story of their own construction with multiple zips and outside seams clearly displayed.... The perverse and the abnormal were valued intrinsically. In particular, the illicit iconography of sexual fetishism was used to predictable effect: rapist masks and rubber wear, leather bodices and fishnet stockings, implausibly pointed stiletto-heeled shoes, the whole paraphernalia of bondage—the belts, straps and chains—were exhumed from the boudoir, closet and the pornographic film and placed on the street where they retained their forbidden connotations.

Similar reversals have happened since: with the transient, flimsy, and tacky artefacts of Nu-Rave (brightly coloured plastic sunglasses, oversized neon accessories, plastic toys) and the reversed meanings of acid house (dummies for example). How then should we regard these reversals in modern material culture? Key here is the degree to which materiality reflects social diversity, and specifically alternative views and perspectives. The point of punk was that it deliberately reversed perspective, twisting it to the point almost of polar opposite. Punk material culture, encountered archaeologically if you will, could be read in a normative, conventional, and literal way, but leaving open the possibility of a contrary view. It is queer, in some respects, turning convention on its head and ensuring the possibility of alternative and perhaps radically opposing views and interpretations. In understanding the meaning of contemporary material culture, context is always critical for interpretation.

Recycling, Retro, and the Study of Modern Material Culture

As we have discussed in Chapter 5, the later twentieth century might be characterized as a time when people increasingly looked to the past with a sense of nostalgia, but also an era in which people felt a melancholy sense of being haunted by the past. We have discussed the rise of official forms of heritage documentation, and indeed, the newfound interest in archaeologies of the contemporary past, as a consequence of this obsession. Another place where this sense of nostalgia/haunting by the past is represented is through contemporary relationships with material culture. Retro, the recycling of outdated fashion or design that can be firmly identified as relating to a particular recent historical period, typifies this relationship between nostalgia and material culture that emerges in the late modern period.

Guffey (2006: 8) sees the beginning of a unique post-war phenomenon in the revival of Art Nouveau design and the sudden interest in the work of artists such as Audrey Beardsley in the mid 1960s, describing it as 'a popular thirst for the recovery of earlier, and yet still modern, periods at ever accelerating rates'. She continues, 'as society has developed it has found new ways to tell its own history. Retro allows us to come to terms with our modern past' (ibid. 8–9).

Critics and commentators have been divided on the meaning of retro. For Jean Baudrillard (1994), retro is associated with the diminution of reality and authenticity, while for historian Raphael Samuel (1994), retro comes to stand for the increased unofficial public involvement in history. Frederic Jameson (1991) is critical of retro, seeing it as a symptom of a society that is 'irredeemably historicist' and has lost the ability to look to the future. Whether positive or negative, Guffey (2006: 17) notes that retro (like heritage) has little to do with the past, but is actually focused on the continual reinterpretation of the past in the present.

We can think of retro as the rise of recycling as fashion rather than thrift. On this linked topic of recycling, it is important for us to comment here on the changes in waste disposal that have occurred in many post-industrialized societies since the 1970s and its relationship to nostalgia and the past. Although recycling precious or rare materials has a history as old as humanity itself, the push after the 1970s to 'reduce, reuse and recycle' saw an increased emphasis on recycling at all levels, including the industrialized processes of recycling plastics, paper, and glass. While on the one hand we can see this as relating at a symbolic level to the nostalgia for, and sense of haunting by, the past that is also responsible for retro as fashion, the new attitude towards recycling has major implications for how we understand the relationship between human use of materials and their patterns of discard. Waste is increasingly being deposited in locations remote from where it is created, and much of it does not make its way directly into landfill, but is reworked and recycled, and finds its way back into circulation. We can no longer assume a direct relationship between consumption and the deposition of waste. Many of these issues are discussed further by Rathje and Murphy ([1992] 2001).

We must see these processes of retro and recycling as intimately linked. Burström (2009; see also Pearson and Shanks 2001) characterizes the relationship as one in which both garbage and heritage are significant for the way they demonstrate the influence of the passage of time on material objects. Both processes influence the ways in which modern artefacts enter the archaeological record, and the potential for objects from the past to be continually reworked in terms of meaning, value and use in the present. There is a cautionary tale here—we can't assume that artefacts date to the periods in which they were manufactured. But there is another, broader issue that this phenomenon reflects, relating to the likelihood for late modern artefact assemblages to be composed of artefacts from a variety of periods, despite the incredibly rapid rate of technological change (see further discussion below). There is a wide-ranging literature on the persistence and reappearance of traces of the past in the present, such as the work of Charles R. Acland and contributors in *Residual Media* (2007). We might also think of the work of science-fiction author Bruce Sterling, whose Dead Media Research Lab is concerned with the problem of how to reuse electronic waste creatively (see <http://www.conceptlab.com/deadmedia/>, accessed November 2009).

Problems of Scale and Rates of Technological Change

Studying modern material culture raises problems of physical scale, the remoteness or number of interconnected material culture items, and the incredibly rapid rate of technological change, which produces a situation in which there is a great deal of variation in the take-up of different forms of technology. We have already mentioned some of the largest late modern artefacts such as the Large Hadron Collider at CERN. Other objects, such as networked computer systems, are interconnected in such complex ways that it is impossible to understand how they function in isolation from the other objects they are connected to. Such artefacts are both enormous and incredibly technically complex. Nonetheless, their study as physical objects from an archaeological perspective has the potential to inform a number of critical questions about the relationships between people and material objects in the late twentieth and early twenty-first centuries.

The pace of change of technology also raises problems for the study of modern material culture. Moore's Law, for example, describes the trend in computing in which the number of transistors that can be placed on an integrated circuit has increased exponentially, doubling approximately every two years (Moore 1965).

This has led to exponential rates of change in the production of computing circuits, which means that some parts of society will be adopting technology at a rapid rate. But because of the operation of the process of recycling described above, as well as the fact that many people do not adopt technology as quickly as it is produced, there will always be a range of different forms of technology in use at any one time, until changes (such as the cessation of the broadcasting of analogue television signals, for example) are enforced. Only when technologies have become essentially useless will they be entirely superseded. So archaeologists of the contemporary past must be able to make sense of a much broader range of types of technology in operation at any one time. It is interesting to note that Moore's Law has theoretical limits that are imposed by the technologies of computer chip production, although there is some argument about when the terminus in Moore's Law might be reached. This idea of technical termini relates back to the concept of survival of the old in the late modern period, a concept that we have emphasized throughout the book as a distinct area of focus for archaeologies of the contemporary past.

The Nature of Recent and Contemporary Conflict

Many of the artefacts that characterize late modernity are those of conflict and warfare (González-Ruibal 2008). We can identify two strongly opposed forces that structure the material culture of conflict and war. In the first process, war has become increasingly industrialized in scale and scope since the early part of the twentieth century. Artefacts in the form of war *matériel* are mass produced, and then typically destroyed or disfigured in the process of being used (see Saunders 2003, 2007). War material culture is centrally produced and distributed, and strongly homogenous in form. The form and design of late modern war material culture is closely linked to processes of nation building (which in turn links it back to heritage).

In the second diametrically opposed process, terrorism and guerrilla warfare is becoming increasingly common. The material culture of terrorism and guerrilla warfare is generally improvised and tends to be ephemeral, dispersed, and 'low tech' to escape increasingly technical forms of weapons and bomb detection. Sustained conflict also often arises between groups with small rather than large cultural differences, and against weak and small as opposed to powerful minorities (Appadurai 2006). While this conflict is also associated with nation building, it is closely aligned to the emergence (or re-emergence) of ethnic nationalisms.

Despite these apparently diametrically opposed forces that are at play in structuring the nature of the material culture of late modern conflict, González-Ruibal (2008: 262) convincingly argues,

> it is precisely this particular and at the same time all-embracing character of the archaeology of supermodernity that makes it a privileged space for reflection on certain concepts that concern archaeology as a whole: mediation, materiality, place and memory, and politics. From World War I to the Chinese Three Gorges Dam, the archaeology of supermodernity is the archaeology of superdestruction of life and matter.

The theme of twentieth and twenty-first century conflict material culture links many of the other issues we have discussed here—for example waste, destruction, and the transformation of one object to another (c.f. Buchli 2002: 13). It is a space for reflection on the nature of late modernity and those things that have been repressed, made abject or remote and unknowable. It demonstrates the potential for archaeologies of the contemporary past to perform both an academic and a therapeutic function (Buchli 2007; Gould 2007; González-Ruibal 2008), to presence absences (Buchli and Lucas 2001*a*) and to force us to question the recent past by making the familiar unfamiliar (Graves-Brown 2000*a*).

Curating Contemporary Artefacts

The curatorial responsibility for artefacts tends to rest with museums and heritage agencies, with good practice determined by a combination of peer review and experience, and guided by museum professionals. But as is typical for this subject, and given its infancy, the archaeology of the contemporary past is somewhat different. The artefacts are not historic and have not been sorted by the passage of time. Everything remains with us, from the obviously important (the first computers, say), to the 'iconic everyday' (mobile phones), to the everyday disposable objects that we routinely discard and replace. Many of the principles of conservation, recording, and storage are probably common to artefacts of any type and age, but choice and selection is another matter. These considerations require value judgements to be taken, and decisions made on the basis of agreeing to collect/curate, for the benefit of this and future generations. Should museums keep every example of a mobile phone for example, or just a representative sample, or simply a couple of key models that define the type? The same with cars—if we can consider these to be artefacts for a moment, as opposed to sites or micro-landscapes, as suggested earlier. Which models should we keep of the thousands that have been produced? In the UK there are statistics on licensed cars by type (including model) and year of manufacture. It can therefore be established precisely how many cars of a particular model remain on the road, and comparison made with manufacturers' statistics for the numbers built. If an early 1970s model of Ford Capri (a fairly iconic car of the time) is one of only very few still in use, what—if anything—should be done about that? Should such rare cars be curated in some way? And how then do these modern artefacts compare to those that have accumulated historic significance and patina? An example is the increased portability of popular music, with shifts in technologies producing waves of transformation and discard, first of records (vinyl) and record players, then cassettes (and briefly 8-Track cartridges) and now, increasingly CDs. Of course the situation is much more complicated than this, with recycling and 'collectibles' ensuring that the market endures. Yet records (and presumably cassettes and CDs) by some lesser-known and less commercially successful bands and musicians have become almost invisible since their heyday. Some bands had a strong and loyal following but lacked commercial success and often also national recognition. By the time these bands and musicians ceased recording, their records—released in their thousands—had become rare to the point almost of being unavailable. Their occasional appearance on eBay might attract significant bids indicative of the bands' now legendary cult status. Typically, such bands have a limited web presence (Wikipedia, for example), and digital downloads of the back-catalogue are not usually available.

Records are perhaps unusual, though the pattern is not. Old technologies and classic household items are often available in facsimile, but originals can be comparatively rare. So in that sense there is little difference between modern artefacts and genuine 'antiquities'. The real thing can be obtained, but attracts high prices. Replicas and facsimiles can be purchased on the open market, and often in high-street stores (Hawkins Bazaar for 1970s toys; Past Times for Victoriana). The only real difference is the way museums treat this material, and the general scarcity of museums of late modernity—although museums that focus on the materiality of the recent past are emerging. The Bakelite Museum at Williton (Somerset) is an impressive example of a museum to late modernity, as is the Atomic Testing Museum in Las Vegas.

CONCLUSION

In this chapter we have explored archaeological approaches to late modern and contemporary artefacts through several case studies. In the first, we saw how an exploration of a mass-produced Ford Transit van helped us to understand more about contemporary attitudes towards modern material culture, and the networks of connection that exist between mass-produced items. In the second case study we explored an approach that foregrounds the agency of late modern artefacts, while highlighting mass customization as an important theme for understanding the global spread of late modern material culture. In the third case study we explored the archaeology of the home as an example of autoarchaeology, or the archaeology of ourselves. All of these case studies focused specifically on mass-produced, everyday artefacts. We suggested that it is the very ordinariness and ephemerality of such items that means they are often overlooked by other cross-disciplinary studies of modern material culture. In the final part of the chapter, we explored some of the problems in the study of modern artefacts for archaeologists, highlighting the themes of reversed meanings, reuse, and retro, problems of scale and rate of change, and the nature of recent and contemporary conflict and curation. Running through these issues we saw similar themes associated with the late modern relationship to the past. In the next chapter we broaden our spatial scale to consider archaeological approaches to late twentieth and early twenty-first century sites.

7

Sites

We gathered at the appointed time, at the confluence of two pedestrian streets in a busy urban centre—thirty or so archaeology undergraduates and me, their teacher. This was an archaeological field exercise, a practical opportunity to apply archaeological methods in an urban landscape: to investigate archaeological sites in the city. I think the students were all a bit bemused. Why here, when there were so many other obviously 'historic' places that could have been chosen? This was an area of recent development, and not even very nice. It was also a closely familiar place, and one they all knew well. Of course these were precisely the reasons I had chosen to bring them here, of all places. Some students seemed more familiar with the place in daytime—they knew where the best bargains were to be had, and good shortcuts between their favoured haunts. Some knew it better at night: the land of clubs and bars unfamiliar to the older amongst us. Either way, it was a closely familiar place but for different reasons, and lacking in obvious traces of a historic past. I divided them into groups and gave each a large-scale map of the area and some coloured pencils. I explained the task: to create an archaeological map of the area, presenting information about human activity, and its material traces. One group was to conduct a surface survey: recording the locations and types of artefacts, not necessarily for the whole area; they could devise a sampling strategy if they wished. Another was tasked with recording, by field sketch, some of the façades of buildings, showing phases, alterations, and repairs. Another yet would create an overview, highlighting by zonation the principal 'character areas', such as residential, retail and commercial, business use, communication, etc. Other groups were to examine traces for specific types of activity that represent, to some degree, the subversion of the order and authority of the urban centre: homelessness and vandalism for example. All knew what they had to do, and all set off, being archaeologists, doing archaeological survey, and recovering evidence for (perhaps even their own) activities of the night before.

INTRODUCTION

Sites are the staple of archaeological investigation, forming the basis of many an excavation or survey project, often within a wider landscape study where it is the relationships between sites that can matter more. Think of any archaeological project or great excavation of the nineteenth or twentieth century, and you have your archaeological site, defined by convention as incorporating either settlement or industrial, religious, or military remains. These sites are often the subject of either a lengthy process of investigation and then post-excavation analysis leading to publication of results, or sometimes a short field evaluation prior to their destruction through development or preservation in situ. Their initial discovery may be newsworthy, and perhaps the result of some significant new development, a new landmark in the making. As we have seen, by convention archaeologists and curators generally treat those places and objects from the past as precious, valued resources for their very historicity and their cultural value, and often (correctly) seek their protection from destructive forces of the present and future. But our view is slightly different. We do not recognize the distinction between that which is old/ancient and matters, and that which is new and does not. Rather we recognize all material culture, the artefacts and sites and the wider landscape, as being suitable for archaeological inquiry and potentially holding value for this reason: not just the objects of the deeper past threatened with destruction, but also the contemporary office building that now occupies the site. Archaeology of the contemporary past even gives recognition to the 'site to be', the places planned for the future, a site that exists only on a planning board or an architect's computer, or as a model, or even in the mind. With the archaeology of the contemporary past, the past, present, and future are woven together in a way that gives the subject complexity, introduces new and unforeseen challenges and difficulties, and equally gives it a heightened sense of social relevance and meaning.

That said, for archaeology of the contemporary past, many of the same rules apply as for earlier periods, although, as we have seen, the sheer numbers of modern sites, and the spatial continuity of human activity and our perception and experience of it, do complicate things somewhat. This continuity blurs the boundaries between what for earlier periods are often clear and discrete entities with convenient borders between what lies inside and what's outside: the site and its environs. But nevertheless we can recognize the existence of late modern sites, even though the ways people use and think about them may defy such simple categorization and spatial delimitation.

In this chapter we present examples of what constitute archaeological sites of the late modern world, both in terms of their existence as distinctive spatial and functional entities, and as places that have seen some form of archaeological investigation, as broadly defined previously in Chapter 3. As archaeologists we like to set up frameworks for the material culture we investigate: typologies or, perhaps more correctly, taxonomies, within which relationships, similarities, and differences can be assessed and made sense of. This chapter is no exception. Here the basic framework is one developed by English Heritage for its 2004 Change and Creation Programme (Bradley et al. 2004), later used as the basis for *Images of Change* (Penrose 2007) and the 'Modern Times' issue of *Conservation Bulletin* (English Heritage 2007a). Table 2.1 provides a summary of the framework into which most of the sites described here should fall, perhaps neatly and seamlessly, perhaps not. Some of the details are in the following indicative account. While there is a UK bias in the examples that follow, that is a reflection of the available literature if not the scope of fieldwork projects undertaken to date.

POLITICS: GOVERNANCE AND DEFENCE

The actions of government, the state, authority and order are clearly imprinted on the landscape, typically embracing education and health authorities, political and military wards. In the UK as in other developed countries these spheres are configured by interrelated yet independent bodies: Parliament (the Houses of Commons and Lords, the elected and unelected lawmaking body); the Executive (to put those laws into effect); and the Judiciary (to adjudicate the law). Its organs are institutional, symbols of authority, recognizable tools of state power (government offices, judicial courts, houses of correction, army installations), and channels of social welfare (schools, hospitals), all arterially joined by channels of movement (roads, corridors, pathways, broader networks). Buildings and infrastructure reflect the legal and administrative organization of government ministries, from health to transport, from rural affairs to culture, media, and sport, and their contribution to the way states and countries look and work. Typically, public understanding of the state is shaped by engagement, interaction, and familiarity with the physical facets of government. It is through its physical manifestation, its design and presentation in the political landscape, that state power is most clearly understood by the majority of the population. In many ways, the extent and range of responses to this political landscape indicate its impact on public consciousness.

As was described briefly in Chapter 2, much of the current focus on the archaeology of the contemporary past owes its origin in part to work on Second World War sites and landscapes, and as a result much of the work in this subject area relates to militarism, and social responses to it. The Defence of Britain project, much of English Heritage's National Mapping Programme (e.g. Hegarty and Newsome 2007), the work of English Heritage survey teams previously part of the Royal Commission on the Historical Monuments of England (RCHME) (e.g. Cocroft and Thomas 2003), and work commissioned by the Monuments Protection Programme and the Listing Team in 1995–2002 (e.g. Dobinson 2001) provide examples of the potential for different approaches and applications, and of the different site types represented within this particular area of activity. It is also an example of how at least part of this development was driven by heritage concerns and the need for understanding as a basis for informed conservation (Clark 2001). Although predating the chronological focus of the second part of the book, the example of Second World War sites in England is worth repeating here, albeit in outline, as it does exemplify a particular methodology and research outcome that have a bearing on approaches to the archaeology of more recent periods. We have seen already how English Heritage's thematic studies reveal the extent to which a combination of documentary and aerial photographic sources can enhance our understanding not only of what survives today, but what was originally built. We know how rare surviving sites are, despite the comparatively recent date and their structural solidity. Some 1,000 Heavy Anti-aircraft gunsites were built in the Second World War, for example. These were robust and extensive sites, with gun emplacements, radar, domestic accommodation, access roads, etc. Yet despite their size and scale, and their wide national distribution, only a very small percentage of these sites survive in a form that is legible to visitors, the majority having been lost due to post-war urban and suburban expansion (Dobinson 2001; Schofield 2002). Key here was their location: these sites were designed to protect cities and industrial centres from aerial attack during wartime, and their location was thus focused around urban areas. These areas expanded significantly during the later twentieth century, engulfing the sites that had previously protected them. There is a certain irony here, and also in the fact that it is aerial photography that has recorded their demise.

This earlier work contributed to a logical expansion of interest in post-Second World War military sites and landscape. For the Cold War, covering the period 1946–89, some historical analysis and limited documentary sources preceded detailed field survey of key sites, providing information on the construction, form, and layout of selected site types. Military architecture of this period, in the UK alone, is vastly complicated, and always reflective of strategic priorities and government spending of the time. It might be suggested that a starting point for recent military studies should be the documentation known to exist in detail amidst public records. For the Cold War, studies have tended to focus more on field recording as a way in, for several reasons. First, for such recent periods, documentation is often not available. It may exist, but often closure or dispersal amongst military units and archives make it difficult to place, let alone access. This is certainly the case for Cold War sites of the former Eastern Bloc. Closure (for example under the UK's Thirty Year Rule) is a factor, but one whose significance may now diminish under the UK's Freedom of Information Act 2000, and equivalents elsewhere. Even where documentary sources are present, they may not necessarily (and often will not) conform to what survives. Perhaps the plans and technical drawings present a template, an illustration (detailed admittedly) that shows what was intended.

What was built may differ from the intended plans for numerous reasons, while subsequent alterations may also have changed the site's appearance in some way. There is another, subtler argument also: that often in archaeological recording and excavation the process is as important as the results. Certainly at Greenham Common and the survey of its peace camps (Schofield 2009*a*), one can argue that the participation and physical act of recording what for many are sacred places, outweighs the significance of the results of the endeavour (Marshall, Roseneil, and Armstrong 2009).

Surveying Cold War military sites in England was undertaken by English Heritage (and predecessors in the RCHME) from 1995 onwards (Cocroft and Thomas 2003). Records were made for a diversity of site types that led to the production of a preliminary classification within which all site types could be placed. The hierarchy is helpful for placing sites in relation to each other, and establishing functional and chronological context. The hierarchy recognizes first 'Cold War military' as a theme, within which are (currently) nine categories (Table 7.1), which divide then into thirty-one groups, and the groups into monument classes. The hierarchy continues, with classes subdividing by type, subtype, etc. Just as with 'Prehistoric Burial', for example, or 'Roman Military', the category 'Air Defence' is subdivided, in this case into five groups (including Radar), which further divide, Radar into three chronologically distinct monument classes: Rotor 1950s, Linesman 1960s–1980s, and Improved UK Air Defence Ground Environment or UKADGE, 1980s. Although recent, many of these sites are now redundant, or have been converted to new (occasionally military) use. The archaeological value of this approach is that it enables sites to be identified to type and date by whatever field remains survive, then allowing observations and assessment on the basis of rarity, representation, group value, and associations, for example (Table 7.2).

At Spadeadam (Cumbria) the monumental architecture of test stands has been surveyed (see Ch. 3), a process that was also the subject of artistic intervention (Cocroft and Wilson 2006). As we have seen, the earthwork remains of the beginnings of an excavation for a missile silo were revealed at Spadeadam (Tuck and Cocroft 2005: 31; Cocroft 2006) (Fig. 3.4). Treasury documents reveal spending for this, but no technical plans or drawings are known to survive.

Table 7.1. Summary of Cold War structures and sites in England listed by category (bold), group (numbered), and class (after Cocroft 2007*a*)

Air Defence

1 Radar
   Rotor 1950s
   Linesman 1960s–1980s
   Improved UK Air Defence Ground Environment, late 1980s
2 Royal Observer Corps
   Visual Reporting Posts
   Underground Monitoring Posts
   Group Headquarters
3 Anti-aircraft Guns
   Anti-aircraft Operations Rooms
   Post-war Heavy Anti-aircraft Batteries
   Post-war Light Anti-aircraft Batteries
4 Surface to Air Missiles
   Bloodhound missile Mark I sites
   Tactical Control Centres
   Bloodhound missile Mark II sites
5 Fighter Interceptor Airfields
   Hardened Aircraft Shelters
   Hardened Airfield Structures

Nuclear Deterrent

6 V-Bomber airfields
7 Nuclear weapons stores
8 Thor missiles sites

United States Air Force

9 Airfields
10 Cruise missile sites

Defence Research Establishments

11 Aviation
12 Naval
13 Rockets, Guided weapons
14 Nuclear
15 Miscellaneous

Defence Manufacturing Sites

16 Defence manufacturing sites

Emergency Civil Government

17 Early 1950s War Rooms
18 Regional Seats of Government
19 Sub-regional Headquarters
20 Regional Government Headquarters
21 Local Authority Emergency Headquarters
22 Civil Defence Structures
23 The Utilities
24 Private nuclear shelters

Table 7.1 (*cont.*)

Table 7.1. Continued

Emergency Provisions Stores

25 Grain silos
26 Cold stores
27 General purpose stores
28 Fule depots

Communications

29 Underground telephone exchanges
30 Microwave tower network

Miscellaneous

31 The Peace Movement

Table 7.2. Summary of assessment criteria for Cold War military sites in England (after Cocroft 2007a)

Survival/condition

1 Structural integrity and survival of original internal configuration, plant and fittings.
2 Monuments have been generally assessed to reflect their original purpose and function, which dictated their form. Nevertheless, reuse for another purpose and time depth may add to the historical value of a structure.
3 Survival of contemporary Setting, Character, Spatial Relationships—Group Value.

Period

4 Representativeness of a particular phase of the Cold War.
5 Centrality to British and/or NATO defence policy.
6 Technological significance: as well as being military structures many sites are important monuments to post-war British achievements in science and technology.

Rarity

7 In nearly all cases the individual monument types may be regarded as rare, with no more than a handful of surviving examples. Many of the structures or sites also carried out unique functions. While rarity and uniqueness are criteria for protection, they will be supported by other, usually technological, reasons.

Diversity

8 Diversity of form—where a given site or structural type might exhibit a number of divergent structural forms, although designed to fulfil an identical or similar function.

Cultural and Amenity Value

9 Education, understanding, tourism, public access.

The study also surveyed features associated with the site's construction, such as builders' yards and navvy camps, representing aspects of the history of the Cold War not previously discussed.

A further and obviously archaeological dimension of the Cold War, and a characteristic of these sites, is what has been referred to as war art (after Cocroft et al. 2006), including signage and graffiti. Such art often survives in former military buildings and establishments and provides information about military sites and culture that is not available through other official sources. These paintings and signs provide information on the way space was used and demarcated and its separation into private and public for example; also on the way art was used to generate *esprit de corps*, and simply to improve living conditions, and to entertain and enliven. War art can also reveal subversive actions and attitudes, either within the service where authority is challenged in subtle ways, or more explicitly by protestors marking buildings and defacing fences with artwork or everyday objects. Art also represents a form of reconfiguration after military and other closed and inaccessible sites are abandoned. The explicit graffiti in the underground military establishment at Bempton (East Riding) displays a very different set of values and meanings than existed originally, challenging the order and authority of its former use (Schofield 2010). At Forst Zinna some 60 km south of Berlin, and in the former East Germany, murals were recorded by the artist Angus Boulton (2006; 2007), and by Buchinger and Metzler (2006), who describe their presence in a transverse wing that connects two wings of a barrack. The murals form several scenes, arranged side by side, their subjects including the founding phase of the Soviet Union after the victory in 1917, the build-up of the Soviet Union during the 1920s and 30s, Hitler's attack on the Soviet Union in 1941, and ends with the launching of a rocket at the Soviet space centre, Baikonur in Kazakhstan. Buchinger and Metzler (2006: 32) describe these murals as part of the 'propaganda furnishings of the barracks and accordingly [they] had to proclaim the glorious past of the Soviet Union and its army as well as the present and future superiority over all contenders'. Portrayals were also intended to express historical awareness and self-esteem and motivate soldiers in fulfilling their duties. They also reflect the 'protected "Soviet world", in which the Soviet officers and soldiers—although stationed in the GDR—lived and worked with only very few, rigidly controlled contacts to the surroundings' (Buchinger and Metzler 2006: 32). Comparing these images and the motivations behind them with those of American servicemen in the UK is something that will merit further attention and provide insight into both social conditions of the time, and, crucially, the places and the cultures in which representations were made.

A less monumental form of archaeological site, but one that equates closely with the traditional camp-sites of prehistory, are peace and protest camps, increasingly now the subject of archaeological attention. One reason for this is the ambiguity of the physical traces that remain, another the lack of documentary records. Archaeological survey is often the most appropriate form of investigation, with its systematic and detailed recording methods and the reflexivity that often now characterizes archaeological investigations of the contemporary past. In particular here is the social proximity of those engaged in various forms of environmental protest and archaeologists as people often sympathetic to those views. At Greenham Common (West Berkshire, UK), artefacts and structures have been mapped for research and resource management purposes (Schofield 2009*a*; Marshall, Roseneil, and Armstrong 2009). The archaeological record at Greenham is fascinating. A series of protest camps were established by a community (the 'peace women') to oppose both the military presence here, and from 1993 the presence of cruise missiles. The camps were named by the protestors after rainbow colours, and dispersed around the base. Even more interesting for archaeology is the fact that these individual camps had their own distinct characteristics, of social fabric, attitudes to the press, and militancy. Yellow or Main Gate was the largest camp and had a special urban desolation that made it grimmer than the rest. Green Gate, established in January 1983, has been referred to as the 'camp of intellectuals', possessed of a 'cosmic atmosphere', a reference to symbolic actions such as weaving webs to represent strength in unity. There was a musicians' gate, while Blue Gate developed a reputation as a community of tough, occasionally rowdy youngsters. Through research conducted at Greenham Common (Schofield 2009*a* and *b*), the intention was to explore archaeological signatures for these distinctive social characteristics. Work at Turquoise Gate (whose character was distinctly 'vegan', and a spin-off from Blue Gate) revealed milk bottles. So, were the women all vegan, or were they reusing the bottles? Or were there children on site that needed cow's milk? And all accounts describe the Turquoise Gate camp as separate from that at Blue Gate; yet in reality material remains are continuous, their distribution blurred with no hard and fast boundary between the two. It seems almost as though the identity of the camp was blurred in reality, yet clearer and more distinct in the way women remember it.

As at Greenham Common, there is symmetry in the archaeological approach taken at the Nevada Test Site, where archaeological investigations of the atomic testing facilities (Beck 2002) were followed by survey of the Peace Camp immediately outside its main entrance (e.g. Beck, Drollinger, and Schofield, 2007). Some of the tensions were similar too, with strong political and cultural oppositions manifest in the approaches of each community towards work on either side of the fence. The former protesters objected to archaeological work inside the fence, while military personnel struggled with that taking place outside. The landscape of protest at Nevada is fascinating and archaeologically challenging, both for its complexity and for the ambiguity of much of what remains. The protest community is also highly dispersed, creating a heavy reliance on archaeological methods and interpretations. Stone arrangements across an area of *c.*2 km by 1 km of desert are diverse in form and numerous with over 600 sites recorded. We will return to this example, and place it within the context of the wider Nevada landscape—the 'nation of odd'—in Chapter 8.

Similar issues arise at the Stanton Moor Protest Camp, established in 1999 within the Peak District National Park (UK) to protest (successfully as it turned out) against the proposed re-opening of Stanton Lees and Endcliffe quarries under the terms of a 1952 planning permission (Badcock and Johnston 2009). The archaeology of the camp, and the survey conducted by archaeologists, reflects the prehistoric archaeology of the local area, including the iconic Nine Ladies stone circle. As was argued at Greenham, these components are both equally a part of this area's archaeological record, and it is now hard fully to appreciate one without the other. The survey methodology was a conventional one: structures and other camp features were mapped and photographed (e.g. Fig. 7.1), including houses/benders, tree-houses, tree platforms, aerial rope walkways, defensive structures, signs, washing facilities, latrine pits, artworks, and garden plots. Camp residents were asked to annotate copies of the survey with place names as well as including anecdotes and memories. This is landscape archaeology in its traditional sense, though highly socially relevant,

Figure 7.1. Tree-houses occupied by protestors at Stanton Moor Protest camp. (Photo: Anna Badcock and Robert Johnston.)

and controversial in the way it challenges conventional views of what would otherwise be a historic landscape confined to prehistoric activity and post-medieval and modern industry.

On the shores of Lake Eyre South (Australia), the Arabunna Going Home Camp has been the focus of recent political activism forged under the theme of 'Caring for Country' and provided a powerful speaking place for both indigenous and non-indigenous activists. As Walshe describes it (2002: 290), Arabunna representatives are urging indigenous people to return to the country, and along with non-indigenous people are urging Australians to consider the impact of uranium mining on the land. Walshe's ethnoarchaeological approach recorded the camp, first established in March 1999 and bulldozed in December of that year. In April 2000 a discrete scatter of objects was recorded over an area not exceeding 17 by 15 m, comprising bolts collected from railway sleepers, a bicycle bell, two vehicle tyres, wheel rim, oil bottle, plastic chair, and one or two other items. The camp lacked definition and specific activity areas, such as a children's art ground and crèche, recalled by a former resident, were unidentifiable. Vegetation can be significant in these instances, where insufficient time has passed to even out the ground conditions pertaining to occupied and unoccupied areas. The former pantry for example was identified by a lush patch of green clover, and the vegetable garden by garlic plants.

As at Greenham Common, this example is significant also in representing an archaeology of the subaltern, whose visibility is notoriously hard to establish, even for the modern period. As Walshe (2002: 292) explains, acts of resistance are spontaneous, transient, and temporary, so it is hardly surprising that resistance sites will be ephemeral 'leaving more of a shadow than a footprint on the land', unlike the object of their opposition that is writ large through strong architectural statements and some of the most monstrous and monumental forms of the late modern period.

PEOPLE AND THEIR LIVES

Much of the developed world is a landscape of housing estates peppered with tower blocks. In the UK we see mock vernacular gables, and Victorian sprawl alongside private closes, and new towns budding out of the old. These places of habitation are joined by motorways and driveways, and in large parts of England are overlooked by angular-steepled churches with abstract stained glass, domed mosques, and Thai-style temples. Aeroplanes stack above, waiting to descend. Across the developed world the post-war social landscape represents at every turn a distinct departure from historical form, and yet at the same time, as many continuities in old forms, old concerns, and old habits. The level of change impressed on the late modern landscape is evident in the generations of residential building or expansion and the increasing physical mobility of its citizens. Cities and towns have morphed into shapes inconceivable in pre-war years, the separation of rural and urban has become blurred and muddled as commuters flit between them. Few spaces are unaffected by the sound of the internal combustion engine, and automobile touring has given way to the steady acceptance of the car as personal space, an extension of home; as one of life's necessities.

One of the most significant impressions on the landscape over the course of the twentieth century has been the road network, and the influence of the motor car. Most people now own one, and people's lives are dominated by the car, and the speed at which it can deliver us from A to B, for work, school, shopping, and so on. The physical traces associated with this dramatic transformation are everywhere, and have been widely studied, often by archaeologists, but also by geographers (Merriman 2004) and others (Beech 2009). Starting at the beginning of the process, the production line itself has been investigated, often at the point at which factories are closed and redeveloped, as the geography of the industry has shifted from its traditional heartland. In the UK, cars are now built in Swindon for example (see below), in place of the traditional and historic rail-works, and in the north-east. The traditional centres of Oxford, Coventry, and elsewhere now host other industries. Between 1986 and 1993 an archaeological survey was undertaken of every one of the *c.*1,500 sites in the UK where cars were manufactured. The study revealed the scale and geographical spread of the industry, and the character of its archaeological remains (after Collins 2002: 169). Results included the fact that the industry was based largely in Greater London and the West Midlands; that 62 firms were making cars before 1900, and 33 continued to do so afterwards. Some 430 new firms entered the industry between 1900 and 1910, and 221 in the 1920s. Of the *c.*1,500 sites, 224 had extant remains at the time of the survey. Equally, no two car factories were alike, with each built in response to a unique series of events and circumstances; and even stripped of their production technology, most car factory buildings retained ample interpretive evidence of their former use (Collins 2002: 172).

The material culture of the car extends also to roadside and ownership ephemera (described in Beech 2009), garages, trunk-roads, often straightened, thus creating lay-bys from former bends in the road, and the cars themselves. Diana Smith (2002) has researched the 'Dodge-tide', a metaphorical play on the idea of a tide remaining static for an unusually long period (Fig. 7.2). In Australia rural watercourses often become sites for the collective disarray of mechanical flotsam, and the Dodge truck is frequently present in these assemblages (ibid. 161). Cars and other mechanical

Figure 7.2. The 'Dodge-tide', in this case vehicles at a Coaldale farm, Alberta, Canada, 2003. (Photo: Tim Smith.)

equipment accumulate in other situations too, on farms as well as on waste ground and urban fallow. And as we have seen in Chapter 6 (and see Bailey et al. 2009; Newland et al. 2007; Stauffer and Bonfanti 2006), cars, like aeroplanes (Morris 2006), can reveal details of their former use, with the potential to reveal much about the conditions of use, and their users, through forensic examination of their component parts and artefacts.

The roads themselves are arguably the main sites, however, especially in terms of their impact on the landscape, and its continued transformation during the late modern period. What should perhaps interest us most are the ways in which the road layout changes to accommodate our use of the motor car. As Minnis (2007: 12) has shown, while much time and effort is expended on speeding up journey times (the UK's comparatively new M6 toll motorway for example), equal effort is now invested in slowing traffic down. Drivers and pedestrians have traditionally been separated, for example, while traffic speed is generally reduced by signage, speed bumps, and chicanes. But in the early twenty-first century this is changing, with its attendant influence on the British suburban landscape. The British government is now promoting Home Zones where road users and pedestrians share space. In a housing scheme at Newhall, Harlow (Essex, UK), traditional traffic measures have been reversed. Trees have been introduced on corners to block views, and road markings indicating priority have been removed. There are no pavements, ensuring that all road users share the same space. As Minnis says (p. 13), the archaeology of roads is showing a significant new dimension to its character: streets lacking in clutter and reducing the visual dominance of the motor car.

There is folk memory to consider here also. One of the authors lives in Wiveliscombe (Somerset, UK), a small town once dominated by a main route from the Midlands to the north coast of Devon and Cornwall. Prior to the construction of the M5 in the 1970s and the Tiverton to Barnstaple link road in the 1990s, the summer months, and especially weekends and holidays, saw vast queues of traffic, snaking along from Taunton westwards, hampered by bottlenecks in the small towns along the route. A delivery lorry parked in the centre of Wiveliscombe or nearby Milverton would have had serious implications for traffic in both directions. Yet in the 1970s the towns were bypassed, or relief roads built, and ultimately the M5 was constructed to ease the pressure on rural communities and transport infrastructure. But it is recent enough for people to remember the inconvenience. And the traces remain: in Wiveliscombe the vestiges of an earlier trunk road are visible, while maps and aerial photographs displayed in public buildings reveal the topographic changes to this local landscape.

One of the attractions of archaeology of the late modern period, and one of the reasons it is often so controversial and challenging, is the close proximity that often exists between our own lives and the places we study. In 2005 and 2006 ARCUS (Archaeological Research and Consultancy at the University of Sheffield) was commissioned by Bovis Lend Lease to undertake a programme of archaeological recording at the Sheffield University Student Halls of Residence in Endcliffe and Ranmoor (Sheffield, UK). Features of archaeological and historic interest were recorded and a report produced (Dawson and Jessop 2007). At one level, this study detaches itself from the students that occupied the halls of residence, describing Building 1 (Ranmoor House), for example as being, 'designed by architects Hadfield, Cawkwell and Davidson, and built in 1968. It is of four storeys linked by covered walkways and bridges to the other buildings

Figure 7.3. Archaeological record of a typical student study-bedroom, Woodvale Flats, University of Sheffield. (Photo: Simon Jessop, ARCUS.)

of Ranmoor Hall'. A description of Building 2 details the form of construction and the materials used. It also refers to the layout, making specific mention of students' study-bedrooms, which of course represent the hall's *raison d'être*. Photographs include images of the study-bedrooms still in occupation (e.g. Fig. 7.3), raising the question of ethical approaches to recording described in Chapter 3. Overall the report is a record of the building, completed *for the record*, prior to the site's demolition and under the terms of national planning policy guidance. The report is also implicitly an assessment of the buildings, and their cultural significance. But what is left unsaid here is interesting in terms of how we undertake an archaeology of the contemporary past and what research questions we should be asking. An archaeologist involved with this study had been an occupant of Ranmoor when a student at Sheffield. For him there was proximity here and a relevance which gave the study added weight and meaning. Dan Ratcliffe said the following about the project:

The strangest thing was taking my children to see where Daddy had lived getting blown up! <http://webcam.cpanel.shef.ac.uk/sorby/>. I don't know if they ever recorded my room (F29) although it was informally asked of ARCUS. Nearly all the rooms were the same, although I think the hall tutors may have had en suites.

It was strange as an archaeologist to see somewhere I'd lived be surveyed in this way. It's the ranging rod in the pictures that seems strangest to me— especially in the pictures of the wardens' residences. There is a slightly 'clinical' feel about it which reminds me of 'scenes of crime' officers, or surveillance camera images.

On the other hand it's good to know that there is a record of what was a very transitory, but probably quite significant home to many people as they made the leap to independent living.

So says an archaeologist, commenting on an archaeological survey of a place where he lived while training to become an archaeologist!

This unlikely situation is reminiscent also of 'The Office', a rapid archaeological survey of the place where one of us once worked, and the artefacts and other traces that remained after English Heritage abandoned it in 2005 (Schofield 2008; 2009c). We will come back to this in the next section.

WORKING FOR PROFIT: INDUSTRY, BUSINESS, AND AGRICULTURE

Much of the landscape has been transformed in the late modern period—city warehouses into bijou flats, mining towns into declining wastelands, rustic and rural farming land into commuter belts. And we farm in new ways—bigger fields; new crops. New 'soft' industry now slots into the crooks of land between major transport infrastructure and over former sites of heavy industry. City centres are no longer domin- ated by a skyline of choking chimneys and hydraulic lifts but of high- tech and high-finance office blocks. Industry has left the city, in many ways outgrown it, and inhabits out-of-town nests—hubs in a global network—delivering its eggs onto the anywhere-anytime motorway system. The advent of the computer changed the way that business, industry, agriculture, and infrastructure were run. Human involvement became less and less necessary as mechanization gave way to automation. Miniaturization was furthered by the invention of the computer chip. The digital age had begun.

A distinctive later twentieth and twenty-first century 'site' is the retail park. Often on the outskirts of towns and cities, and close to major road or motorway junctions, some have taken on the significance almost of shrines, special places in the landscape where people congregate at certain times of the year to participate in the annual rituals of Christmas shopping and the January sales. In the social context of Daniel Miller's (1998a) seminal study of shopping, Paul Graves-Brown examined the landscape archaeology of the Trostre Park retail centre on the outskirts of Llanelli, south Wales. This the author describes as a landscape/observational study, 'treating the site as if it were an historic or prehistoric landscape' (2007b: 75). This is a place Graves-Brown likens to a concrete island, surrounded by busy roads, farmland, and industry; a focus of consumer activity surrounded by no-man's land anonymity. It is a place people travel to by road; to reach it on foot is virtually impossible. Interesting here is the way the plan has been circumvented because of the inconvenience that it has created amongst visitors. An informal use of space can be seen at Trostre, in the form of paths that cut across planted areas (Fig. 7.4). The intention is not so much to confront authority as to circumvent the shortcomings of a planned environment: 'In wishing to get from A to B people appropriate what their environment affords. Normally speaking we tacitly accept the many boundaries and non-spaces that are created in the urban landscape, but when the sanction of these barriers becomes inconvenient we overcome our tendency to conform' (ibid. 79). Such places and paths are never formally mapped, but simply 'become'. And it is interesting in a world where so much is planned, and so much is hard, permanent concrete, that the highly ephemeral can often prevail, holding particular value to the society whose subversive actions have created these landscapes in the face of authority.

On another scale, and perhaps more landscape than site, at least in the way we conceive it as residents or visitors, is Swindon (Wiltshire, UK),

Figure 7.4. Creating paths. Parc Tawe Swansea, looking north, with the eroded central reservation in the foreground. The actual pedestrian crossing is about 100 m to the right, which is some distance from the pedestrian entrance pictured. (Photo: Paul Graves-Brown.)

the archetypal nineteenth-century railway town that witnessed huge transformation in the post-war years (Falconer 2007). Up until 1960 Swindon was a railway town, with significant drawdown of the industry after the last locomotive was built there. But its twentieth-century legacy has not been merely one of heavy industry and then decline, as is the case elsewhere, but one of urban and industrial renaissance, notably through the production of cars (as we have seen, part of a shift of emphasis away from some Midlands towns to the south and north) and the electrical and electronics industries. An archaeological gaze provides two particular but complementary perspectives: the landscape, through the changing shape, size, and character of the urban area, and sprawl along the M4 corridor (the 'Sunrise Strip', after Finn 2007); and in the architecture, the particular building types associated with these new industries, and the new post-1960s housing to accommodate workers. The place and its material remains had been transformed concomitant with the town's fortunes. Swindon is now home to what is reputedly the largest heritage campus anywhere, with English Heritage, the National Trust, and the Steam Museum sharing a reinvigorated landscape of former railway workshops and offices.

Archaeological survey has recently been concluded for the Trent Valley sand and gravel industry, representing a thematic and regional survey of aggregates, arguably the quintessential industry of the twentieth century that literally shaped the world we now inhabit (Cooper 2008). There are three principle stages of an industrial process evident amongst the collection of sites and infrastructure: 'working landscapes' and 'worked-out landscapes', which often then later become 'reclaimed landscapes'. The monuments and sites of the industry occur widely across the region and beyond, relating to preparation, extraction, transportation, processing, and use. As an industry it is extraordinary in the scale of its impact and the diversity of surviving structures. As is often the case with this archaeology of the contemporary past, there are also interesting relations with more conventional archaeological remains and conservation. The Aggregates Levy Sustainability Fund has for some years funded archaeological research (including this study) effected by gravel extraction, and the publication (ibid.) covers examples of this. The relationship between archaeology as traditionally defined, and the archaeology of processes that have caused its destruction is an ambiguous one, but fascinating nonetheless. It is certainly no reason to ignore the archaeology of our own lives, and the destruction (sometimes even through archaeological practices) that causes the removal of what came before. Archaeology is concerned primarily with processes of change after all.

The work space, alongside and sometimes more so than the home, has become a characteristic of the late modern world. Offices are often purpose-built, anonymous, and lacking in characteristics that have any regional or local distinctiveness. They are often also of short lifespan, falling into decay and ruin prior to redevelopment in times of economic confidence, and redundancy in times of crisis and crunch. The interiors too are often unwelcoming. A few years back it was decided that the one space within the office where colour and character had been introduced, in the adornment of people's personal workspaces and desks, was to be discouraged, partly to do with the emergence of 'hot-desking', and shared space, but also one suspects to create further uniformity and business-like surroundings, and remove distractions and the unprofessional character of a place where work was the primary focus. The office was not a place for fun. As with war art, earlier, one might expect to find traces of subversion in such an environment, in addition to the wastefulness that now exists within society. A study of the former offices of English Heritage, at 23 Savile Row, London, immediately after the building was finally abandoned but prior to the developers moving in, provided an opportunity to assess this (Schofield 2008; 2009c). Graffiti was encountered for example, but positive, not critical, and a great deal of humour left behind as all personal mementoes and keepsakes were removed. The study was of interest particularly for what was left, and in the context of changing conceptions of tolerance and convention within the workplace. Pot-plants were left behind for example, following a memorandum that the owners of the new accommodation forbade their tenants to keep them; and what appeared to be significant documents were discarded, but only because digital technology had made multiple hard copies redundant and unnecessary. Attempts at decoration were also evident, introducing a serenity and beauty to the otherwise rather functional and dead space of the office (Fig. 7.5). The office was a changed place. Even over a short period of time the workplace has transformed, and its archaeological traces reflect that, if we can be bothered to look for them.

This study of 'The Office' is an intimate record of a particular place that holds significance for some of those that worked there. The majority of offices are in fact mundane places, which are rapidly and repeatedly transformed as internal space is reconfigured to adapt in changing times, or as tenants come and go. The building itself and the space are ordinary, even though the lives and activities that occur within them may not be. Yet some buildings can attain significance for what took place there: an ordinary place with extraordinary associations. The IKEA shed, for example, in southern Sweden, where Ingmar Kamprad began selling items before extending to a global enterprise, or the garage in Menlo Park (US) where Google was conceived and developed prior to its global expansion, or the Palo Alto and Los Altos garages in which Hewlett-Packard and Apple

Figure 7.5. Blue bottles creating a place of enchantment and serenity in an abandoned office. (Photo: John Schofield.)

were first developed in 1938 and the 1970s, respectively (Emirzian 2006). Sharr (2006; also Clark 2008) considers the mountain ski-hut above the village of Totnauberg in the Black Forest (Germany), used by Martin Heidegger, noting how the inhabited space, and not the inside of Heidegger's brain, was the site in which a crucial element of thinking took place. In his essay 'Can a Place Think', Clark follows Andrew Benjamin (cited in Sharr 2006: p. xx) in concluding that 'there is an important link between geography (place) and modes of thinking'. Such observations beg the question, 'What benefit might an archaeological approach bring to these particular iconic buildings?'

Much of this chapter is focused on familiar places, or at least familiar types of place: the office and student halls of residence, for example. These are places we know about, at least experientially: we have lived these places; we have stories to tell about them; and our psycho-geographical senses can ensure a carefree navigation whenever these places are encountered. But there are sites that demonstrate just how difficult it can be when the place is unfamiliar,

Figure 7.6. Bust amidst the ruins of Piramida (Norway). (Photo: Bjornar Olsen.)

whether culturally, geo-politically, or environmentally. We have already made brief mention of Andreassen, Bjerck, and Olsen's (forthcoming) examination of Piramida ('The Pyramid'), a deserted Soviet mining town in the high arctic archipelago of Svalbard, being Norwegian territory but occupied by a Russian mining company from 1946 until its abrupt abandonment in 1998 (Figs. 7.6 and 7.7). Imagine an abandoned city where average summer temperatures are 5 degrees Celsius, and a winter average of minus 12 degrees; where permafrost extends between 100 and 400 m below the surface, and four months of midnight sun balance an equivalent period of complete winter darkness. Yet these were the conditions faced by Soviet miners that lived in this thoroughly modern town, with a standard of living higher than most other places in the USSR.

The authors describe their 'thing' approach to Piramida—equivalent to the recognition here of an archaeological study being different to any other motivation by virtue of the primacy afforded to material culture. And what material culture. Post (total) abandonment, most

Figure 7.7. The music room at Piramida. (Photo: Bjornar Olsen.)

books remain on the shelves of the town library; musical instruments lie in the cultural palace awaiting the return of the musicians who played them; bottles and glasses sit empty at the hotel bar; in the museum Andreassen et al. (forthcoming) describe a 'stuffed polar bear [that] still looks in vain for some imaginary prey, ostensibly unmoved by the fact that it recently has been shot yet again through the museum window'.

Such things are recorded here in a 'preliminary and experimental way'. As with Strait Street (outlined in Ch. 3 and again in Ch. 8), much emphasis was placed on just being there, trying to grasp and sense the place. The intervention was low-tech: using notebooks and cameras as the main form of documentation. But, 'most important was the bodily experience of actually being present and to encounter the imposing materiality of the site' (ibid.). As we saw in Chapter 3, this is often the best way with archaeology of the contemporary past: an experiential approach can work, conveying a sense of what the place is like, in situations where detailed survey is just too vast an undertaking. There is room for both, however. A detailed study of the remote Cold War military testing site at Orford Ness (Suffolk) has recently been completed by English Heritage, while a more 'experiential, traveller's account of the Ness' was also undertaken, separately but at around the same time, by a researcher who felt such methods 'formed a crucial part of the material available for analysis there, even bordering on it being its own form of analysis' (Davis 2008: 143). This too was referred to briefly in Chapter 3.

PLEASURE AND LEISURE: THE PURSUIT OF HAPPINESS

People today are internationally known as hobbyists: the landscape of weekending and after-work activity has historically displayed regional undulation. However, changing economic emphasis and technological development has started to reshape our landscapes of leisure. In the twenty-first century car ownership transports the pleasure seeker to any number of leisure sites while, paradoxically, technology offers an imagined array of televised landscapes and virtual worlds to entertain within the home. The advent of disposable income has equated leisure with consumption: units of leisure time and activity are bought and sold, and the leisure market is one of the biggest and fastest growing economies. The consumption of leisure—the almost laborious way in which we enjoy free time—has led to the inexorable boom of leisure's market share, from the contemporary obsession with the gym and pursuit of the body beautiful to the reinvention of the past for modern-day amusement.

The archaeology of leisure and pleasure has embraced a diversity of activities characteristic of the twentieth and twenty-first centuries, with distinctive monument and building types and material culture. The seaside resort for example (Brodie and Winter 2007), sport and conservation, including the creation of national parks for public benefit and enjoyment. Sites in this context might include sporting stadia, theme parks (although these are discussed in Ch. 9), and places associated with film and television (both created for screen media, and given significance through it, e.g. Brown 2009).

In his chapter for the *Defining Moments* book (Schofield 2009*d*), Brown (2009) describes his involvement with the television programme Celebrity Big Brother, sifting through contestants' rubbish in an attempt to distinguish whose was whose. We have known for some time that film sets, left where they were created as representations of reality, can benefit from archaeological attention. Although predating the focus of attention in this book, the lost city of Guadalupe, 170 miles north-west of Los Angeles, was located by archaeologists at the turn of the century. This was the city created by Cecil B. De Mille for his 1923 film *The Ten Commandments*, and set the standards of production design for the rest of the industry, with its 10-storey buildings, 25-tonne sphinxes, and avenues wide enough to race chariots. Once the film was completed, De Mille buried the city in 18 miles of dune that run along the Pacific coast (Fagan 1991: 16; see <http://www.lostcitydemille.com/pics.html>, accessed November 2009). Ong El Jemel and Matmata in Tunisia are further and more recent examples of film sets (in this case for *Star Wars*) viewed now as heritage or tourist destinations, and where much of the sets remain (Fig. 7.8). In his essay on De Mille's film set, Fagan questioned the relevance and validity of this sort of archaeology. Indeed the question put to him, that perhaps this was a waste of time and lacking in credibility, when other more significant archaeological sites merited attention, was dealt with robustly. Fagan explained how this was the only structure of its kind, and for that reason alone was worthy of attention, with the aim of preserving key artefacts. Second, the site can be used for training archaeologists, he says, implying there is something quirky or not really archaeological about it. Is it better to let trainee archaeologists loose on a modern site than a 'precious' older one? Nevertheless he notes the complicated jumble of rubble, lumber, and metal that requires careful dissection if anything is to be learnt about the set's construction. The third reason, and again not a convincing argument for the merits of archaeology of the contemporary past, is the fact that the excavation team are movie historians, for whom the investigation of the set is part of the movie-making enterprise. Survey and excavations revealed some of the site's architecture as well as information about the rate of erosion and finds, including cough mixture bottles in which alcohol was hidden during Prohibition. While Fagan clearly supports the excavation, in concept

Figure 7.8. Part of the *Star Wars* film set in Tunisia. (Photo: Rod Short.)

and execution, he sees it as something other than mainstream. Our argument would be that the stage set 'classical city' is as archaeological as the classical city itself, and in each case archaeological information can be uncovered about life in that city, its social conditions, the methods and phasing of its construction, and the reasons for its formation and for its demise.

In a recent study of Europe's leisure landscapes, authors including John Urry review the huge impact leisure has had on European landscapes in the late modern age, as contemporary Western life has given rise to all sorts of mobilities, flexibilities, and incentives that can fuel the changes we are witnessing today. In his own essay Urry (2008: 26) describes how 'people's fantasies of a place, rather than the performances it actually affords, are a constant theme in tourist tales, as evocatively captured in the book and film *The Beach*'. Indeed, he goes on, 'as quickly as places are produced as a particular kind of place, so they are consumed, wasted and used up as they become frequently "toured" by people seeking various kinds of "leisure landscapes". Travel practices can thus move on and leave places behind. One era's leisure spectacle is mundane in the next' (ibid.). We will see an example of this in Chapter 9, as parks such as the American Adventure theme park in Derbyshire, UK, are created and repeatedly transformed and updated, and ultimately fade.

Urry's review of 'Leisure Places' concludes with a summary of the six main types of leisure places in Europe. He identifies first the paradise beaches of the Mediterranean, 'strange, liminal places [that] became highly desired, the beach signifying a symbolic other to factories, work and domestic life', and where the 'icon of the tanned body indicates the body as mask or sign' (ibid. 27). Second are those places transformed from run-down deindustrialized cities into a new post-industrial spectacle. He cites Emscher Park in the German Ruhr area as an example, where former industrial sites and buildings have been converted for pleasure uses. Third are those places with historic cores that stem from a desire to signify a previous industry or political project, places such as St Petersburg, for example, whose historic core includes Soviet-period buildings introducing a conflict over whether, where, and how they should be erased or celebrated. Fourth are those places that attract without any kind of visual spectacle, but which may appeal to one or more of the non-visual senses, for example smell (the fishing town of Grimsby, UK), taste (Lyon, France), or sound (Memphis, US). Fifth are places that have lost their powers, apart from those that attract vast numbers of visitors. As Urry (ibid.) puts it, 'Rome and Venice . . . seem overwhelmed by the performances and practices of tourists that make their public spaces into "dead" spaces where there is only "leisure".' And finally are the various dark places of death, disease, and suffering turned into leisure spectacles, such as Northern Ireland's 'troubles tours' for example, and Stasi prisons in Germany (Fig. 7.9).

Leisure thus provides a complex panorama of sites and landscapes that adopt or attain relevance and meaning because of the attractions they provide to visitors, attractions that are a factor of late modernity, both in terms of the propensity of people to take holidays, and be able to afford to do so, and for the historic (and often recently historic) actions and activities that have created the attraction in the first place. Urry (p. 26) sums the situation up thus:

Figure 7.9. The Stasi prison complex at Hohenschoenhausen, Berlin—now a visitor attraction. (Photo: John Schofield.)

There are many different leisure landscapes which are contingent, not fixable and given, but uncertain and unpredictable within the swirling vortex of global travel. Many places can suddenly find that for a time they are places of desire. Places move closer or further away from global centres. Places are not fixed and unchanging, but depend upon what can be performed within them, by "hosts" and by various kinds of "guests". They are often on the move upon this global stage.

We will focus now on some of the less tangible elements of the recent past which, we argue, also merit the attention of archaeologists studying this late modern period: the archaeology of popular culture, and popular music in particular. In 2000 a brief overview was published on this topic (Schofield 2000), with three case studies intended to demonstrate the range of site types and material culture, and their potential for archaeological research: the field archaeology of festival sites, akin almost to medieval fairs; the material culture of musical style-tribes or subcultural groups, notably punks and their propensity for reversing meaning, transgressing an object's proper place in society (outlined in Ch. 6); and then the intangible element: the music itself. The main point of this investigation was the degree to which music is representative of the place as well as the people who created it, through lyrics of course, but also the wider soundscape that is created. The band Joy Division, for example, captured the essential character of Manchester in the late 1970s, described as the 'alienated, terrible glee of a decayed city' (cited in Cohen 1994: 123), while in Detroit (US) Motown production techniques were said to have 'developed a rhythm based on the clattering mechanical beat of Detroit's assembly lines...and created rudimentary sound effects with chains, hammers and planks of wood, or by stomping on floorboards' (Perry and Glinert 1996: 191). This particular example of late modern archaeology incorporates materiality therefore, but also immateriality, and it is the two elements together with their wider social context that make this example relevant and interesting.

An example of the gradual acceptance of this particular archaeology of leisure and pleasure is English Heritage's National Monument Record (NMR), a representative inventory of England's cultural heritage, which now increasingly incorporates modern sites, including clubs and other venues for popular music, mainly from the 1950s and 1960s, but also including early jazz clubs from 1919 (Page 2007). This desk-based project focused initially on London but has expanded to include regional examples in Liverpool associated with the Beatles and Merseybeat. Entries have included the Cavern and the Casbah Club, the latter including murals by Beatles members, and sites relating to the rare 1960s and 1970s phenomenon of Northern Soul including the Wigan Casino. But the main focus has been Soho of the late 1960s. Examples include the seminal Mod haunt, the Scene Club (now a car park), the Flamingo, where the all-nighter was pioneered, and La Discothèque, one of the first true discothèques in Britain.

In the United States sites have been listed on the National Register for their post-war popular musical association. An obvious example is Graceland, listed in 1991 (Stager 1995) for its close association with Elvis Presley. Less obvious was a nondescript two-storey building in Chicago, designated by the Commission on Chicago Landmarks due to its use between 1957 and 1967 by Chess Records, one of the principal music labels associated with the development of American blues and rock 'n' roll (Samuelson and Peters 1995). This was accepted for designation, despite subsequent alterations to the building. In fact it was the music specifically that swung things in favour of acceptance: 'mere mention of the song "Johnny B. Goode", recorded by Chuck Berry at the Chess Studios in 1958, was an immediate touchstone to most of those involved. At one City Council meeting, an alderman ... noted, "Yeah, I always liked that song", and voted for designation' (ibid. 121).

Taking this subject a step further, a recent study in Liverpool has investigated the city's popular cultural associations, investigating the social context of music-making in the city, documenting what people describe as their influences and how the music created in the city reflects these. But it is also about the places where music is made, produced, performed, and sold (Schofield, Kiddey, and Lashua forthcoming). The study examines the city streets where buskers perform for passers-by; the venues large and small where they perform for paying audiences; the recording studios and record shops. Asking musicians to produce maps that illustrate the physical extent of their influence has produced some interesting views on sense of place in a socially deprived urban context. Young hip-hop artists, for example, appear to focus more on neighbourhood (the 'hood'), and the cribs (homes) within it; while others draw greater influence from some of the city's landmarks and historic venues (Cohen, Lashua, and Schofield 2010). The main product of music-making (the music itself) is intangible, as increasingly is the medium through which it is distributed and heard (as records and CDs are replaced by downloads); but the physical places—as we saw from the NMR records, above— remain and are increasingly important to the communities for whom Liverpool's diverse musical heritage holds significance, significance that continues after the buildings are abandoned and where they remain 'thickly woven into local leisure practices' (Edensor 2005: 50).

CONCLUSIONS

We began this chapter by stating that sites, either per se, or in landscape context, form the staple of most archaeological inquiries, and that, for the contemporary past, this is no different. The chapter has outlined some of the site types that have been investigated by archaeological methods, to which can be added a wide range that have been studied in what one might call an archaeological way, albeit by researchers from other disciplines. An abandoned factory making garden statuary in Watford (UK) was studied by the self-titled Institute of Contemporary Archaeology in 1966 for example, the 'Institute' being a group of collaborative artists called Boyle Family (see further discussion in Ch. 4). It is a subject area that can be difficult to envisage though: a prehistoric landscape of sites can be imagined, explored, mapped, and studied. As archaeologists we can normally recognize the material traces of a site versus the more scattered traces of 'off-site' activity (e.g. after Foley 1981) that surrounds it. We can use archaeological research methods to investigate connections between sites, for example in the form of material culture common to both, and which may have been traded or exchanged. And in the case of palimpsests, of course, we can split the complexity of the map into simpler chronologically distinct layers. For the late modern period things are at once more challenging, and also in a way easier. One challenge concerns boundaries, that the boundaries between and around sites are more difficult to draw, partly because there are physical and social boundaries and partly because a boundary to one may not be recognized by others. Smokers and non-smokers may see their office building in different ways: for one the built form creates the boundary; for others the extra-mural smoking area is part of the building. A similar distinction may be seen between car-drivers and people who walk to work, or cyclists and everyone else. Only a cyclist often knows where the cycle sheds are. So there are complexities there too. Another challenge is the sheer number of sites, and the number of people whose experiences of those sites can be very different. In an urban area this is particularly acute, where office workers who commute in, residents, street cleaners, addicts, children, and homeless people will all have very different experiences of a central business district or of a particular building or landmark within it. In rural areas, long-term residents, holiday-makers, migrant workers, and conservationists will experience the same place in quite different ways. All will view the landscape and its sites through different lenses or filters, valuing them in terms of different criteria, and all within the context of their own experiences, prejudices, and unfamiliarities.

Given this degree of complexity and ambiguity, how can we hope to begin to make sense of sites and of landscape, the subject of our next chapter? One tool that researchers have found able to cope with this complexity is 'GIS'. Geographical Information Systems have the capacity to hold and manipulate all these data, and to respond to the very specific questions that researchers, planners, politicians, and others might wish to ask. The map base is accurate to the time the survey was conducted. Often now, with satellite imagery and so on, maps and aerial photography are current. But earlier map layers exist too, so change can also be displayed over time through GIS. Further information can be included as layers, superimposed, faded in, etc., notably high resolution aerial photographic mapping. Together these resources provide maps or photographic records of the late modern world which can then be broken up by incorporating or interrogating datasets. Postcode data linked to business premises for example, or income, can display evidence for the social and economic fabric of a city or of rural areas. Particular types of business activity can be mapped, as can roads and structures connected to roads and associated infrastructure. And even where the relevant information is not readily available, digitizing it is a comparatively straightforward task. This takes us into the next chapter. The point here is that the information exists, but rather than thinking about lists of sites, as we might for certain approaches to prehistory or the Roman period, perhaps derived from published gazetteers or local authority Historic Environment Records, we instead treat the digital map, and the images derived from Google Earth, and postcode directories, etc. as our source material. In a way therefore, the landscape becomes the site. By combining these various sources, the possibilities for studying the material culture of the contemporary world, and specifically the places and things within it, are almost literally endless.

8

Landscape

The students were restless. A classroom full of third year archaeology undergraduates, at the start of their final semester, anxious now to move to the next stage: employment, gap-year travels, further studies. It was a restlessness also born out of the unfamiliar: a building on the main campus they were not used to, a new 'Heritage' course, and a visiting lecturer they had never seen (and quite possibly never heard of) before. The building was a tower block, with extensive views to the east over suburban developments of the inter-war years, and post-war housing, in addition to light industry, a smattering of retail, much of the university campus, and a common. Views also extended to the distance, beyond the city limits: to fields and churches. The students become even more restless as I open the class by asking them to leave their seats and look out of the windows. Some find it amusing; others are just baffled. They are asked to look below and around them; to cast their eyes to the horizon, and to describe what they see in terms of what they consider to be cultural heritage. Silence. I am patient in these situations, to the point where the silence becomes more embarrassing to them than me. 'The Common', someone says. I ask why, and she comments, intelligently and accurately, on the historic status of commons, and the fact that it has escaped development. Others are encouraged by the exchange. 'I can see a church.' 'There is an estate which is protected.' 'Indeed', I respond, noting that it is a conservation area, and I am sufficiently informed to tell them why. Eventually they run out of 'historic buildings and places' to identify and all falls quiet. I then talk a little about how views of the historic environment have shifted over the past fifteen to twenty years, away from only focusing on special places, to a recognition of the wider landscape: a more holistic view has become more prominent. I also explain how the term 'historic' has extended to include not only the ancient, but also the only recently passed. I talk a bit about this, and about heritage being what we inherit and what we pass on, not only what we select and choose *to pass on. They look and think once more. Again, silence. Again I exercise patience. Eventually someone says what I have been waiting to hear: 'Everything. It is all heritage.' 'Excellent,' I say. If I'd had gold stars to give out she'd have had one. We return to our seats and another year's 'Heritage' course begins.*

INTRODUCTION

As we saw in the previous chapter, many close comparisons exist between the archaeology of the contemporary past and that of earlier periods, most obviously in the way we conceptualize and investigate sites as places or loci of human activity through the material traces left behind. We saw how this approach, this archaeological methodology, applies equally to prehistoric settlements and abandoned office spaces that we ourselves have occupied. Another comparison concerns the question of landscape, and the ways in which human activity occurs within and across landscape; how it can be influenced by the properties of landscape, whether physical or social; how the present landscape is the result of actions, activities, and attitudes in the past, and their collective and cumulative impact over time; and how we can helpfully study human activity at this broader scale. We are not talking here about particular landscapes that become fossilized at a certain time, coincident for example with their abandonment or some natural catastrophe: the Roman townscape of Pompeii for example; the Palaeolithic land surfaces at Boxgrove (West Sussex); or nuclear testing facilities of the western United States, closed or downgraded at the end of the Cold War. Rather, for the contemporary past, we are (or at least should be) referring to landscape in a more holistic sense: the everything, the everywhere, and of course—what makes it so interesting and so relevant that we examine this as archaeologists—the everyday. This scale of inquiry, the sheer amount of stuff within the contemporary landscape, and the new technologies that make it possible now to begin making sense of all this material, is one of the main challenges and benefits of exploring the archaeology of the late modern world.

This chapter returns initially to the principles of historic landscape characterization or 'HLC', first discussed in Chapter 3, to think further about investigations of this kind, and how, for example, national and international patterns of change and use can be studied archaeologically. Then, thinking outside HLC, some more focused case studies follow, from Malta, for example, and an extended discussion of Nevada, the latter as an archaeological and experiential account of a fascinating yet bizarre landscape of extremes, and the materiality that exists there, often abandoned and unloved even in a place where 'modern' so clearly matters. There is obvious overlap between this and the previous chapter, and the question of when sites or places become landscape is perhaps a valid one. It is not one that concerns us here, however. Some of the examples in this chapter (e.g. Malta) could equally be considered sites or places, while some sites or places (Piramida for instance) may equally be thought of as landscape. First though, we return to characterization and specifically its relevance for documenting and interpreting the late modern landscape.

MORE ON CHARACTERIZING LANDSCAPE

We know how we characterize landscape (Ch. 3), and why (Clark, Darlington, and Fairclough 2004). But here we focus on another question: to what extent do the results of historic landscape characterization (HLC) and similar regional- and national-scale analyses provide an archaeological assessment of the contemporary past? Are historic landscape characterization maps and databases of benefit to studying the archaeology of the late modern world?

Let us begin with the European Landscape Convention or ELC (European Landscape Convention [2000] 2008), which provides a relevant context for this discussion and the examples that follow. The Convention usefully defines landscape as an 'area, as perceived by people, whose character is the result of the action and interaction of natural and/or human factors'. Thinking about the everyday and the everywhere, this Convention applies to all areas, including what it refers to as 'natural, rural, urban and peri-urban areas. It includes land, inland water and marine areas [and] landscapes that might be considered outstanding as well as everyday or degraded' (ibid. 406). Although unsaid, the implication is clear, that landscape is something contemporary as well as something 'historic'. And as with the European Landscape Convention, HLC has wide geographical application, in other European contexts for example (e.g. Fairclough and Rippon 2002) and in the United States (Dingwall and Gaffney 2007).

Closely allied to both HLC and ELC is English Heritage's Change and Creation programme, and its successor, the publication *Images of Change* (Penrose 2007). Both are inquiries into the impact of later twentieth-century themes and processes specifically on the English landscape, although its general principles can be applied to any late modern landscape especially in the developed world. As archaeologists we learn, first and foremost, that things change: that places rarely stay static for long, and it is interesting to note how the twentieth century has largely been a century that introduced this concept of stability, of arresting change, largely through the growth of a conservation movement (Fairclough 2009). In the UK, National Parks were established, alongside Areas of Outstanding Natural Beauty, Sites of Special Scientific Interest, Conservation Areas, Scheduled Monuments (in 1882 in fact, though the concept was significantly extended in the twentieth century), and Listed Buildings, essentially to control change, but often to prevent it. In the US and Australia, these developments occurred during the same period, although under different guises. In the US, the earliest national parks and historic monuments were gazetted by Congress in a reasonably piecemeal fashion, before being brought together under the umbrella of the new Federal bureau of the National Parks Service in 1916. In Australia, although a number of national parks were gazetted and individual properties lobbied for protection, formal agencies charged with the protection of heritage emerged later in the twentieth century. Whatever the history of conservation in each country, the processes that changed the historic environment, as defined by convention, were perceived to be 'destructive processes', processes that destroy or diminish the idyll that existed before. But therein lies a contradiction. As archaeologists we celebrate and study change; yet often operate in a system laden with processes that seek to prevent it (see further discussion in Pearson and Shanks 2001: 91ff.). The principles of Change and Creation were to extend the archaeological gaze into the present; to recognize that change happens, and that as archaeologists we are uniquely placed to investigate change, of whatever age it might be: early prehistoric or the late modern. Change and Creation asked the simple question: 'why wait?' Why wait fifty years before taking an informed view of the heritage of late twentieth-century date? The programme rejected the notion of objective distance that underlies this urge to delay or postpone our treatment of things until they become 'historic', extending even to a celebration of subjectivity and personal engagement, and stressing that landscape is a mental construct, an idea, a feeling that anyone can create. Change and Creation, ultimately, rejected the view that recent landscape change equates only to 'loss': the removal of hedgerows, the hollowing out of town centres, and concreting the countryside (Penrose 2007: 9). Change means creation too, building something new for the present and for the future, though ideally containing some references, at times only subtle, to what existed in the past.

The town centre is a good example. Traditional views of heritage would consider the present state of urban centres as having been deeply affected by social and economic changes of the later twentieth century. Areas of traditional and historic terraced housing were lost or removed from towns in the north of England in slum clearances of the 1960s and 1970s, concomitant with the removal of industrial buildings and infrastructure. Towns were subjected therefore to significant change resulting in a 'doughnut' effect: as the historic cores were removed, new town centres characterized by 1960s architecture were designed, and any remaining 'historic interest' existed only on the periphery (Fig. 8.1). Characterization does not make judgements about such changes. It does not opine on whether this process of change is a good thing or not. It merely presents the pattern, and in this case it is a repeating pattern. As archaeologists investigating this evidence we can see what it is, and interpret it in terms of social processes now, just as we will in the future, by studying the fabric, by map regression, and—if need be—incorporating planning authority archives, interviewing architects and planners, and studying

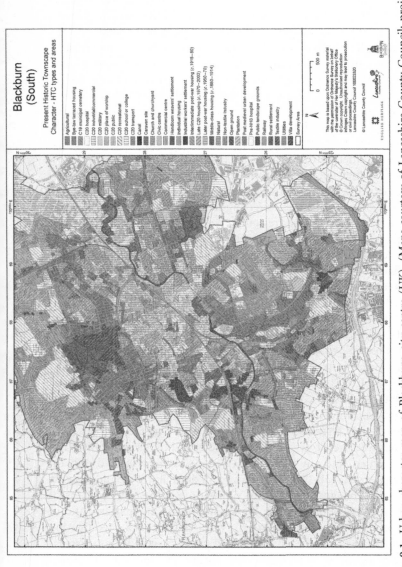

Figure 8.1. Urban character map of Blackburn city centre (UK). (Maps courtesy of Lancashire County Council; project supported by English Heritage, Lancashire County Council, and Blackburn with Darwen Borough Council.)

planning policy guidance and its evolution, the types of method that were discussed in Chapter 3. The archaeology of the late modern urban centre is a fascinating topic for study, and one for which landscape characterization provides a helpful starting point. It is not simply a story of an outer ring of historic fabric enclosing or bounding inner-city 'dross-scapes'; it is about phases of development: recognizing areas with distinct characteristics of particular age, and the result of a particular combination of social, economic, and political circumstances. This is the archaeological view. The view of others (e.g. architectural historians) will be different, for the simple reason that change, and the material traces indicative of change, is what archaeologists understand: it is our focus, our specialism. Architectural historians and to some extent others such as cultural geographers and artists, do not usually give primacy to that longer-term perspective. It is why an archaeological view of landscape is different, and it is why we can sometimes sidestep the value judgements implicit in some other approaches.

Following Change and Creation, *Images of Change* (Penrose 2007) extended the study of contemporary landscape from something largely theoretical to a series of examples, with a view to exposing more obviously the merits of an archaeological gaze. In a sense this study represented an archaeological 'field guide', these words being dropped from the book title only at a late stage in its production. It recognized categories of things within the context of social, economic, and political processes, and within those categories it recognized classes and types of site (see Table 2.1). The view was national: the implication being, however, that many of the classes and types listed and photographed were widespread, and not necessarily only within England. For instance, the class of activity referred to as 'homelessness' described a diversity of site types that exist in both urban and rural contexts in both developed and less developed countries. As Penrose states (p. 44):

High unemployment in the 1980s and cuts in social provision, such as mental health institutions and social housing, left a human imprint on townscapes. Visibility grew, in the shape of rough sleepers in shop and office doorways, makeshift townships in peripheral wastelands, queues for soup vans, kitchens and charity hostels.

'Cardboard City', a concrete maze of underpasses beneath Waterloo's bullring roundabout...became a media-celebrated residence to 200 of London's homeless. Temporary boundaries, walls, rooms and beds were erected from discarded cardboard and other flotsam of the city's commercial life. This was a physical symbol of the permanence of transience—in a city where skyscrapers stood empty. It remained so until eviction orders were given in 1998.

It is not sites and places so much as the broader patterns of change that concern archaeologists engaged with characterization studies, and it is a view therefore best seen either from the air, or expressed as GIS layers on maps. In fact, maps are a good example of how the principles of characterization work, and of how it is theorized. The standard 2 cm: 1 km map in the UK, issued by the Ordnance Survey in its Landranger series, is a map of the present landscape, within which can be 'read' evidence of its former use, in field patterns, road layout, and the footprint of urban and suburban development. It is often said, to the point of cliché, that reading a map is like reading a book: that one can 'read' the landscape almost as one does text. It is the same with an aerial view and with an HLC map such as Fig. 8.1. In Hayden's (2004) US-based study *A Field Guide to Sprawl*, she describes 'reading the landscape from an airplane'. She describes first how landscape history is the 'broadest way of looking at how a society shapes its space over time' (ibid. 13), and how 'aerial photographs reveal the scale of existing and new development. In an era when a truck stop can be larger than a traditional town, aerial images convey the vast spread of much twenty-first century development and can bring up-to-the-minute data on the progress of construction' (p. 14). Her *Field Guide* identifies the types of sprawl, through a language of fantastically descriptive terms, and stunning aerial images. 'Privatopia', for example:

A community-of-interest development (CID) where residents are legally bound to obey the covenants, conditions and restrictions (CC&Rs) of a homeowner association may be called a privatopia. Author Evan McKenzie coined the term to emphasise how these associations assume many of the powers of private governments, providing such basic services as police, fire or trash collection. They may use CC&Rs to regulate paint colours, landscaping, and tenant behaviour. Some are gated communities, where all persons entering must pass a security gate. (p.84)

In the early days of English Heritage's Monuments Protection Programme (MPP), a national review of England's archaeological resource, conducted in part to enhance its protection (Schofield 1999), it sought snappy and clear definitions for every class of monument evident within the archaeological record. Hayden's descriptions for classes and types of sprawl in the United States are closely comparable, and would certainly form a useful starting point for any late twentieth-century equivalent. In all, fifty-two distinct types of sprawl are identified in Hayden's study. It would be interesting to see a map of the US, or a state within it, with these various types highlighted: to see, geographically, what impact they have had on the landscape, and to what extent these forms are now predominant at broad scales of analysis. Some of the groundwork for such an analysis has already been put in place by the Centre for Land Use Interpretation (CLUI), based in Los Angeles, which has been engaged in mapping land uses across the US as part of their land-use database project. The American Land Museum exemplifies this approach. As the website states, the CLUI is the lead agency in the establishment of the American Land Museum,

a network of landscape exhibition sites being developed across the United States. The purpose of the museum is to create a dynamic contemporary portrait of the nation, a portrait composed of the national landscape itself. To establish this far flung museum, the country has been divided into separate zones called Interpretive Units. Each unit is to have a museum location to represent it, providing regional programming for the area it represents. Interpretive Units were created out of the continuous national fabric through an accumulation of criteria, and finally actualized through the process of combining 'districts' and 'regions.' Regions are general topographic and land use areas with gradual or transitional boundaries. They generally follow physiogeographic features (such as mountain ranges, and drainage systems), as well as cultural, economic, and historical development patterns. Regions could be described as being defined from within, rather than from without, as the edges of these regions are often indistinct, overlapping and dissolving into one another. Unambiguous boundaries were then drawn around these regions, following the existing political boundaries that separate states. The cluster of states define the District that makes up each Interpretive Unit. (CLUI 2009)

Figure 8.2. CLUI Wendover Residency Complex observation tower, overlooking the historic Enola Gay Hangar at the Wendover Airfield, during a spring snowstorm. (Photo courtesy of Steven Rowell for the Center for Land Use Interpretation, 2007.)

As an example, the area around Wendover, CLUI's home base on the stateline between Utah and Nevada, is described largely in terms of its late modern characteristics (Fig. 8.2):

Chemical industries pump brine into massive evaporation ponds, using an elaborate system of canals to channel the water, and levees to contain it. The valuable compounds removed from the evaporite come from the surrounding landscape, from minerals which melted from the mountains and collected in the deep packed powder of the flats over millions of years, within this basin without drainage to the ocean.

The military has used over three million acres in the region for bombing and training activities, and more than a thousand square miles of land outside of military reserves has undocumented and unexploded bombs buried in its soil. Rocket engines, explosives, and propellants are manufactured at two large industrial sites in the region, and explosions from the disposal and testing of munitions at nearby military grounds still shake and crater the landscape.

Large-scale extractive industries in the region create new topographies of pits and tailings mounds, causing changes in the landscape that are clearly recorded by the contour lines of successive editions of topographical maps.

Hazardous waste disposal facilities have followed the path of least resistance to this area, where the toxic and radioactive detritus, the negative byproduct of industrial processes, comes from far away cities, and lies entombed in shallow troughs, closing parts of the landscape off from access to humans for thousands of years. (CLUI 1996)

Such is the character of Wendover.

This wider view is closely comparable if not indistinguishable from that adopted by archaeologists. It is a view that will also be familiar to geographers and planners, increasingly now at an international scale of policy-making and implementation: people who seek to identify the character of the present landscape and the processes that underpin it, and to project and effect future change. The New Economics Foundation, for example, completed a study in 2004 that described the transition towards 'clone town Britain', where local identity was disappearing from the nation's high streets, and all places becoming the same, in the shops that were present, the character of street furniture and form, the piped music played there, even the accents and dialects heard amongst shoppers (New Economics Foundation 2004). Similarly, the European Environment Agency's 'Urban Sprawl in Europe' study mapped trajectories of change, examined the drivers for change, and modelled future change across Europe. Since the mid 1950s for example, European cities have expanded on average by 78 per cent, whereas the population has grown by 33 per cent, meaning that European cities have generally become less compact. The dense, enclosed quarters of the compact city have been replaced by free-standing apartment blocks and semi-detached and detached houses (Uhel 2006: 11). Taking a narrower time slice, in the ten-year period 1990–2000 the growth of urban areas and associated infrastructure throughout Europe consumed more than 8,000 sq. km—a 5.4 per cent increase during the period (ibid. 10). Much of this sprawling development occurs on the coast: during the period 1990–2000 urbanization of the coast grew some 30 per cent faster than that of inland areas, with the highest rates of increase in the coastal zones of Portugal, Ireland, and Spain (p. 16).

All these studies investigate the present landscape in relation to recent processes of change, and potential future change ('futurologies').

This is familiar territory for us as archaeologists. The time period may be unfamiliar to archaeologists in the conventional sense, and the reasons for the study largely socio-political, yet the data and the trends have strong resonances with landscape archaeology in a more conventional sense and setting.

INTERSTITIAL PLACES

Interstitial places are the in-between places, those that don't really fit, that defy easy categorization. They are the places that are better understood for what they are not: they are not commercial, residential (in any conventional sense), retail, or conservation areas. They are the places planners typically ignore (SLOAPS—Sites Left Over After Planning) or simply aren't aware of, or the places they try to 'improve', to 'tidy up' and make safe. They are places where many people simply will not go. They feel unsafe or threatened—but mostly the fear is merely of the unknown. Greg Keeffe (forthcoming) has described some of these areas as the cities' 'compost heaps'. Just as every garden should have a compost heap, where all the rubbish gets thrown, so these areas exist also in every city, and arguably in every settlement. One does not necessarily want a compost heap in one's garden, as it doesn't look or smell so good. But it is essential. It provides the means to ensure a productive garden. It is a rich and fertile area. So it is often with urban compost heaps: the 'crappiest' of environments are the most productive—low rents create ghettos of artists requiring low-cost but spacious accommodation—which encourages other creative industry. These are the places therefore that generate cultural achievement, through music and the arts. Bands and musicians often come from these areas, their lyrical content extraordinarily perceptive of the environs in which they originate. One thinks of the Arctic Monkeys for example, and their origins in inner-city Sheffield and its estates of predominantly low-income and socially deprived inhabitants.

In his book *The Location of Culture* (1994), Homi Bhaba also suggests that culture is most productive and creative at the margins, in contexts where it is most ambivalent and transgresses boundaries.

His work is a consideration of the potential for post-colonial theory to mediate practical social change through its emphasis on breaking down the binary oppositions between colonized and colonizer, and instead emphasizing the creative value of cultural hybridity. In this sense he is writing of a different form of interstitial space, the space of colony and post-colony, but his ideas are no less relevant to an understanding of all such spaces on the margins. For many, such spaces are the places of home, work, or perhaps where people simply 'exist'. We might think of the spaces of homelessness here, for example (e.g. Zimmerman and Welch 2006). We have noted earlier, following Buchli and Lucas (2001*a*), that the subaltern is a key theme for the archaeology of the contemporary past, and is notoriously hard to locate. In considering the archaeology of the contemporary past it is in these interstitial areas that we can begin the search and where traces are most likely to be encountered. Two such landscapes, and an archaeological approach to them, are described here.

Strait Street

Valletta is the capital city of Malta, which is centrally situated in the Mediterranean, *c.*90 km off the coast of Sicily. It is the main town on the island, and a World Heritage Site, for its impressive fortifications and colonial architecture. It is central also to the tourist experience of Malta. Few stay in the city, but most visitors from the island's resorts, and on visiting cruise ships, will tour the city at least once during their stay. Malta is Catholic for the most part, and city authorities and planners seem to manage the place in a very particular way, a way that effectively hides any aspect of its past that is deemed shameful, even alternative. One such place is Strait Street, a long, straight, and narrow road (part of which is also known as 'The Gut') which runs the length of the town and was once an area of bars, lodging houses, dance halls, and fast-food outlets (Fig. 8.3). Fountain Street, which extended beyond Strait Street at its far end, was a centre for prostitution, with trade evidently extending into Strait Street, at least at its lower end. Strait Street was where sailors came on shore leave, in vast numbers. The authorities were not

Figure 8.3. General view of Strait Street, Malta. (Photo: John Schofield.)

happy, and with the island's independence in 1964, and the decline in the numbers of visiting servicemen between 1964 and 1979, when the navies finally left, the street effectively closed down. Such was the stigma attached to the place that it has remained empty ever since, the locked doors sealing the fabric within and the memories and stories that accompany it. In 1965, *Titbits* magazine included the following description of Strait Street under the title 'The street that shames Hero Island':

British tourists should steer clear of Malta till the island's government take this advice: stamp out the vice in a street that is the shame of Malta—Straight Street [*sic*].

This is an area of vice and prostitution that ranks with the world's most notorious sin spots....

Officially, the problem does not exist. The Gut is not mentioned in the newspapers, on radio, TV, by parliament or even in polite conversation....

[The Gut] is a dirty, squalid alley that is packed from noon to early morning with prostitutes who sell themselves for the price of a drink....

A street where teenage British sailors are accosted by women old enough to be their grandmothers. (Saxon 1965: 30)

Dench (1975: 109) has assessed the impact of this article, exploring further the contradiction between Malta's strong identification with the Catholic faith and the activities associated with Strait Street. To Maltese priests, Dench explains, deviant sexual behaviour and vice are almost unmentionable—even uttering immoral words is unacceptable, with fifty-eight men committed to prison for doing so as recently as 1960–5. Recourse to a prostitute is a mortal sin, like other sexual acts outside marriage, for which absolution is necessary. Open reference to vice is considered utterly offensive and respectable Maltese try to close their eyes and ears to the topic (Dench 1975).

Local response to the *Titbits* article was unsurprising therefore, exciting 'a curious sensitivity in which evident consternation combines with half-hearted and equivocal denial that such a thing might be possible—in Malta at any rate' (ibid.). The magazine was banned in Malta, though a few copies circulated. Local people were incensed to the extent that public comment became necessary. Clearly a vigorous denial would have been a nonsense, as the article's allegations were true. Yet passive acceptance would have been painful and offensive to many, and would have led to calls for Malta to be 'cleaned up'. So the issue was fudged, by stating that it did not merit public scrutiny. '[E]yes were averted, and the vague belief entertained that the authorities have matters under satisfactory control' (p. 111).

A study of Strait Street in 2004 to 2009 revealed the extent to which material components of the bars, music halls, and other places had survived despite forty years of closure, as well as the receptive attitude and support of local residents (Schofield and Morrissey 2005, 2007). The project has its origins in a chance encounter with Strait Street in 2002, a comment by a Maltese military historian about the significance of the street as a good 'run ashore', and the fact that many people that once worked in Strait Street remained there, often living in poverty, forgotten by the authorities. The project sought to make this invisibility visible; to reveal the hidden histories of Strait Street and to do so primarily through material traces, in particular the abandoned bars and music halls that line the street, and their contents. Access was difficult, and proved possible only through direct encounter with those that once owned the premises or worked there. The project was thereby

Figure 8.4. Interior of Rocks Bar, Strait Street. (Photo: John Schofield.)

extended from one that concerned principally the material traces of the Street, to the close combination of material traces and testimony—the tangible and intangible heritage in post-colonial context. In Chapter 3 we described the social-anthropological practice of 'bimbling', of giving people the opportunity to re-experience their connections with landscape and to reminisce, prompting 'other life-course memories associated with that individual's relationship with place' (Anderson 2004: 258). To gain access to the places therefore first involved being seen in the Street, and becoming a familiar sight there; to practise 'bimbling' with those that we met; and to 'see' through the opportunities bimbling opened up. And what was seen, ultimately, were the interiors of some twenty bars and music halls, some empty and ruinous shells, some now converted to other uses including domestic and industrial space, and some retaining much evidence for their former use, often quite deliberately (e.g. Fig. 8.4). The bar signs in Strait Street are disappearing fast, the subject of souvenir hunters, but also in some cases the original bar owner retaining 'his' bar sign, because it is part of his own heritage, even though the association with the place is lost as a result. Artefacts are less common than we had anticipated, again largely because anything associated with the Street is highly collectible—tokens, beer mats, bottles, mirrors, etc.

Of particular interest is the attitude of people to this project. All the preparatory work suggested this study would not be welcomed in the city. A letter to the *Times of Malta* requesting assistance received one anonymous reply: 'If you have some respect for the [G]eorge [C]ross Island, skip the idea of shedding light on Strait Street.... Yours truly, A.D.' (anon. letter, n.d). A map included with this reply suggested Fort St Elmo as an alternative area of interest where, it appears, various attacks on tourists had recently occurred! At least one local resident thought this was no coincidence.

A jeweller who once owned a bar in Strait Street strongly indicated that Strait Street was a respectable place, that prostitution never occurred there, and that any study should be sure to make this point. He then posed for photographs in his shop, surrounded by religious icons.

On visiting Strait Street, and talking to those that still occupy this alternative and neglected city space (one of Keeffe's compost heaps, perhaps), the attitudes were very different. There was surprise that anyone should be interested, combined with a willingness and an enthusiasm to guide us through their landscape, to point out which bars were which, and to tell their stories. Some people really stood out, people who retained many of the bar's fixtures and fittings despite closure, and the artefacts and gifts given by sailors. Tony and Anna Pace of Rocks Bar showed off their bar and the objects within it, including their photograph albums of busy nights here and at Tico Tico, another bar they owned. They had ships' photographs, signed and framed for them; and a ship's flag carefully folded and stored away. These were precious objects, and clearly triggered fond memories.

In walking along Strait Street it was mostly men that were encountered, though some women who once worked in the bars of Strait Street spoke with enthusiasm about their life and work. Of the men, Joseph Buttegieg stands out. He told of his father, who owned a bar at the bottom end of the street, building all its fittings himself. He then ran the business successfully for years. After closure and his father's death, Joseph opened it again, but this time as a workshop, keeping all the fixtures and furnishings intact. He showed off the art-deco style bar his father had made, and spoke very warmly of him and of his achievements.

There was pride amongst these people, contradicting the attitudes of authorities towards this hidden-away space, this compost heap tucked away in the far corner of the World Heritage city of Valletta. This is unquestionably an alternative view of public archaeology and of landscape, involving a public who have simply never been asked what they think. Without this project, and without the involvement of Victor Scerri, whose accounts of people's lives on Strait Street have become a regular feature of the Maltese language newspaper *it-TORCA*, Strait Street might have been irrevocably changed without any reference at all to those that actually *live* there, or who did so with great joy and enthusiasm until the 1970s when most bars closed down. Why should their views not be heard? And more to the point, why are their views not pre-eminent in assessing future plans for this area? It is their street after all.

Now talk is of Strait Street becoming the city's cultural quarter, with a return to bars, exhibitions, galleries, street theatre, live music, and so on. Currently the street appears largely empty. The bars are all locked up and have been for three to four decades. A problem is often that nobody knows who owns them as, following independence, bar owners transferred their business to places such as London's Soho, and simply locked up and left. There is now no connection with the former owners, and no prospect for making one. But assuming that problem can be overcome, those that once worked in the street and now live in damp and decrepit accommodation above the bars could have a better quality of life. Some improvement and investment is needed; a community centre could be generated for those who have no central place to congregate of an evening other than a statue in the main square. In 2008 the *Times of Malta* featured an article that discusses the street's future prospects. Emmy Bezzina wrote, on 10 May, of 'A vision for seductive Strait Street'. She notes how 'fascination is one of the hallmarks of this narrow stretch of street, harboured on both sides by protective long buildings which provide an idyllic array of shades and shadows throughout the day', and that 'the Valletta local council should wake up and undertake a truly worthwhile rehabilitation project for our capital city'.

On 2 September in *The Malta Independent Online*, Michael Carabott wrote about Valletta's pedestrian zone, which is gradually extending into streets adjacent to Strait Street. 'The new system', he notes, 'allows pedestrian access to Strait Street, which is fast becoming the cultural street of Valletta with various exhibitions, wine bars and restaurants.'

Things are changing therefore. The landscape is a complex and challenging one, for all its past troubles and contradictions, and for the cultural achievements of its artistes and musicians. Most significant though is the recognition of the values attached to this place by those who once lived and worked here, and—in some cases—live there still, often in very poor conditions. Strait Street matters, and finally, slowly, that fact is being realized, and it is a process that is, in the words of Andreassen, Bjerck, and Olsen (forthcoming), 'thing led'. It is the material objects and physical spaces that have enabled this account to be made, and stories told. Had the street already transformed into the inevitable cultural quarter, such depth and detail would never have been recalled, the stories would have been lost, and with them, identity and heritage. In such situations archaeology can make a difference.

Nevada: the 'Nation of Odd'

In Chapter 3 it was explained, through work at Piramida (Norway) and Orford Ness (Suffolk, UK), how part of the methodology for documenting contemporary places and landscape can involve experience and encounter. In the case of Orford Ness, the remote, coastal Cold War experimental site in Suffolk, Davis presented an 'experiential, traveller's account... which method of description I feel to be a crucial part of the material available for analysis' (2008: 143 and Ch. 3 above). At Piramida Andreassen, Bjerck, and Olsen (forthcoming) noted that, of the methods adopted to record and document the place, 'most important... was the bodily experience of actually being present and to encounter the imposing materiality of the site'. This section is an attempt to extend these principles to a landscape of distinct character, partly through direct experiences of an often remote and other-worldly landscape, and partly through the travel-ogue of writer David Thomson (1999), some of whose words and insights are presented in the following account. Through words, thoughts, and experience we here attempt a rather different form of characterization of this land—the 'nation of odd'—and we do so by dividing the account thematically. But unlike Penrose's (2007) and Hayden's (2004) accounts, we have adopted very different terms of reference, being the four elements that truly define the state: earth, air, fire, and water.

Nevada is a part of the world one can easily get drawn into—in part as a willing traveller and enthusiastic voyeur of all the state has to offer; and in part sucked in, drawn towards the plug-hole with thousands of others, ready to be disgorged or spat back into the mainstream after a few days away. Nevada is an 'other world', a place where other rules apply, unfamiliar rules, rules that contravene everything we as archae-ologists think we know about the process of change, about landscape history, time depth and the past, about survival. But at the same time it is a landscape full of fascinations and contradictions, darknesses and disappearances—where permanence is ephemeral, and the ephemeral permanent, thus challenging some of the conventions of how we think as archaeologists. Fortunes are made and lost here, sometimes in minutes. Legends are made and broken. People get ill; people die because of the landscape and the extremes with which it challenges those that encounter it. The affluence of The Strip borders the poverty of 'Naked City', where showgirls once rented cheap rooms and topped up their even tans around hotel pools. This is Hell, and it is El Dorado. Indeed, the 'helldorado' days of the Rat Pack are part of the heritage, fondly remembered by the older generation.

We could be talking only about Las Vegas, but we are not, and that is part of the fascination—the scale at which these distinctive and unusual characteristics are evident. We are talking here about Nevada state. For, as David Thomson has said,

the desert and desertedness are the true character of the state, and there is no proper getting to Vegas without crossing the desert first. That is how you can see its glow reflected in the sky, so that you wonder if it is burning already. And ... in Nevada, there is burning for a moment, like a struck match, and being on fire for eternity.   (1999: 5)

He goes on to observe how it is natural yet perverse for humans to create a society out of the desert, just as there are forces in the desolation that are ready to disown the attempt. There should be no long-term interference with the desert. And so, when pictures first came in from Mars in 1997, showing a seemingly unlimited expanse of geological rubble, Nevadans were not surprised. They know that landscape and what it means for human history (ibid.).

The first thing to say about Nevada is that the intensity of the experience, its profundity, waywardness, and extremism, are all clearly evident all over the state. From the Burning Man Festival to the Extra Terrestrial Highway with its rumours of alien abductions and the Little A'Le'Inn; from the atomic testing programme to the land art of Michael Heizer and others; from Las Vegas's famed Strip to the rapid pace of development at the ever-expanding city limits (Figs. 8.5 and 8.6); the willingness to gamble vast sums—leading variously to the generation of instant personal fortunes, or in some cases to suicide. Heritage is clearly in evidence here: museums exist to Atomic Testing and Liberace; the cities of Paris, New York, Rome, and Venice are faithfully recreated; there are white lions; Michael Jackson allegedly had his own suite of rooms at the Luxor Hotel; the Great Pyramid where visitors can explore Tutankhamen's tomb; legal brothels and gangster burials lie deep in the desert; and, in the 1950s, there was the enthusiastic acceptance of the Atomic Testing Programme, with ladies sporting 'mushroom cloud' hairdos and—in Marilyn Monroe's case—a mushroom cloud dress. When an institution is identified, a place that has historic, cultural, and popular cultural interest, so it is removed with barely a thought, barely a trace—with the sole exception of wedding chapels, where one can marry in a Polynesian paradise or accompanied by a chorus of Elvis impersonators. All these examples, we would suggest, are characteristically wayward, profound, intense, and pretty extreme.

This for us is an archaeological journey, one in which things and places predominate, and through those things and places we can briefly explore some recurring themes to illustrate the various processes at work in Nevada, each causing us to reflect a little on the ephemeral and transient nature of the Nevadan landscape. Why archaeological? The simple answer to this is 'because those making the journey are archaeologists' and, as David Clarke famously said

Figure 8.5. The 'Strip' at Las Vegas, viewed from Henderson. (Photo: John Schofield.)

Figure 8.6. New buildings at Las Vegas's city limits. (Photo: John Schofield.)

(1973: 6), 'archaeology is what archaeologists do'. But the more complex of explanations is perhaps more helpful. Our view of this landscape is focused very firmly on the material traces within it, and the evidence within this landscape for the historic processes that have shaped it. We are interested here in the presence of traces and scars of human activity from the late modern period (and most obviously atomic testing and some of the now demolished themed casino-hotels of the 1950s), and on the contribution those scars and human actions have made to forming the distinctive landscape character of this region. To what extent was the land artist Michael Heizer influenced by the landscape's physical form, for example, and by the presence of nuclear testing within it; and to what extent are the land-forms left at Peace Camp influenced by earlier human occupation of the region, and by Michael Heizer's representations; and how does Las Vegas itself reflect the wider history and shape or grain of Nevada? These are questions others can ask, but the argument we present here suggests that archaeology has a particular contribution to make, recognizing the ways in which things interconnect, taking a wider holistic view of the region, and understanding the process of change and the links that suggest some element of continuity here.

Let us begin in the desert—the desertedness; the EARTH. Here we see the ephemeral in all its various guises. The monumental architecture of the Nevada Test Site (Fig. 8.7), vast constructions some of them, built to perform or test the impact of particular scientific experiments between 1951 and 1992 (Beck 2002). How the earth moved for the Sedan test, for example, on 6 July 1962, only a few months before the Cuban Missile Crisis. A device yielding 104,000 tons was exploded 635 feet under the ground. Over 12 million tons of earth were vaporized or moved. But despite the horrors of its construction, and of the implications, it is a beautiful monument to the Cold War—beautiful in its form, its symmetry, and its sheer monstrosity. How the earth moved here had knock-on effects. It influenced what happened in Las Vegas, sixty miles away. Hotels were designed to be earthquake-proof, meaning that they could withstand tremors set off by underground tests at the Test Site. But more recently, following the Test Ban, rumour has it that no such measures were insisted upon. So what happens if testing restarts—how

Figure 8.7. Testing facilities in the desert, at Nevada Test Site. (Photo: Harold Drollinger, Desert Research Institute, Las Vegas.)

will the new hotels such as Stratosphere Tower fare? There was also an implication for domestic architecture. Johnson (2002) has described how buildings in the 1950s not only ignored but castigated the advice of the Federal Civil Defense Administration, defying the brutish, survival-minded lessons taught by civil effects testing. This was a reactionary response—the use of floor-to-ceiling plate glass windows, for example, and open-framed, thin-walled, rambling ranch-style architecture—hardly the sort of thing to protect the occupants during an attack.

Michael Heizer is a land artist of repute. His family were Nevadans since the 1880s, with professional backgrounds that incorporated geology, archaeology, and engineering. His interest in the physicality of the environment is obvious in all his work, constructed at a remote desert site forty miles from the closest habitation. Heizer started to do largescale land art in Nevada in 1967. In his *Double Negative*, he replaced over 244,000 tons of soil to create a vast cut in the desert. The work is one of emptiness, challenging the gigantic scale of the natural world.

Heizer lives in a caravan on an animal farm including dogs, cats, horses, and oxen as well as scrapers, freight lorries, tractors, trailors, and fertilizing machines. He lives alongside his constructions—his monuments to late modernism, in their remote desert setting.

At Peace Camp, sixty-five miles from the edge of Las Vegas, and directly opposite the one known entrance to the Test Site, occupants from the 1950s—most in tents and caravans—left their temporary desert home as they found it—not a trace from which archaeologists could record their presence. Or at least that's what people said. Some, including those supportive of archaeological intervention at the Test Site, could not accept that anything surviving at Peace Camp would be of interest to archaeologists. Others simply said there was nothing there. But leaving as found was not something that occupants of Peace Camp took at all literally. What remains in the desert are over 600 features, stone arrangements that in earlier prehistoric contexts would be interpreted as a ritual landscape par excellence, with stone circles, formations, geoglyphs, cairns, and rock gardens—words inscribed on the desert floor, and odd, unexplained interventions such as the 'shadow children', representing a visit to Peace Camp by Hiroshima veterans (Beck, Drollinger, and Schofield 2007). The monuments of Peace Camp also reflect those that were here—the diverse religious and cultural community that coexisted, in such an inhospitable environment, making their contribution to protect the earth from annihilation. Buddhists, Christians, New Franciscans...and the Western Shoshone, whose traditional lands these are, and whose concern for the earth is powerfully and profoundly expressed. The earth here has been transformed, on one side of the fence by the emerging militarism of the late modern age, and on the other, by the peaceful concerns of traditional owners and their allies. In a sense this archaeological record is an ephemeral one—it will gradually erode and fade back into the desert, as Nevada's many ghost towns and boom towns have done in the past...but some trace will remain, for a very long time.

The desert air feels crisp and clean in Nevada. Indeed AIR is high on everyone's agendas in Nevada. Wherever you are: cars, malls, casinos, hotel rooms, shops—your air is conditioned. When Las Vegas first emerged as a desert town in the 1930s, 'swamp coolers' revolutionized living in the desert. Although noisy and unattractive, the invention made the conditions bearable. But the air was not always that clean, and maybe it is not still. While the materiality of nuclear tests remains, along with those that protested against them, there is also a darker legacy in the environmental pollution that resulted from this phase of experimentation.

Valerie Kuletz is an academic and a researcher as well as being the daughter of a weapons scientist. She grew up in the Mojave Desert. In 1998 Routledge published her book *The Tainted Desert: Environmental and Social Ruin in the American West*, in which she describes the Nevada Test Site as perhaps the most profoundly devastated area of nuclear landscape on earth. Groundwater in some aquifers on the Test Site is contaminated by tritium 3,000 times in excess of safe drinking water standards, as well as by plutonium and other radioactive isotopes. Since 1951 radioactive releases from the Nevada Test Site have emitted more than 12 billion curies into the atmosphere, and in high fallout areas near the Site, childhood leukaemia rates are 2.5 times the national average. A map shows the impact on the wider US landscape (ibid. 71). Contrast the situation here with the Los Alamos Laboratories. At Los Alamos the story is one of scientific mastery, achievement, success; the harnessing of infinite energies embedded within the core of the material world. The Nevada Test Site on the other hand enjoys no such tale of triumph. According to Kuletz (p. 71), this is the darkest zone on the nuclear landscape, the proving grounds for this mastery of energy. The image of the brilliant scientist is nowhere to be seen, replaced by the mere technician. The mushroom cloud looms large over the backdrop of an unpopulated Nevada desert. But the cloud dissipates, leaving no visible reminder of its deadly by-product. As Kuletz (p. 76) puts it:

While Atomic Vets, Utah Mormons and the Indians of the Great Basin and Mojave deserts are not usually outspoken critics of the federal government, their stories make visible the secret nuclear landscape and the power relations that have created it. Collectively their bodies map the nuclear landscape, and their scars reveal the hidden costs of nuclear technology, military secrecy, and national sacrifice.

Fire: we have never attended the Burning Man Festival, at Gerlach in upstate Nevada. In David Thomson's travelogue—*In Nevada: The*

Land, The People, God and Chance—he described his arrival at the festival and noticing the camp from the road:

Tents, cars, camping, RVs, all stretched out in rows. It is a great campsite but there are no facilities. Every bit of food and water, every sound system, every piece of performing art, every grain of mind-altering substances—all have to be driven into this place where the temperature will reach ninety degrees at least and then fall precipitously at night. And maybe twenty thousand people—hippies, if you like, crazy kids, freaks, pagans, ravers, and not many of them Nevadans—will be there for three, four, five nights and days, going naked, fucking like bunnies, stoned out of their minds. And maybe having the kind of intense experience that can never be ruled out in desert places. (1999: 10–11)

The last part of this description is important: the idea that deserts create a particular intense experience interests us. The extremes presumably cause this: the challenge of just surviving here, let alone living with any degree of comfort. Tourists who run out of fuel in Death Valley do actually die there, having arrived ill-prepared for any sort of crisis. Perhaps it is the intense experience, or the promise of such intensity, that draws so many people to Vegas for short periods: for gambling, marriage, sex, and adventure. Equally, the silence and light of the desert makes for a profound experience, especially amongst those used to higher densities of population, and urban living. As Thomson said, it may form you, save you, or leave you unfit for much else. There is also an extremism and waywardness of visiting such truly out-of-the-way places. But consider especially the significance of fire. The searing heat. The unease that comes from discovering small roadside fires on remote desert roads. The inferno that engulfs the Burning Man at the climax of the festival. The fact that cremation makes up 20 per cent of burials in the United States, but 55 per cent in Nevada. All moments of crisis in a landscape of extremes.

Las Vegas guzzles WATER. The site was selected for settlement because of the springs and artesian wells that proved so productive. But for modern Nevada to exist it needed more, and that came from the creation of Lake Mead and the construction of Hoover Dam, the water from which is not just there to ensure survival of people, but survival of the very concept of Las Vegas—the ornamental lakes and dolphin pools, swimming pools, glasses of iced water, the lush lawns and golf courses with their sprinkler systems, and, of course, the big attractions of the Strip: the sea on which the pirate ship battle takes places several times each day; the canals of Venice on which gondolas glide, and the spectacular dancing fountains at the Bellagio. For comparison, the farming industry in Nevada in 1991 used 90.3 per cent of available water while producing 6,000 jobs and annual revenue of $168 million. The hotel owner Steve Wynn retorted that he employed more people at his Mirage hotel than the whole farming industry and that the hotel and gaming industries used only 9.3 per cent of water. So why shouldn't he be wasteful, or indulgent?

Of all things that should endure, surely Hoover Dam stands out. It was described by Richard G. Liddiard in 1942 as being to 'Americans what Chartres Cathedral was to Europeans, what the Temple at Karnak was to Egyptians. The clean, functional lines, the colossal beauty, and impersonal mass and strength of the dam itself are as symbolic as real' (cited in Thomson 1999: 195). It had real implications for Nevada. This was no longer a dead land, neglected. It had been lifted up by national enterprise and attention. And Nevada had been dignified. But as David Thomson (1999: 231) has said, the real significance of Hoover Dam lies elsewhere.

The constructions of the area often seem flimsy or temporary. Phoenix is no more convincing than Las Vegas as a city that has taken root in the ground. Their style has to do with transience and illusion. But Hoover Dam has a strength that is directly emotional. You can imagine the Southwest empty of people because of one hazard or another. You can imagine yourself coming up the river in an open boat and seeing that almighty wall. And somehow the dam works, even if the people have gone.

We do not attempt to analyse these processes in any detail; merely to record some of the paradoxes, the processes at work, and to think a little about their implications for the various ways we construct and investigate the past. This has been a journey through an unusual, queer, uncompromising, and—at times—deadly landscape, where the basic elements of earth, air, fire, and water appear predominant, or at least their predominance is more noticeable than elsewhere. Finally, then, we come to rest in Las Vegas, and the sadness of seeing a favourite hotel demolished in 2004.

Figure 8.8. The Glass Pool Inn sign and site. (Photo: John Schofield.)

Las Vegas is constantly and rapidly expanding far into the desert, while within the city limits, buildings go up and down without a sense of the monumental or seemingly of loss or trauma (*contra* Read 1996). They are plays upon the imagination, as much set-like as solid. It is as if the desert base and background inspired building with a sense of impermanence or potential makeover. You may not admire that, but as an approach, it is modern, intriguing, and suggestive of many truths in our culture (Thomson 1999).

In 2004 the Glass Pool Inn was demolished. Glass Pool Inn was an institution, but had seen better days. It had become undeniably seedy. Perhaps it always was. People loved the way their business cards advertised their status as 'The World Famous Glass Pool Inn'. Its location on the Strip and opposite the mega-hotels of Mandalay Bay and the Luxor did for it in the end, and now only the sign remains (Fig. 8.8). But it was famous, for a time: beginning with the 1955 crime drama *Las Vegas Shakedown*, over time the motel became one of the city's most photographed destinations. From motion pictures (*Casino, Indecent Proposal,* and *Leaving Las Vegas*) to television shows (*Vega$, Crime Story,* and *CSI: Crime Scene Investigation*) to music videos (from artists such as Robert Plant, ZZ Top, and Bon Jovi, among others), the motel's signature glass pool served as a backdrop for various productions. Photographers also brought their cameras, including Annie Leibowitz, who once captured Brad Pitt there for *Vanity Fair* magazine.

The windows on the Glass Pool are what made it stand out—and the theme of surveillance, watching and observing, is another recurring one in Nevada—something we recognize as a characteristic of our age. In Vegas as in Nevada surveillance occurs *in extremis*. Readers may recall Louis Theroux testing the security of Area 51 as part of his *Weird Weekends* television series. No sooner had he stepped over the line, in a vast landscape of nothing at all, than a jeep appeared with armed soldiers to dissuade him from going further. How did they know? To cite David Thomson (ibid. 134–5):

Miles of videotape come in every day from all over Las Vegas, not just the cameras that record transactions and missed meetings in the public places, but the cameras that watch over all the gaming tables and can call back the fall of cards, the shy distress of some players, and the deft cheating of others. The cans of surveillance, supposedly, are catalogued and stored in the warehouses on the edge of the city. So many minutes; so much short-lived action and excitement; and always the steady, listless beat of time peeling away. And so in the crushed spirit of a watched society, every mirror, every glass surface becomes the front for a clerical scrutiny—a little man, eating a sandwich, absorbing and being bored by your nakedness.

Sadness at the demolition of Glass Pool Inn is not enduring however. Here change is good—it is what makes Las Vegas special. And timelessness appears inherent, part of the essential character of the place.

This example returns us to Chapter 3 (Methods), to the earlier part of this chapter, and to the European Landscape Convention. Reading the landscape in this experiential way is for us a legitimate form of archaeological investigation, taking the principles of landscape characterization on the one hand, and in particular its emphasis on the holistic and everyday nature of landscape, and the question of perception on the other, and constructing a model that recognizes the grain of a landscape, its occupation and patterns of use, the time depth evident within it, the processes that have shaped it, however ancient or modern they might be, and the material culture that survives. As with Strait Street, the story here is one of landscape, but a landscape in which people are central to its understanding. The difference between an archaeological approach and that of other disciplines is that material culture is more often the starting point, leading us then to the people who created and used it. Kuletz (1998) tends to see things in what we would describe as this archaeological way, mapping the visible and invisible nuclear landscape of the American Midwest. As any good archaeologist would, she presents this map as a series of 'layers', beginning with the uranium region, which shows the transformation of land under nuclear colonialism. 'Its story spans forty-plus years of uranium booms and busts, concerns millions of acres, massive environmental pollution still left unreclaimed, and generations of Indians dying of cancer' (p. 37). But as she says, this particular part of the landscape does not exist in isolation. It is part of a larger terrain, 'part of a number of interconnected transformative processes that emerged in the post-war West and Southwest' (p. 37). Science cities form another layer, being those laboratories and scientific institutions, many created from scratch in remote places deemed to be 'uninhabited'. The Los Alamos Laboratory in northern New Mexico is one such science city; the Mojave Desert is another. These zones are effectively character areas, albeit defined at broad scale, and as is typical of character areas, links and connections exist between them, either as continuities in form or function, or discontinuities and disconnects. But that itself is what often characterizes the late modern landscape. As with Las Vegas and Nevada, it is generally a landscape of surprises and challenges. This is why investigations at this broad landscape scale can work, as they do of course for earlier periods.

CONCLUSIONS

This chapter has extended our archaeological gaze out from the minutiae of objects and places to the wider landscape of which they are a part. Landscape is about networks of sites and their interrelations, their connections with the land, and with topography, and the degree to which we could analyse the relations people had with landscape, through phenomenology for instance. For archaeologists of the contemporary past all these issues equally apply, but with the additional complexity of often knowing more about the material record, more about relations with the land, and more about social meaning: about how people interact with and perceive the landscape. We also now have our own reflexive passions and persuasions manifest, for example, in the desire to conserve large areas of landscape, or at least participate in decisions that affect their futures: the speed of suburban growth for example; decisions on whether to build (or not build) iconic tall buildings that will dominate skylines and perceptions of the future. And thanks to new technologies, the situation is one in which we can all participate, through an increasingly democratic and participatory planning process, at least in parts of the developed world. We can all have a view therefore, and we can do something about it. We can change things, or at least contribute to a process that manages change. Indeed as archaeologists we are uniquely placed to comment. Change is something archaeologists know all about.

In the final chapter in Part II, we broaden our scope even further, by turning to some of the most distinctive landscapes of late modernity, following on from the work in Chapter 5 which established non-places, imaginative landscapes, and the virtual as key areas for an archaeological inquiry into the contemporary past.

9

Non-Places and Virtual Worlds

As I pass through security screening and into the departure lounge, all thought shifts from the journey that has brought me here to the series of carefully orchestrated steps that will lead me from this place to my destination. I look around for the sign that will direct me towards my departure gate, checking my watch and noticing that I have less than an hour before boarding. I walk through the Duty Free store, past the aisles of discounted spirits and perfumes, indistinguishable liquids with only the bottle size and design to differentiate them. I join the queue to buy a cup of coffee and small bottle of water from Starbucks, before taking my seat in the far corner of the lounge, closest to what the sign tells me will be a twenty-minute walk to my departure gate. Out of the corner of my eye, I notice a scrap of pale blue carpet peeling away from the furniture fittings below my feet, to reveal a small triangle of green carpet underneath. In being presented with this insight into the building's stratigraphy, I think about other places where its particular histories are laid open, only to realize there are none. This is a place where history is banished beneath layers of fresh paint and carpet, where memories are erased like old furniture fittings, and where only the here and now seems to maintain a foothold. Not a scrap of peeling paint remains to tell the story of its former colour schemes, former histories, or traces of lives past. 'No place for an archaeologist,' I think, rising to my feet and starting my approach to departure gate G15 . . .

INTRODUCTION

In previous chapters we have considered how we might take an archaeological approach to the contemporary or very recent past in what would be recognized to be a fairly conventional series of archaeological 'realms'—artefacts, places, and landscape. In this chapter, we will explore some of the ways in which an archaeological approach might be taken to some of the most distinctive features of late modernity. In Chapter 5, we explored a number of these features, highlighting non-places, the work of the imagination, and the virtual as key areas for archaeological inquiry. This chapter takes up some of the challenges of these new materialities (and, indeed, the new 'virtualities') of late modernity, considering the ways in which an archaeological approach to the contemporary world might help illuminate aspects of late modernity that have not previously been well understood. As in previous chapters in Part II, this chapter is broken into a number of sections reflecting broad themes relating to the distinctive features of late-modern everyday life—non-places; virtual worlds; experience economies and the work of the imagination; and hyperconsumerism and globalization.

NON-PLACES

In Chapter 5 we looked in detail at Augé's (1995) concept of the 'non-place'. Augé uses this term to describe a whole series of spaces in contemporary society—airport lounges, shopping malls, motorways—that he suggests are to be distinguished from 'places', in the sense in which these spaces are not relational, historical, or concerned with the establishment of a sense of identity (all those things that characterize the traditional social anthropologist's interest in 'place'). These 'non-places' are primarily associated with the experience of travel or transit, and reflect the simultaneous time–space expansion and compression that he associates with late modernity. We suggested that such places rely not only on aspects of their generic design, but also on a series of 'technologies of isolation' that work together to produce a characteristic feeling of solitude and the emptying of consciousness discussed in Augé's work. These technologies of isolation—the headphones of the in-flight entertainment system that one wears in the aeroplane, the iPod in the ears while working out at the gym, the isolation of the car as we drive along the motorway, the silent banks of heads immersed in e-readers and mobile entertainment devices on public transport, both produce and are produced by a sense of hypermodern alienation that we can identify as a fundamental aspect of the late modern experience. But how might we approach such places archaeologically?

Let us start by taking an archaeological approach to the study of air travel. As with any journey, we first must decide where to start. Shall we begin with the global web of airports, regulated and synchronized with each other through international networks of travel and commerce involving air traffic controls, legal regulation, and globalized business firms, not to mention the millions of passengers who travel through them every day? At the level of the individual airport, itself a vast shopping and commercial hub, a microcosm of the globalized city? With the aeroplane, the site and technology of air travel that is the reason for the airport's existence? With the passengers, part of a network of inputs and outputs that flow through the space of the airport? Or with the millions of individual artefacts that make up the archaeology of air travel? Or should we consider all these aspects simultaneously, while focusing on individual sites and places, and on the artefacts found there? The sort of approach outlined in Chapter 5 to actor-networks and John Law's (2004) work on research method and 'mess' provide a tool to help us do this.

For want of a better place, we could begin with a consideration of Heathrow airport in London, or LHR as it is known by its airport code, one of 17,576 possible unique three-letter acronyms, of which approximately 9,000 have been assigned by the International Air Transport Association to airports throughout the world (Fuller and Harley 2004: 156). Airports Council International data states that London Heathrow airport is the world's third busiest airport in terms of passenger traffic, having received over 68 million passengers in 2007 (Airports Council International 2008). In 2009, ninety-two airlines serviced Heathrow, with flights departing to 187 international destinations (BAA 2009).

The airport is a complex artefact. Its operations represent a series of networks through which objects and people flow from one space to the next. It is complicated as an archaeological case study because it not only includes fixed infrastructure (runways, terminals, associated transport infrastructure, fixed machinery) but contains various objects that are constantly in motion but which never leave the space of the airport (trucks for moving goods on and off aeroplanes, luggage trolleys) and other objects that are always in a state of transit through the space (luggage, food and other items for sale, aeroplanes, passengers).

Our consideration of the work of Latour (Ch. 4) has suggested we must look to the transitions, shifts, movements, and the interstitial spaces to explore the places where the social becomes traceable and to understand the relationships between the particular and the whole. Fuller and Harley (2004: 38) propose that the airport represents a sort of laboratory for considering relationships between technological and cultural processes and systems of social movement, and that the operations of the airport are transforming notions of national and global citizenship and humanity through allowing for a sort of 'transit-life'. They suggest that one way of thinking about the airport is as a series of transformations from processing to holding and non-sterile to sterile. Passengers and their luggage are registered, cross-referenced, processed, and held in several cycles before shifting into terminal airspace. Landside and airside spaces are considered to be non-sterile and sterile respectively. Thus, what the airport *is* depends on where you are within it, and the means by which you are travelling through it (ibid. 17; see Fig. 9.1).

Let us look in more detail at how one moves through the space of LHR, and the various transformations that occur from the passenger's perspective. There are five terminals at LHR, each serviced by various public transport hubs. Assuming one is travelling from Terminal 4, one enters the terminal and progresses to the check-in desk. Movements are constantly mediated by signs. Matching the numbers on the e-ticket with those on a screen, the passenger progresses to check-in, a place in which the bodies of aircraft passengers are linked and cross-referenced to their luggage and to a seat on the aircraft. At this stage, passengers become 'distributed persons' (cf. Strathern 1988, 2004; Wagner 1992; Gell 1998)—they become simultaneously not only their physical body, but also their luggage and the space on the aircraft on which they will ultimately fly. Their fortunes from this point become intimately linked with those other distributed pieces of their personhood. This is the first

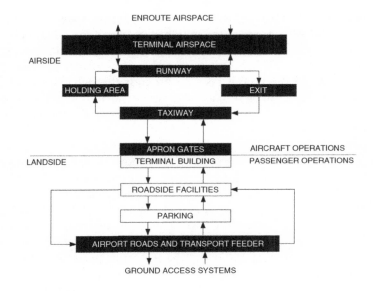

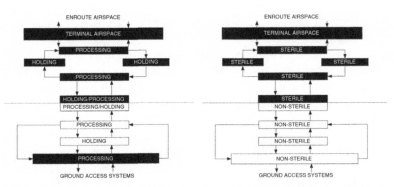

Figure 9.1. Various ways of conceptualizing the space of the airport as a system. (Redrawn by Rodney Harrison from Fuller and Harley 2004: 16–17.)

transformation in the steps leading towards a citizenship of what Fuller and Harley (2004) refer to as 'transit-life'.

Now we are at a crossroads. We could, like the narrative with which we began this chapter (and the one that forms an introduction to Augé's *Non-Places*), follow the passengers as they make their full transition into the sterile space of the airport transit lounge, but we might be more interested in following one of the other manifestations of the passengers' personhood in the form of their luggage. Indeed, from the luggage's perspective, the security and passport controls and the time it takes to progress through the transit-side shopping mall can be seen as obstacles intended to slow the progress of passengers so that their bags can be made to reach their aircraft at the same time as they do—a sort of race to reassemble the distributed person in his or her proper place on the aircraft. Within most modern airports, the time allocated to move the bag from check-in to departure gate is directly determined by the amount of time it will take the passenger to make the same journey (Ashford, Stanton, and Moore 1996: 186). A series of automated bag-handling systems move luggage from check-in through a network of conveyor belts and junctions, onto unmanned destination-coded vehicles (automated trucks for loading and unloading baggage) that utilize automatic barcode identification, through explosives screening, further sorting and automated processing, with diversions for fast-tracking urgent bags to the departure gate before they are loaded on to the aeroplane. At Heathrow Terminal 4, some 70,000 bags are transported this way each day (BAA 2009).

Our passengers must now pass through security screening and into the Departures area. Here they make the transition that their baggage has already made, from non-sterile to sterile space. Once again, the transition and passage are mediated by way of a series of signs that direct passengers to the appropriate security screening booth. Passing through security, passengers remove all but their inner layers of clothing while their hand luggage is x-rayed and scanned. On entering the departure lounge, passengers enter what is essentially a shopping mall (see Fig. 9.2). Nothing is private in the airport, but all thought and experience becomes internalized and focused on the passenger as consumer. Within the departure lounge, the focus is on the provision of well-known multinational goods and services that will be familiar to passengers as members of the global citizenship of transit-life. These multinational companies seek to reassure and encourage the global passenger through clear use of well-known branding and familiar shop design. Fast food restaurants and retail chains generally incorporate strong design

Figure 9.2. The airport as shopping mall: London Gatwick North Terminal. (Photo: Rodney Harrison.)

elements that make both their brand and function easily recognizable. For example, fast-food restaurants will be designed in such a way that customers will recognize that they should consume their food quickly then move on (Piotrowski and Rogers 2007: 157). This is achieved through the use of tall bar facilities and banquette-style seating in preference to tables, fixed benches rather than chairs, and plastic materials that are durable, anonymous, and easily cleaned.

There is obvious repetition in the layout and provision of services at airport terminals. One of us spent eight hours at Sydney airport (SYD) in transit from Adelaide (ADL) to LHR. When he exhausted the shopping mall at the terminal, a helpful shop assistant explained that there was another terminal, some twelve minutes walk away. The journey involved a series of tunnels and numerous escalators, eventually leading to another terminal, with its own shopping mall and restaurants. However the shops and food outlets were exactly the same, in more or less the same layout, and selling precisely the same things. Even the internal arrangement of goods in the shops was the same. Only the staff were different, though presumably also perceived to be somewhat interchangeable.

This focus on the provision of standard, uniform, and predictable goods and services has been termed 'McDonaldization' by the sociologist George Ritzer ([1995] 2004; see also Ritzer 1998, 2003, and 2006). Ritzer points to the ways in which various aspects of the philosophy and operational rationale of the American fast-food restaurant have permeated all sectors of society, especially those relating to the provision of goods and services. He defines the 'dimensions of McDonaldization' as efficiency, calculability (the emphasis on quantity rather than quality), predictability (the assurance that products will be of the same quantity and quality in all outlets), and control through non-human technology (Ritzer 2004: 12). It is this final point that might concern us most as archaeologists of the contemporary past. Customers are controlled through the imposition of signs and other visual clues that help to motivate the behaviours that are expected of them; for example, bins are left by doors to remind customers to clear up after themselves when they leave the restaurants (ibid. 116). The physical design elements of restaurants encourage customers to eat quickly, or not to sit in the restaurant at all (drive-through windows). Colour schemes are chosen to motivate customers to move on as quickly as possible (p. 117).

In the vast shopping mall in which our passenger arrives through customs in the departure lounge at LHR Terminal 4, he or she is confronted with a number of retail outlets and restaurants of well-known franchises, both 'national' (Harrods, WH Smith, JD Wetherspoon) and 'international' (HMV, Starbucks). Our passenger would encounter the same retail outlets and restaurants whether in Terminal 4 or in any of the other four departure lounges at LHR. As we saw at Sydney airport, all these outlets, and the design of the airport itself, work together to produce an architecture of generic transit; they work on the body to produce a simultaneous sense of familiar alienation. The surfaces are frequently cleaned and painted so that they acquire no sense of historicity—such places exist only in the present and do not celebrate their connections with the past but seek to mask them wherever possible. The role of the archaeologist in such contexts is not only to explore the ways in which the bodily sensation of 'transit-life' is made manifest, but also to reveal the specific histories of these places and the ways in which they are concealed from the public. The peeling carpet, the layers of paint, and the traces of previous styles of airport furniture all carry a sense of the specific history of the airport departure lounge, signalling to the passenger that he or she is in 'this' place rather than some other. Drawing attention to these artefacts and traces reinstates a sense of the past in these places that manufacture for themselves only a living present.

Let us skip forward in time to the point at which the passengers and their distributed material culture are reunited in flight. Here too, there is a strong potential for archaeological analysis. We might think of an analysis of the material culture of air flight and the differences between the material assemblage of First Class and Economy class. While most of the artefacts are fixed within the aeroplanes themselves, the artefacts associated with inflight meals seem an appropriate place to start such an analysis, representing as they do the most widely experienced portable material artefacts of air travel. A comparison of the breakfast trays that were handed to customers on an Air Canada flight between London and Toronto in January 2009, for example, illustrated some major differences. Within the economy meal were a large number of plastic wrappers and utensils that are used and then discarded, either by the airline itself (if the items are all handed back to the flight attendant) or by the passengers should they choose to take any of the items off the plane with them. However, the Executive First Class tray contained almost exclusively items that could be washed and reused, and very little in the way of material that could be taken off the plane by the passenger and/or end up in landfill. A tub of yoghurt was the only item common to both. Even within the same flight, we see the proliferation of very strong differences in the material signatures of First and Economy class travel, which is created through the differentiated use of materials (plastic vs. stainless steel cutlery; plastic vs. crockery plates; paper vs. cotton napkins; disposable vs. reusable items) as well as their presentation.

This focus on one aspect of the material culture of air flight suggests other areas for future archaeological research. How do individual airlines differentiate themselves whilst also giving the passenger a comfortingly generic experience? How do these conflicting desires, to distinguish your brand whilst producing a generic transit-life 'non-place', resolve themselves through material culture? What is the role of the archaeologist in understanding this distinctively late modern phenomenon?

This section has suggested some approaches to the archaeology of non-places with specific reference to LHR Terminal 4. As one of the key features of late modern societies, both the ways in which generic spaces of transit are produced and the ways in which they are experienced emerge as key areas for an archaeology of 'now'. We will now turn to consider another of the specific spaces of late modernity, the space of the virtual and its associated new communicative technologies.

VIRTUAL WORLDS

In Chapter 5 it was argued that one of the key aspects of late modernity revolves around the proliferation of communicative technologies and their associated impacts on the experience of time and space, what Jean Baudrillard refers to as the development of a 'hyper-reality' (1994, 1995; see also Tiffin and Terashima 2001). Central to these changes has been the rise of Computer Mediated Communication (CMC) and virtual experience, part of the work of the imagination as a social force discussed by Appadurai in *Modernity at Large* (1996; see further Ch. 5). What role does archaeology have to play in the exploration of the internet, new communicative technologies, and virtual worlds? While anthropologists have begun to explore the ways in which CMC is giving rise to new forms of virtual communities and the sociocultural implications of new communication technologies (e.g. Hine 2000; Miller and Slater 2000; Fabian 2002; Wilson and Peterson 2002; Eisenlohr 2004; Zongming 2005; Boellstorff 2008), there has been little discussion of an *archaeology* of virtual communities. Graves-Brown (2009*b*), in a provocative look at how an archaeologist might approach the internet, suggests that we should consider computer software to be an 'intangible artefact'. Web pages, he points out, are not simply documents, but behave as 'tools' in the sense in which 'they actually *do* something'. Given that 'tools' have always formed a focus of traditional archaeological inquiry, the fact that web pages can be considered to be tools suggests that archaeologists may indeed have a role to play in understanding them. Noting that these virtual tools are coterminous with humans as part of complex actor-networks, he suggests:

the design of the tools that we use in the virtual world, and the nature of their relationship to real world analogues, can have important implications for our understanding of the nature of twentieth- and twenty first-century society. This suggests that archaeology, with its depth of understanding of material culture, can have an effective role in the exploration of the virtual.

These issues were considered as part of Harrison's (2009*a*) archaeological investigation of the virtual settlement of 'Second Life' (SL). Virtual settlements have expanded rapidly in response to the development of computerized technologies that allow for the creation of interactive synthetic environments in which users are sensually immersed and that respond to user input (Sherman and Craig 2003: 6). As a medium, virtual reality (VR) has three defining characteristics—it operates in real time, so that feedback is not noticeably delayed from the perspective of the user, it is interactive, and is based on the use of three-dimensional spatial models (Whyte 2002: 3). While many early VR mediums employed stand-alone computer-based technologies, the widespread availability of the internet and broadband technologies that allow large amounts of data to be downloaded relatively quickly has meant that internet-based VR has grown rapidly in the last decade. This has led to the development of what are commonly known as virtual worlds (but which might be better termed virtual 'settlements') and virtual communities. Rheingold (1993: 5) defines virtual communities as 'social aggregations that emerge from the Net when enough people carry on ... public conversations long enough ... to form webs of personal relationships in cyber-space'. Jones (1997) distinguishes between such virtual communities and their virtual settlements, defining a virtual settlement as 'a cyber-place that is symbolically delineated by topics of interest and within which a significant proportion of interrelated interactive group-CMC occurs' (ibid. 6). He posits that a virtual settlement must meet a minimum set of conditions, requiring a minimum level of interactivity, a variety of communicators, a certain level of sustained membership, and a public common space where interaction may occur. While Jones is at pains to point out that the virtual communities are not created by new technologies, it is important to note that the development of virtual communities and settlements is reliant on the technology that realizes the possibility of VR.

While it has its antecedents in the work of Anderson (1983), the anthropology of online communities (e.g. Hine 2000; Miller and Slater 2000; Fabian 2002; Wilson and Peterson 2002; Boellstorff 2008) is a relatively new field of research. Indeed, there is some argument as to whether the concept of an 'online community' is even a useful one (e.g. Rheingold 1993; Hakken 1999). One important aspect of the anthropology of virtual communities has been to emphasize 'the link between historically constituted socio-cultural practices within and outside of mediated communication and the language practices, social interactions, and ideologies of technology that emerge from new information and communication technologies' (Wilson and Peterson 2002: 453), and the blurred boundaries between online and offline worlds (Miller and Slater 2000: 5). Wilson and Peterson (2002) distinguish between those studies concerned with offline social, cultural, and historical processes (e.g. Garfinkel 2000) and those more concerned with the development, diffusion, and reception of new technologies and media (e.g. Latour 1996). Agre's (1999: 4) work has considered the relationship between online and offline identities, suggesting the ways in which 'social and professional identities are continuous over several media, and . . . people use those several media to develop their identities in ways that carry over to other settings'. The connection between offline and online identities and the cultural significance of the internet and its relationship with nationalism, gender, and class is the focus of Miller and Slater's (2000) ethnographic study of the internet in Trinidad. Other areas of anthropological and sociological concern in the study of the internet have included communication and language shifts (e.g. Eisenlohr 2004), and the relationship between ideology and social and linguistic practices in cyberspace (e.g. Crystal 2001; Wilson and Peterson 2002: 461).

The only detailed ethnographic study of SL is Boellstorff's *Coming of Age in Second Life* (2008). This study, which approaches the online settlement of SL as a traditional ethnographic field, considers changing notions of personhood associated with the emergence of virtual settlements, and draws out the connection between virtual and actual worlds. Boellstorff (ibid. 29) emphasizes the fact that, contrary to the widespread use of terms such as 'post-human' to describe the notions of personhood generated by virtual worlds, 'virtual worlds reconfigure selfhood and sociality, but this is only possible because they rework the virtuality that characterizes human being in the actual world'. The connection between actual and virtual personhood thus emerges as a critical concern for both the anthropology and archaeology of online communities.

Harrison (2009*a*) draws on the work of Jones (1997) to suggest a new way of understanding virtual communities through the study of their cultural artefacts. His outline of a new discipline of 'cyber-archaeology' extends not only to the actual technologies employed by virtual communities (computer hardware, the internet), but also to the objects they create within virtual settlements. He suggests that it is possible to understand aspects of a virtual community through the study of its virtual material culture, and to explore issues of 'virtuality' that would be of concern to archaeologists and those with a focus on material culture. Discussing the ways in which virtual material culture is produced and the complex network of transactions in virtual material culture that can be 'read' by exploring the history of virtual objects in SL, he shows how objects carry information about who made them and when they were created, and ways in which this information can be interrogated at any time by selecting the object and 'inspecting' it with a series of mouse clicks. Objects and gestures are frequently queried by SL users, to find out who 'owns' them. The 'history' of the creation of any object is contained in its code. All SL objects are composed of a series of three-dimensional shapes, created using a limited three-dimensional modelling tool or the more sophisticated Linden Scripting Language (LSL) which is used to give objects within SL autonomous behaviour. Once an object has been created by a user in SL, it is registered as 'created by' and 'owned by' particular residents. The owner and the creator of the object maintain certain rights over the object, and the creator of an object may mark it as uncopyable, unable to be modified, or unable to be transferred to another resident. Objects which have been marked as able to be copied, modified, or transferred preserve a history of all such actions carried out on them. These constitute an amazing digital archive of the traffic in virtual objects throughout SL, and allow one to build up a picture of the ways in which objects have been modified and used throughout their virtual lives.

It is the concern with stratigraphic layering that makes such an investigation of virtual material culture a form of archaeological excavation. Indeed, one could imagine using a Harris Matrix to record the changes and layers of ownership of objects in SL, for example. This would produce a grid that would allow the transformations of objects and their ownership in SL to be compared across time and space.

In addition to this ability to look in detail at the ways in which objects have been created, used, modified, and moved around the virtual settlement, the significant digital archives produced by SL allow the potential for a study of the ways in which the 'meanings' of objects and places have changed through time. For example, one artefact conserved in the SL History Museum is a small statue of a hippo (Fig. 9.3). A wide range of mythology surrounds hippos in SL, although it appears that more recent users may not be aware of this mythology as it relates to 'old' social practices dating to earlier versions of the virtual settlement.

The tale of the hippo began simply enough in a forum thread by Darwin Appleby in which he strikes a long lasting topic about hippos, which became one of the longest lasting threads on the SL forums. It was then carried over into the grid when Hikaru Yamamoto started a zoo in which a small hippo family could be found. This small yet humble family loved to be fed by visitors and soon became a crowd favorite! Soon enough hippo statues and avatars began to appear throughout the grid...Some may have forgotten about the beloved hippo, but to others the hippos shall never die... HIPPO was also the name of a Linden-made object that you could put keywords into and it would detect other people wearing HIPPOs that had the same keywords in them as well. Example: Oz Spade has 'cats' in his HIPPO, Bob Boberson has 'cats' in his HIPPO, Oz walks past Bob, and both of their HIPPOs light up. The HIPPOs still work, but are not used by many residents, becoming one of those things that 'never really caught on'.   (Second Life Wikia 2009)

While this particular artefact is clearly intended to be humorous, it does demonstrate the way in which certain types of technologies in

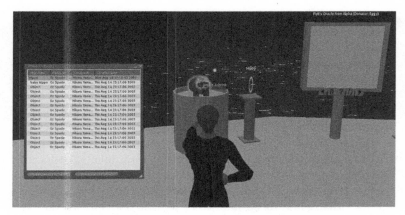

Figure 9.3. Screenshot showing an Avatar 'inspecting' the Hippo statue in the Second Life History Museum to study its history, which is shown as a series of time- and date-coded 'layers'. (Photo: Rodney Harrison.)

SL, as in the real world, become defunct not only because their function is taken over by new technology, but also because they go out of fashion or do not prove to be socially popular.

Harrison (2009a) concludes with a discussion of the explicit programme of heritage conservation in Second Life, suggesting that the way in which virtual communities use (virtual) material culture and heritage to create a sense both of belonging and of 'place' emerges as a new area for study. Indeed, as Paul Basu (2007: 97) has noted, 'it is somewhat paradoxical that the internet, this global-ising technology *par excellence*, should prove such an effective facili-tator of individuals' localising strategies'. However, Harrison (2009a) is critical of the rather limited palate of forms of heritage in SL. He argues that the ways in which SL functions as a space that both relates to and changes individuals' sense of personhood and being in the (actual) world suggests that we should be concerned with the trend in SL towards homogenous 'official' heritage discourses that allow little space for the development of alternative or subaltern forms of heri-tage within such virtual environments.

Bartle (2003: 1) has described virtual settlements as 'places where the imaginary meets the real'. But how does the virtual influence the 'real' world? One example is the material legacy of the Year 2000 problem and the ways in which its associated millenarianism was expressed in both incidental and designed material remains of global Millennium celebrations (Harrison 2009c). Concerns about global technological catastrophe and the end of the world at the end of the last millennium centred on international fears surrounding the 'Millennium Bug', fears that were manifested in monumental building programmes that looked to the past to emphasize stability and the absence of change. These fears were spread through the electronic media and proliferated on the internet, creating a virtual panic that we can read in the archaeological record of monuments produced to mark the beginning of the new millennium.

The 1999–2000 calendar changeover became a focus for fears around what came to be known in popular parlance as the 'Year 2000 problem', the 'Millennium Bug', or simply 'Y2K', which described potential errors that might occur in critical computer systems due to the practice of storing year dates with two digits rather than four.

> The Year 2000 computer problem is globally considered as one of this century's most critical issues, so much so that the world community has joined forces to resolve the problem.... [A]t the end of the twentieth century, many software applications will stop working or create erroneous results when the year switches from 1999 to 2000.... [D]ate sensitive embedded chips could (also) stop working... [These] embedded business systems control traffic lights, air traffic control, security systems, time clocks and hospital operating systems. (Reid 1999: 1–2)

Predictions regarding the effects of the Year 2000 problem ranged from the inconvenience of the failure of computer software programs to the collapse of critical services such as power and water. A very successful information campaign on the potential hazards of the Year 2000 problem led to most organizations and businesses upgrading computer software and hardware so that very few problems were experienced when the clock struck midnight on 31 December 1999 (CNN 2000). However, by this point the global preparedness for the Year 2000 problem was reported as having cost well over US$300 billion (BBC 2000b).

It is now difficult to recall the scale of fear surrounding the Year 2000 problem, and the way in which it connected in the popular imagination with other millenarian uncertainties. *The Y2K Personal*

Survival Guide (Hyatt 1999) recommended stockpiling water, food, and basic groceries for all families and included suggestions for households in developing their own alternative sources of power and heating. There were a number of newspaper and television reports of individuals building bunkers or shelters in which they intended to weather the impending apocalypse. This meant that in addition to the excitement of the dawn of a new millennium for many, New Year's Eve 1999 was filled with a sense of apprehension and trepidation. Harrison (2009c) argues that this setting of widespread confusion regarding the impact of the Year 2000 problem produced a lasting legacy in the UK in the form of monuments and material remains associated with the work of the Millennium Commission, which in 1993 embarked on one of the most expensive monumental building programmes of the late twentieth century.

A range of monuments was constructed at the end of the millennium, many of them funded by the Millennium Commission (see further Harrison 2009c). For example, throughout Britain, tens if not hundreds of modern 'standing stones' were erected, mirroring the form of Neolithic standing stones, circles, and monuments. They evoked a Neolithic past, reimagined as a Golden Age in which fears of humanly generated environmental and technological disasters were absent. The Millennium Experience, a series of temporary displays and events throughout the year 2000, housed in the Millennium Dome on the Greenwich Peninsula, presented the future as post-apocalypse, while overall, the work of the Millennium Commission can be seen as looking to the past through the emphasis on projects associated with existing heritage sites and precincts. In addition to these physical memorials, all computer software and hardware produced after this period conserve artefacts of the fear of collapse of critical infrastructure and computing systems at the end of the last millennium, fed not only by legitimate concerns about the computing problem, but also by broader uncertainties about the future that manifested at this time. This is apparent in the insistence on storing dates within software and hardware as four digits rather than two.

This brief example illustrates the rich potential for an archaeological approach to the internet, new communicative technologies, and virtual reality. The virtual has become increasingly important as new media and communicative technologies have transformed existing forms of communication and social relations. As discussed in Chapter 5, Appadurai (1996) has argued that the electronic mediation of communication, coupled with mass migration and transnationalism, works on the imagination in innovative ways. The imagination itself takes on a new role in late modern society, allowing the individual imagination to become linked with what Appadurai terms a 'community of sentiment', that allows the imagination to have agency in ways it has not previously throughout history. In the section that follows, we will consider the ways in which the work of the imagination and the new experience economy of late modernity might be explored archaeologically.

THE EXPERIENCE ECONOMY AND THE WORK OF THE IMAGINATION

In *The Experience Economy*, Pine and Gilmore (1999) argue for a shift from a service-based to an experience-based economy, in which goods and services have come to be valued not so much for their function, but in terms of their engagement of the senses and the experiences that surround their purchase and use (see also Sundbo and Darmer 2008). Some authors have related this shift in the nature of consumption to other conditions of late modernity, in particular the new modes of capitalism involving more flexible forms of capital accumulation and distribution. In Chapter 5 we noted that the manifestations of the experience economy—casinos, museums, entertainment spaces—have formed a major theme for archaeologists of the contemporary past. For example, archaeologist Martin Hall and social anthropologist Pia Bombardella have written on the entertainment spaces of the new South Africa (Hall 2001, 2005, 2006; Hall and Bombardella 2005, 2007), and archaeologist Cornelius Holtorf (2005*b*, 2007, 2009) has undertaken research on contemporary entertainment spaces such as archaeological theme parks and resorts in the US, UK, continental Europe, and South Africa. We will consider their work here in more detail to explore some of the ways in which archaeologists can contribute to an understanding of the experience economy of late modernity.

Theme parks are generally considered to represent the most fundamental manifestation of the experience economy (Clavé 2007: 155), and are central to the discussion of the emergence of 'experience' as a commodity. Although there was a long tradition of amusement- and trolley-parks, which provided picnic areas, mechanical rides, and other forms of entertainment (themselves evolving from a tradition of travelling fairs and expositions), the opening of Disneyland in 1955 is considered to represent a watershed in the sense in which it represented one of the world's first fully themed amusement parks, which has subsequently acted as a model for the development of not only other theme parks, but themed attractions such as shopping malls, casinos, hotels, and restaurants (e.g. see papers in Sorkin 1992; Mitrašinović 2006). Bryman (2004: 2) refers to this process as the 'Disneyization' of society, and notes that this process has several dimensions. The first dimension he refers to as 'theming'—where institutions or objects are given an overall narrative unrelated to their history or function. The second he describes in terms of hybrid consumption—'a general trend whereby the forms of consumption associated with different institutional spheres become interlocked with each other and increasingly difficult to distinguish' (ibid.). The third relates to the area of merchandising, where goods and services that bear images and logos are produced for sale. The fourth dimension relates to performative labour, where frontline service work is increasingly viewed as a form of performance and a certain display of mood is linked to the performance of that service. This is perhaps most clearly embodied in the phrase 'service with a smile'. Ryman argues that Disneyization extends the principles of McDonaldization in a new way, in the sense in which it is concerned with promoting consumption but swaps the homogenization of experience with the increasingly spectacular context in which consumption can take place. Indeed, Mitrašinović (2006: 35) goes further, to argue that homogenization is a necessary prerequisite for 'theming' to work, by creating a blank template prior to the requisite fusing of what had previously existed as separate domains of human culture and experience.

There are several ways in which archaeologists might approach the study of theme parks. The first is a consideration of the themes used by theme parks themselves. As Holtorf (2007, 2009) points out, many theme parks draw on historical, archaeological, or heritage-related themes. He (2009: 58) suggests that by exploring these themes and the ways in which they are utilized within the context of particular theme parks, we might explore the potential for a 'new archaeology for a new society'. A second avenue of investigation relates to an analysis of the material culture of the theme park itself. If we are to consider theme parks as a microcosm for understanding the experience society, then an analysis of its material world should help us to understand how the experience economy operates. An archaeological investigation of theme parks could take place at the level of individual artefacts, sites, or whole landscapes. Because most theme parks still operate as functioning entities it is not possible to excavate them, but instead, archaeologists have subjected them to analysis through an exploration of their material culture and physical architecture. Working in such circumstances, archaeologists are concerned with both the physical layering of buildings and artefacts in space and the layers of meaning that such places produce.

GrandWest Entertainment World and Casino, Cape Town, South Africa

Hall and Bombardella (2007) provide an analysis of the GrandWest Entertainment World and Casino in Cape Town, South Africa. Their procedure illustrates how an archaeologist might approach such a space. Disneyland and other theme parks have been described as heterotopias—places that exist in parallel to the everyday and that provide a vision of a utopia (e.g. Marin 1984). Like other theme parks, GrandWest exists as an entirely self-contained fantasy world. The entertainment complex comprises two hotels, a casino, restaurants, food court, bars, ice skating rink, bowling alley, cinema complex, rides, and concert venue. Of particular interest is the 'Magic Company', 'a gateway to a world of fantasy and fun-filled adventure—particularly for little people... housed in a 17th century Fort, with a replica of Jan van Riebeck's historical ship anchored outside' (Sun International 2009*a*). Hall and Bombardella (2007: 247) note that GrandWest is a gated complex, enclosed by high fencing with visible CCTV and security staff. This not only creates a sense of security, but of isolation from the world outside. They describe it as a 'night out in a simulated town' (ibid.).

GrandWest is built around a theme relating to the heritage of Cape Town. The main architectural elements used to establish the theme include

- a reconstruction of the 'Fort of Good Hope', referred to as the 'Magic Castle' and containing a mini-funfair, rides and arcade games;
- a series of commercial buildings set around a lake containing reconstructed eighteenth century 'Cape Dutch' style architecture;
- reconstructed nineteenth century streetscapes and façades which form the outward facing perimeter of the complex; and
- 'The District', which comprises the casino, restaurants and commercial buildings built around a reconstruction of Cape Town's District Six, including narrow streets, washing lines with washing hanging on it, and vernacular façades. (Hall and Bombardella 2007: 247–250)

Hall and Bombardella (2007) note that there is little attempt to offer a realistic reproduction of the majority of these elements, and they exist as an eclectic mix of architectural styles and time periods, juxtaposed to create a homogenous and nostalgic representation of Cape Town's past. The 'theming' is established not only through this architectural connection, but through a continuous narrative connection between attractions within each of the four areas. For example, the streets within 'The District' are named after actual streets within District Six. These streets host themed bars and events that contribute to the overall heritage-themed 'experience' at Grand-West. 'If you're feeling the need to let your hair down and dance the night away, travel no further than Hanover Street. Boasting two bars, themed events, live bands, a large dance floor and showcasing the best of Cape Town's DJ talent, Hanover Street is a hot and happening club in the heart of The District' (Sun International 2009*b*). This theming leads to an integration of all experiences into a single overarching 'story'. Consumption forms a part of all aspects of this experience.

However, as Hall and Bombardella (2007: 256–7) note, this is not a coherent story, but one that draws on the power of nostalgia, reflecting 'a global trend in individualised entertainment that promotes consumption through desire for a state of life seen as better than the present, but ever just out of reach ... which unintentionally produces a new set of referents for an imagined past, a bizarre, concentrated mélange of romanticised Cape Malay and white suburban villa Baroque, with a bit of colonial militarism thrown in'. This suggests, as in the work of Holtorf discussed above, that theme parks should be considered as places that offer alternative ideas of history, the reconstruction of which might be a legitimate archaeological concern in its own right. This connects with Jameson's (1991) characterization of late modernity as a form of pastiche, a merging of all discourse into an undifferentiated whole as a result of this process by which the cultural sphere had become entirely colonized by the culture industry, which he saw as a reflection of a crisis in historicity (see Ch. 5). So what does this archaeological record of the mythologized Cape Town at CapeWest tell us about late modern societies?

Hall and Bombardella (2007: 257) note that CapeWest offers new formulations of race 'as the old racialised divisions of apartheid are reassembled as socio-economic classes'. The symbol sets of artefacts that form the material culture of 'The District', for example—the street signs, washing lines, narrow streets, and vernacular façades—represent a new articulation of older racialized representations of District Six under apartheid. Many readers will be familiar with the recent apartheid and post-apartheid history of South Africa, a system of racial segregation in which the state classified and kept separate white, coloured, and black citizens, enforced by the National Party government of South Africa between 1948 and 1990. The system of apartheid was dismantled over the period 1990–93 and finally removed in 1994 during the country's first general elections with universal suffrage, at which time it elected the African National Congress (ANC) as the governing body. Under the presidency of Nelson Mandela, post-apartheid South Africa sought quickly to establish itself as a new nation in which: 'Each of us is as intimately attached to the soil of this beautiful country as are the famous jacaranda trees of Pretoria and the mimosa trees of the bushveld—a rainbow nation at peace with itself and the world' (cited in Manzo 1996: 71). In their discussion of heritage in plural societies, Ashworth, Graham, and Tunbridge (2007: 194) suggest that South Africa's 'rainbow nation' demonstrates an attempt to develop a mosaic society in which a new past must be created to reflect the new circumstances of the present. They point to the use of the heritage of apartheid in the post-apartheid era to contrast with the modern situation to develop a vision of history in terms of a linear narrative from 'bad past' regime to 'good contemporary' one, and to develop the theme of the struggle for freedom (see also Coombes 2003: 120ff.).

Hall and Bombardella (2007: 254) argue that the District emphasizes representations of District Six's residents as having a penchant for drinking and partying, and primarily representing a lower socio-economic status, through the citing of bars and other adult entertainments such as the casino in this area, and the use of the washing lines as shorthand for social class. 'Replicating the unique vibe of Cape Town's Old District Six with buildings inspired by those found on the original streets, The District lies at the heart of GrandWest's dazzling nightlife—offering a banquet of culinary delights from an impressive selection of Cape Town's finest restaurants, along with an infectious mix of local and international music.' The multicultural nature of District Six is reflected in the presence of Indian, Thai, Italian, and Japanese restaurants. It does not accurately reconstruct aspects of District Six's ethnic make-up, but merely replaces it with a shorthand for ethnic diversity and 'other-ness'.

This brief exploration of the 'archaeology' of GrandWest provides us with one approach to the archaeology of the experience economy where theme parks remain in operation. Another approach is possible to the remains of *abandoned* theme parks, which would lend themselves to conventional excavation and archaeological recording techniques. This approach can be illustrated by the archaeological survey of the former American Adventure theme park in Derbyshire, England.

The American Adventure Theme Park, Derbyshire, England

The American Adventure theme park was built around the rehabilitated site of the former Shipley Coal Mine, and opened by Derbyshire County Council in 1985 as 'Britannia Park' (this history of the park is based on Udder Creative 2009 and Squires 2006). The original

Britannia Park sought to celebrate 'the best of Britain', and contained several 'British Genius' pavilions showcasing British design and a miniature railway, both of which were later reused by the American Adventure theme park. Its other attractions included 'Small World', a series of small-scale replicas of international landmarks, and 'Adventureland', containing several fairground rides and attractions. Britannia Park seems to have been dogged with problems from the start, and only remained open for twelve weeks, after which it was closed due to poor attendance. The site reopened in 1987 as the American Adventure, one of the UK's first fully themed parks. It was based on a Wild West theme, with one half of the park dedicated to Native Americans and the other to cowboys and 'pioneers'. The new park design made full use of the lakeside setting, reworking Britannia Park's 'British Genius' pavilion into a fibreglass 'Mount Rushmore' style mountain with carved faces (which would later become known as the Aztec Kingdom) as part of Pioneer Playland, a replica of the Alamo, the 'El Paso Arena' in which horseback stunts were performed, and a series of fairground rides and other attractions. Themed shops and restaurants, a Wagon Wheel themed Ferris wheel, log flume ride, and mine train rounded out the park's offerings.

Over the next twenty years, various new rides and exhibits were introduced (Fig. 9.4). By 1989 the miniature railway did a complete circuit of the lake and a number of new rides had been added to the park, including 'Spaceport USA' and the 'Missile' rollercoaster, at a cost of £4 million. In 1993 a new 'Stars and Stripes' theme was introduced, and many of the rides and exhibits were restyled in a way that was consistent with the revised theme. Over the late 1990s the park changed management several times, and began shifting away from its American theme by rebranding itself as 'Adventure World'; however, by the turn of the century, it was again being marketed as 'the American Adventure'. Over the period 2000–6 there were some new additions to the park's rides and attractions, but many of the older rides were closed and the park itself began to run down. It is possible to track these changes in the fortunes of various park attractions through an analysis of theme park maps, many of which have been archived on enthusiasts' websites. Squires' account of the park in 2006 is helpful in understanding the nature of the park's downturn in this period:

Figure 9.4. The American Adventure park map, *c.*1999. (Courtesy Richard Duszczak Cartoon Studio Ltd.)

It was increasingly obvious that over time, less and less attention had been paid to maintaining the existing rides. Amongst other things, Nightmare Niagara's tunnel had long stopped turning (apparently the tunnel disorientated people, rendering them unable to brace themselves as necessary for the drop ahead), The Missile's track had gone from deep grey, to sort of grey, to brown, The Rocky Mountain Rapids had lost all or most of its features, and everything on park could be described politely as needing a repaint.

At the end of 2006 the park closed for the last time. When Derbyshire County Council were contacted in 2009 a purchaser for the site had not been found, and the bulk of the rides had been removed and sold to other theme parks. Enthusiasts' websites track the movement of these rides and their components—anecdotal accounts suggest that Twin Looper (originally opened as the Iron Wolf in 1995) was relocated to a park in Poland where it has been renamed the 'Tic Tac Tornado', while other rides were relocated to Suffolk and Leicestershire (Udder Creative 2009). This suggests that the distributed nature of theme park artefacts and the network of connections between them is an important area for future research on the nature of the experience economy and its material culture.

An archaeological survey of the site was conducted in 2009. The survey focused on recording the extant surface features on the site. By the time the survey was undertaken, most of the buildings had been demolished and almost all useful materials had been removed. The only standing buildings were sections of the original entrance buildings, the Aztec Kingdom and Neptune Theatre, Pier 49, and various temporary buildings and staff buildings located close to the old entrance. While the park had been in operation, most of the abandoned rides and attractions had simply been left within the park grounds, as discussed by Squires during its final year of operation in 2006:

perhaps the best part about the park is the signs left of the past: Nightmare Niagara's station remains, as if a tribute to its own former purpose; all the buildings around Space Port still remain to be seen, as they were the day they closed in October 2004; buildings which have not been used in a decade still stand, as there is no need to demolish them. And the park make no effort to close off these now abandoned areas, so they lay there, for anyone feeling a little nostalgic to explore.

This meant that it was not a simple matter in matching the archaeological remains to the theme park maps, as many of the maps do not show places or attractions that were not in operation at the time the maps were drawn. The palimpsest nature of the park's archaeological remains reminds us of how extreme the differences between design plans and the material record might be, even when exploring places relating to the very recent past (as discussed in Ch. 3). Nonetheless, various activity areas were able to be matched from their material remains on the ground when compared with 'historic' site maps obtained from the internet and when later compared with historical aerial imagery obtained using Google Earth. The resulting archaeological survey plan is shown in Fig. 9.5, and photographs taken during the survey in Figs. 9.6–9.7.

We might consider abandoned theme parks to represent an archaeological record of the failure of the experience economy and an artefact of changing fashions for different themes. Gonzáles-Ruibal (2006), for example, has suggested we should focus our archaeological

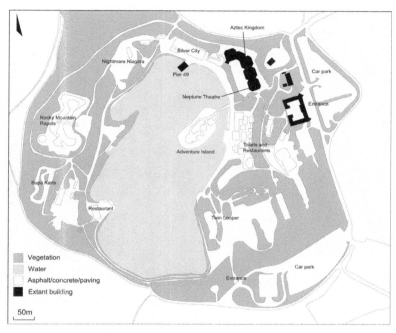

Figure 9.5. Archaeological survey plan, former American Adventure theme park, May 2009. (Drawing: Rodney Harrison.)

gaze on the ruins and rubbish of modernity to explore the places where modernity has failed 'to deconstruct the weakness and contingency of our notions of the "modernist super-artefact"' (2006: 196). Here, we might be tempted to see the changing fortunes of Britannia Park and the American Adventure theme park within the political context of Britain in 1985 and 2006 respectively. In 1985, Britain was in the midst of the miner's strike, the end of which was widely interpreted as a heavy political blow for the trade unions in their battle against Prime Minister Margaret Thatcher's Conservative Government policies. The idea of a theme park that celebrated all things British, sited on a former coalmine site, may have been difficult for some members of the UK public, and certainly the local community, to reconcile. A Wild West fantasy theme, on the other hand, may well have had the sort of escapist subject matter that would have

Figure 9.6. The remains of the Aztec Kingdom and Neptune Theatre in 2009. (Photo: Rodney Harrison.)

appealed under such political and social circumstances. The failure of the park in mid 2006 similarly came at a time when there was an upwelling of anti-US sentiment in the UK as a result of unpopular US foreign policy relating to the US-led Afghanistan War. Within such a context, an American theme would probably have been unpopular with English customers. While anecdotally there appear to have been a range of particular circumstances that led to its closure, when considered in a broader political and social context, we can see that the failure of such artefacts of the experience economy may relate as much to the individual fortunes of their management as to the changing fortunes and popularity of their themes themselves.

The archaeology of 'theming' clearly has important implications for understanding the nature of late modernity and the role of the imagination in the experience economy. A more detailed analysis of archaeological phasing at the American Adventure theme park would be required to explore the ways in which the theme of the

Figure 9.7. A pair of 3D glasses found near the remains of the Neptune Theatre. (Photo: Rodney Harrison.)

park changed in more subtle ways, but even at a broad level, it has been possible to link the changes in theme and the park's fortunes themselves to broader social and political currents and historical shifts in fashion and taste. The archaeological analysis of these artefacts of the experience economy emerges from this discussion as an important new area of research within the archaeology of the contemporary past, and one that deserves more attention and detailed analysis in the future.

DISCUSSION: FUTURE DIRECTIONS FOR AN ARCHAEOLOGY OF LATE MODERNITY

In this chapter we have looked at what it means to take an archaeological approach to some of the most distinctive aspects of late modernity. In doing so, we have focused particularly on non-places, virtual worlds, experience economies, and the work of the imagination. In Chapter 5 we identified several other themes that might be explored archaeologically, which we will consider briefly here.

Hyperconsumerism and Globalization

The relationship between globalization and consumption was raised as an area of concern for an archaeology of the contemporary past by Buchli and Lucas (2001*b*). We might think here of an archaeological approach to Amazon.com, based not only in a study of its warehouses, but also its websites, distribution networks, and products. The network metaphor that was explored in relation to Actor-Network theory in Chapter 5 seems particularly relevant here. In thinking through an archaeological approach to hyperconsumerism and globalization, the areas for research outlined by Majewski and Schiffer (2001: 31–3) in relation to the study of consumerism are worth repeating. These include

- structural and behavioural aspects of the emergence, growth, and maintenance of consumer societies;
- effects of consumerism on the life histories of specific products;
- advertising and communication;
- explaining apparent alternatives/reactions to consumerism;
- commercialisation processes of consumer services and societal practices;
- ideological expressions of consumerist societies.

As we discussed in Chapter 4, many of these questions relating to consumption are shared amongst other disciplines with an interest in modern material culture. Nonetheless, they form the foundation for an archaeological approach to this distinctive feature of late modernity.

The Final Frontier? Archaeologies in Orbit

At the time of writing there are estimated to be approximately 13,000 humanly made objects in orbit around the Earth (ESA 2009).

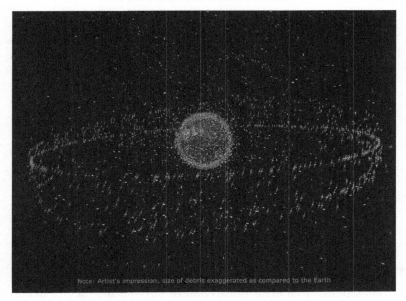

Note: Artist's impression; size of debris exaggerated as compared to the Earth

Figure 9.8. Distribution of catalogued objects in space being tracked by ESA. (Courtesy ESA.)

Fifty years of space activity have placed over 6,000 satellites into orbit, of which only around 800 are still in operation. These inoperable satellites and other sources have contributed to the development of a layer of 'space junk' in orbit around the earth which is so thick that the European Space Agency must monitor it to avoid collisions with operating space craft (see Fig. 9.8). Such objects are of interest to archaeologists as artefacts of space exploration (Gorman 2005), as part of the broader archaeological study of the Cold War (Gorman and O'Leary 2007), and are linked to other important late modern processes such as transnationalism, decolonization and globalization (Gorman 2009*a*).

Gorman (2009*b*) notes, however, that describing the spatial and chronological relationships of objects in orbit forms a problem for Earth-bound archaeologists, who work from a geodetic or Earth-centred perspective. She suggests that to begin to conduct archaeology in space, contemporary archaeologists must adopt new space–time models that are sensitive to the altered space-time which exists beyond the Earth. The geodesic manifold, despite its complex mathematics, gives us a kind of map of space on which to plot the movements of artefacts, in which some points stay still over time and others swirl in continuous movement. Gorman's analysis suggests some interesting new directions for the archaeology of the contemporary past, and tackles some of the conceptual problems of doing archaeology in orbit. The logistics of such an archaeology still require further consideration, but her work points to an important emerging issue for archaeologists of the contemporary past in engaging with archaeology that exists beyond the Earth.

CONCLUSION

It was suggested in Chapter 5 that we need to see archaeology of the contemporary past in historical context—to consider the role of new communicative technologies and economic and social change associated with the late modern period as giving rise to a series of social conditions that have made it desirable not only to historicize the immediate past but also to analyse and comment on it. This chapter has considered instead the ways in which an archaeological approach might help us better to understand some of the most distinctive features of late modernity. In the first part of the chapter, we explored the archaeology of non-place and transit, considering the potential for archaeology to inform our understanding of the materiality of non-places. Following this, we considered the contribution archaeology might make to the study of virtual worlds and the ways in which new communicative technologies are transforming the relationships between individuals and their communities, landscape, and material culture. Finally, we explored different approaches to the archaeology of the experience economy, both to those artefacts that are still in use, and to those that have been abandoned. We have focused particularly on those issues that might be able to be approached archaeologically—the idea of a supermodern present 'haunted' by the past; the production of 'non-places' and the disassociative spatial elements of postmodernity that produce a sense of melancholy and nostalgia; generic objects and spaces and their association with mass production and mass customization; and speed, experienced as the acceleration of time. What emerges strongly from this chapter is the key role that the archaeology of the contemporary past might take in this interdisciplinary area of research on the nature of late modernity and its associated temporal and spatial shifts.

10

Discussion and Conclusion

This book has been written at a time when late modern societies are experiencing a period of enormous social and economic upheaval. Some commentators have suggested that late modern societies should be seen as defunct, or at best in decline. This forecast of the end of late modern societies looms larger than it has ever done before. But, in what ways will this influence the archaeology of the contemporary past as a discipline, and its agenda as we have charted it in this book? In many ways, the need for an archaeology of the late modern period has become even more urgent in the light of these changes. Any discipline that allows us to look at the nature of late modern societies from a different perspective will help us to understand the critical points at which societies change, and to put this information into practice in the future.

But what if we are in a period that heralds the onset of a new form of society? Will the archaeology of the contemporary past simply become another period study, like the archaeology of the Neolithic for example? Although we have focused much of our discussion on the nature of late modern societies, we argue that we need an archaeology of 'now' as much as we need one that explores social responses to the very recent past that got us here. The central theme of this book is the need to develop an archaeology that allows us to be more self-aware and critically reflexive by understanding the nature of contemporary society and its engagement with the material world, *as well as* our recent and deeper past. It is this single point that is at the core of our argument—that we need to use the approaches of archaeology not only to study the roots of our society, but also to understand our present lives. Thus archaeology becomes not only a discipline for recording objects, places, and practices that are extinct or have fallen into ruin, but develops a series of tools alongside its more conventional ones for scrutinizing objects, places, and practices within our own society that are still in use. This sort of critical self-awareness will allow us to overcome some of the most destructive aspects of modernist philosophies, and to develop an archaeology that focuses on ethics, politics, diversity, and multivocality. Even in the brief time since Thomas (2004) called for the development of a 'counter-modern' archaeology, such an archaeology seems infinitely closer to realization.

Critical to the process of developing a 'counter-modern' archaeology of the contemporary past will be an awareness of the present as a surface—a physical stratum that contains not only the present, but all its physical and imagined pasts combined (Olivier 2000; Witmore 2004; Gonzáles-Ruibal 2008: 262). Alfredo Gonzáles-Ruibal (ibid.), paraphrasing Christopher Witmore (2004), puts it elegantly—the past 'percolates'. As we have argued, the role of the archaeology of the contemporary past is to start from the present and work backwards in time, being sensitive to the influence of the materiality of the past which constantly intervenes in the present. This approach runs counter to the modernist roots of professional archaeology, which takes for its frame an evolutionary perspective (Thomas 2004) that necessitates the search for origins in the deep past, and the analysis of material, social, and economic change by tracking their progress forwards through time. We argue for the need for an approach that begins in the present, with the imminent (and immanent) past, and is not constrained to a linear perspective, but is sensitive to the intervention of many different pasts in the present. Thus, an archaeology of the contemporary past might *also* be an archaeology of the late Palaeolithic, or any other period that intervenes in the present. The main objective of the discipline is to understand the nature of contemporary, everyday life, and its relationship to what has come before it.

There is a temptation in times of economic and social change to seek out the roots of social problems in external phenomena, such as new technology. This impulse goes back a long way, and its lineage can be seen in art and literature from many different time periods. We are reminded of Mary Shelley's *Frankenstein*, for example, written in the context of widespread concern about the nature of social changes produced by the introduction of mechanized looms in Britain during the nineteenth century. A discipline that is firmly rooted in the analysis of contemporary and modern material culture will allow us to explore whether such social changes are indeed a product of new technology and its associated speed and rate of change, or whether explanation of social change might be better sought elsewhere. The archaeology of the contemporary past is indeed an archaeology for our times—a new approach that allows us to look at some of the most pressing social and cultural circumstances of the contemporary world in a different way. This is a counter-modern archaeology for a postmodern age.

In the book, we have developed an extended argument for the need for an archaeological approach to the very recent and contemporary past, and have explored a series of case studies that demonstrate how this might be undertaken. In Part 1 we looked at the history of archaeological approaches to the recent past, showing how it developed from early ethnoarchaeological studies as part of the New Archaeology, and found further impetus in the new-found interest in critical approaches both to archaeology itself and to the relationship between material culture and social change, as part of the post-processual response to this. We then charted its emergence as a new subdiscipline in the years following the new millennium, noting that its growth was coincident with a growing interest in the heritage of the recent (modern) past. We considered the nature of the field methods employed by archaeologists working in this new subdiscipline, and its relationship to other academic disciplines. We also considered the writings of a series of scholars whose work has focused on the nature of late modern societies, both to help to explain the emergence of the subdiscipline at this particular time, and to develop a set of themes on which to focus our attention in Part 2.

In Part 2, we outlined a new approach to the archaeology of the contemporary past, focusing particularly on late modern, post-industrial, developed societies. We began by looking at a series of reasonably conventional archaeological domains—artefacts, sites, and landscape—before broadening our perspective to take in some of the more distinctive features of late modern societies. We highlighted the themes of non-places, virtual worlds experience economies and the work of the imagination, and hyperconsumerism and globalization as particular areas for attention, while noting that other distinctive features of late modern societies are yet to be explored archaeologically.

Throughout the book, we have looked at aspects of the nature of late modern societies and their urgent need to engage with the recent past. We explored the idea of *speed*, experienced in late modern societies as the acceleration of both space and time, which leads to a sense of the present being 'haunted' by the past, and the spectre of forgetting it. One approach to this sense of *haunting* is to develop institutionalized ways of ensuring that the past is not forgotten, which we recognize as 'heritage'. Another way of responding to this sense of haunting by the past is to commercialize and objectify it, through retro and kitsch. This urgent sense of the past receding ever more rapidly is argued to be one of the most convincing reasons for understanding the emergence of the archaeology of the contemporary past as a subdiscipline and an area of broader public interest. We discussed the role of archaeology as a form of exorcism, and its redemptive potential in helping to recover, and create, public memory, particularly in areas where it is troubled and contentious, and in response to the super-modern violence of the twentieth and the early twenty-first centuries.

A prominent theme that emerged from the literature review was the role of archaeology in *presencing absence* within contemporary society, and the idea of archaeology as a form of *material witness*. We have noted that the nature of the media and its control by external forces means that late modern societies have rendered much of their recent past unknowable, either by processes of active concealment or passive forgetting. Rather then promoting multiple perspectives on the present, the saturation of media coverage has often led to the rapid development of a dominant, authorized account, a 'plague of fantasies' (Žižec 1997) that is difficult to challenge. Archaeology has a role in such circumstances in bringing to light material evidence that can challenge, provoke, and confront, and around which to develop multiple perspectives on the recent and contemporary past. As a discipline focused on material evidence and concerned with revealing and bringing to light that which has been hidden, archaeology has a distinct role to play in developing alternative perspectives on the recent and contemporary past as a form of material witness. This theme is one that has developed prominently amongst those who work within the field of forensic, rescue, or human rights archaeology; those who use the archaeological record as an engagement with the politics of the present. But equally important is the role of archaeology in drawing attention to the *unspoken*, the abject, the poor, and the subaltern. By telling the stories of those on society's very margins, archaeology can develop for itself a critical social function in twenty-first century society.

The *therapeutic* potential for an archaeology of the contemporary past has also been a prominent theme in writings on the topic, and one of the core justifications for its emergence as a new subdiscipline. The extremely violent nature of the twentieth and early twenty-first centuries, placed alongside the modernist projects of state control, has produced a contested history in which many have been left feeling aggrieved, be it politically, socially, economically, or physically. The industrialized nature of the wars of the twentieth century, and the rise of ethnic violence and globalized terrorism in the twenty-first, has produced a critical need for a historical *intervention* in the recent past. González-Ruibal (2008: 262) speaks of the simultaneous therapeutic and critical power of an archaeology of the recent past not only in reconciling the past with the present, but also in acts of disclosure that can 'bring healing to those who have suffered supermodernity's violence'. Similarly, Buchli (2007: 116) calls it an engagement 'with raw and extremely painful nerves... profoundly melancholic contexts that are unresolved and in which archaeology materialises these troubling absences and serves as a therapeutic device'. The archaeology of the contemporary past has a key role to play in reconciling late modern societies with their recent pasts.

We have considered the role of archaeology in understanding the nature of *non-place* and the isolation, solitude, melancholy, and nostalgia that are associated with this most distinctive spatial and temporal aspect of late modernity. We reflected on the claims of some scholars that we should understand the nature of late modern society as a 'dream' or experience society, exploring the archaeological manifestations of theming and the prominence of the imagination as a social force in a world dominated by new communicative technologies. We also looked at the ways in which archaeology can help us understand the nature of *virtual* communities, and the relationship between 'virtual' and 'actual' worlds.

As an archaeology of 'us', the archaeology of the contemporary past has an important role to play in developing an inclusive approach to the recent past and present. We have discussed the archaeology of the contemporary past as a form of 'autoarchaeology', and explored some examples of archaeologists who have investigated their own recent histories as a very stark example of this. But the broader point relates to developing a more inclusive archaeology, in which we overcome the modernist philosophies that seek to divide and understand ourselves through a construction of difference, to develop instead a critically reflexive practice that helps us to understand our own society through the study of ourselves. An archaeology of the contemporary past must break down the fundamental divisions between subject and object, researcher and 'other', and reconstruct itself as a new, inclusive archaeology for a multi-vocal, postmodern age.

Like any form of archaeology, the archaeology of the contemporary past must be seen as a political activity, and as a critical intervention in the present. This idea becomes even more obvious when working on the contemporary period, in the way in which it forces us to turn the archaeological lens on ourselves. But in addition to this role, the archaeology of the contemporary past can also produce significant social commentary and suggest solutions to social problems that are based in the material record itself. Rathje's Garbage Project (e.g. 2001; Rathje and Murphy [1992] 2001) is an example of a long-term research project with specific environmental implications and social goals. Similarly, work on housing and homelessness has demonstrated the potential for an archaeology of the contemporary past to engage with important social issues of broad public concern. Archaeology can no longer afford to ignore its social context and the public whom it seeks to educate. Indeed, the archaeology of the contemporary past necessitates a dissolution of these boundaries between 'expert' and 'community' to recognize the diversity of late modern societies, and the role each one of us plays in producing them. Perhaps this is a key difference between archaeology of earlier periods and the archaeology of the contemporary past. While for earlier periods it might be argued that there are clear and uncontested claims about who the 'experts' are, in the case of the contemporary past we are all 'experts' and we all have a claim. The realization of a radical democratization of the past that is opened up by working on the archaeology of late modern societies has much broader and more important implications for the way in which we undertake the archaeology of *all* time periods. Such a realization has the potential to radically transform archaeology as a discipline in the twenty-first century.

References

Acland, C. R. (ed.) (2007), *Residual Media* (Minneapolis: University of Minnesota Press).

Agre, P. (1999), 'Life after Cyberspace', *European Association for the Study of Scientific Technology Review* 18: 3–5.

Airports Council International (2008), 'Interesting Statistics', <http://www.aci.aero/aci/aci/file/Press%20Releases/2008/Interesting%20Stats_2007.pdf>, accessed 8 June 2009.

Anderson, B. (1983), *Imagined Communities: Reflections on the Origin and Spread of Nationalism* (London: Verso).

Anderson, J. (2004), 'Talking Whilst Walking: A Geographical Archaeology of Knowledge, *Area* 36(3): 254–61.

Andreassen, E., Bjerck, H., and Olsen, B. (forthcoming), *Persistent Memories: An Archaeology of a Soviet Mining Town in the High Arctic* (Trondheim: Tapir Akademisk Forlag).

Appadurai, A. (1986), 'Commodities and the Politics of Value', in A. Appadurai (ed.), *The Social Life of Things: Commodities in Cultural Perspective* (Cambridge: Cambridge University Press), 3–63.

—— (1996), *Modernity at Large* (Minneapolis: University of Minnesota Press).

—— (2001), 'The Globalisation of Archaeology and Heritage: A Discussion with Arjun Appadurai', *Journal of Social Archaeology* 1(1): 35–49.

—— (2006), *Fear of Small Numbers: An Essay on the Geography of Anger* (Durham, NC: Duke University Press).

Ashford, N. H., Stanton, P. M., and Moore, C. A. (1996), *Airport Operations* (New York: McGraw-Hill Professional).

Ashworth, G. J., Graham B., and Tunbridge, J. E. (2007), *Pluralising Pasts: Heritage, Identity and Place in Multicultural Societies* (London: Pluto).

Attfield, J. (ed.) (2000), *Wild Things: The Material Culture of Everyday Life* (London: Berg).

Audouze, F. (ed.) (1992), *Ethnoarchéologie: Justification, problèmes, limites* (Juan-les-Pins: Éditions APDCA).

Augé, M. (1995), *Non-Places: Introduction to an Anthropology of Supermodernity* (London: Verso).

—— (2002), *In the Metro* (Minneapolis: University of Minnesota Press).

—— (2004), *Oblivion* (Minneapolis: University of Minnesota Press).

Augoyard, J. F. ([1979] 2007), *Step by Step: Everyday Walks in a French Urban Housing Project* (Minneapolis: University of Minnesota Press).

BAA (2009), 'Heathrow at a Glance', <http://www.heathrowairport.com/portal/page/Heathrow%5EGeneral%5EOur + business + and + community%-5EHeathrow + Lowdown%5EHeathrow + at + a + Glance/08ba07077d3d2-010VgnVCM100000147e120a____/448c6a4c7f1b0010VgnVCM200000357e-120a____/>, accessed 9 June 2009.

Badcock, A., and Johnston, R. (2009), 'Placemaking through Protest: An Archaeology of the Lees Cross and Endcliffe Protest Camp, Derbyshire, England', *Archaeologies* 5(2): 306–22.

Badger, G. (2007), *The Genius of Photography: How Photography Has Changed our Lives* (London: Quadrille).

Bagwell, M. (2009), 'After the Storm, Destruction and Reconstruction: The Potential for an Archaeology of Hurricane Katrina', *Archaeologies* 5(2): 280–92.

Bailey, G., Newland, C., Nilsson, A., and Schofield, J. (2009), 'Transit, Transition: Excavating J641 VUJ', *Cambridge Archaeological Journal* 19 (1): 1–27.

Ballbé, E. G., and Steadman, D. W. (2008), 'The Political, Social and Scientific Contexts of Archaeological Investigations of Mass Graves in Spain', *Archaeologies* 4(3): 429–44.

Barker, B., and Lamb, L. (2009), 'The Archaeology of Poverty and Human Dignity: Charity and the Work Ethic in a 1930's Depression Era Itinerant's Camp on the Toowoomba Range Escarpment, Queensland', *Archaeologies* 5(2): 263–79.

Bartle, R. A. (2003), *Designing Virtual Worlds* (Indianapolis: New Riders).

Basu, P. (2007), *Highland Homecomings: Genealogy and Heritage Tourism in the Scottish Diaspora* (London: Routledge).

Bath, J. E. (1981), 'The Raw and the Cooked: The Material Culture of a Modern Supermarket', in Gould and Schiffer (1981), 183–95.

Baudrillard, J. (1968), *Le Système des objects* (Paris: Gallimard).

—— (1994), *Simulacra and Simulation* (Ann Arbor: University of Michigan Press).

—— (1995), *The Gulf War Did Not Take Place* (Bloomington: Indiana University Press).

BBC News Online (2000*a*), 'Millennium celebrations "a huge success"', BBC News Online, 2 January 2000, <http://news.bbc.co.uk/1/hi/uk/587189.stm>, accessed 22 February 2008.

—— (2000*b*), 'Y2K: Overhyped and oversold?', BBC News Online, 6 January 2000, <http://news.bbc.co.uk/1/hi/talking_point/586938.stm> accessed 22 February 2008.

Beck, C. M. (2002), 'The Archaeology of Scientific Experiments at a Nuclear Testing Ground', in Schofield, Johnson, and Beck (2002), 65–79.

—— Drollinger, H., and Schofield, J. (2007), 'Archaeology of Dissent: Landscape and Symbolism at the Nevada Peace Camp', in Schofield and Cocroft (2007), 297–320.

Beech, J. (2009), '1 June 1935: The Introduction of Compulsory Testing of Drivers in the United Kingdom: The Neglected Role of the State in Motoring', in Schofield (2009d), 55–64.

Bell, M. (1997), 'The Ghosts of Place', *Theory and Society* 26: 813–36.

Bender, B. (2001a), Introduction, in B. Bender and M. Winder (eds.) *Contested Landscapes: Movement, Exile and Place* (Oxford: Berg), 1–18.

—— (2001b), Landscapes On-the-Move, *Journal of Social Archaeology* 1(1): 75–89.

Bennett, T. (1995), *The Birth of the Museum: History, Theory, Politics* (London: Routledge).

—— and Watson, D. (2002), 'Understanding Everyday Life: Introduction', in T. Bennett and D. Watson (eds.) *Understanding Everyday Life* (Oxford: Blackwell), pp. ix–xxiv.

Bhabha, H. (1994), *The Location of Culture* (London: Routledge).

Bijker, W. E. (1995), *Of Bicycles, Bakelites and Bulbs: Toward a Theory of Sociotechnical Change* (London: MIT).

—— Hughes, T. P., and Pinch, T. (eds.) (1989), *The Social Construction of Technological Systems* (London: MIT).

Binford, L. R. (1978), *Nunamiut Ethnoarchaeology* (New York: Academic Press).

—— (1983), *In Pursuit of the Past: Decoding the Archaeological Record* (London: Thames & Hudson).

Blake, C. F. (1981), 'Graffiti and Racial Insults: The Archaeology of Ethnic Relations in Hawaii', in Gould and Schiffer (1981), 87–99.

Boellstorff, T. (2008), *Coming of Age in Second Life: An Anthropologist Explores the Virtually Human* (Princeton, NJ: Princeton University Press).

Boulton, A. (2006), 'Film Making and Photography as Record and Interpretation', in Schofield, Klausmeier, and Purbrick (2006), 35–8.

—— (2007), 'Cood bay Forst Zinna', in Schofield and Cocroft (2007), 181–92.

Bourriaud, N. (2002), *Relational Aesthetics* (Paris: Presses du Réel).

Bradley, A., Buchli, V., Fairclough, G., Hicks, D., Miller, J., and Schofield, J. (2004), *Change and Creation: Historic Landscape Character 1950–2000* (London: English Heritage).

Bradley, R. (2005), 'Discovery and Excavation', *Scottish Archaeological Journal* 27(1): 1–11.

Bril, B., and Roux, V. (eds.) (2002), *Le Geste technique: Reflexions méthodologiques et anthropologiques* (Ramonville Saint-Agne: Éditions Erès).

Brodie, A., and Winter, G. (2007), *England's Seaside Resorts* (London: English Heritage).

Brown, B. (2001), 'Thing Theory', *Critical Inquiry* 28(1): 1–22.

Brown, M. (2009), '2 October 1925: From Ally Pally to Big Brother: Television Makes Viewers of Us All', in Schofield (2009*d*), 47–54.

Bryman, A. (2004), *The Disneyization of Society* (London: Sage).

Buchinger, M-L., and Metzler, M. (2006), 'The Soviet Murals in Forst Zinna near Jutebog (Germany), a Cycle of Paintings in the Barracks of the 57th Construction Battalion', in Schofield, Klausmeier, and Purbrick (2006), 28–34.

Buchli, V. (1999), *An Archaeology of Socialism* (Oxford: Berg).

—— (2002), 'Introduction', in V. Buchli (ed.), *The Material Culture Reader* (London: Berg), 1–22.

—— (2007), 'Afterword: Towards an Archaeology of the Contemporary Past', in McAtackney, Palus, and Piccini (2007), 115–18.

—— and Lucas, G. (2001*a*), 'The Absent Present: Archaeologies of the Contemporary Past', in Buchli and Lucas (2001*e*), 3–18.

—— —— (2001*b*), 'Models of Production and Consumption: Archaeologies of the Contemporary Past', in Buchli and Lucas (2001*e*), 21–5.

—— —— (2001*c*), 'The Archaeology of Alienation: A Late Twentieth-Century British Council House', in Buchli and Lucas (2001*e*), 158–67.

—— —— (2001*d*), 'Bodies of Evidence', in Buchli and Lucas (2001*e*), 121–5.

—— —— (eds.) (2001*e*), *Archaeologies of the Contemporary Past* (London: Routledge).

Buehler, P. (2009), Modern Ruins, online at <http://www.modern-ruins.com/>, accessed 15 June 2009.

Burström, M. (2007), *Samtidsarkeolog: Introduktion till ett forskningsfält* (Lund: Studentlitteratur).

—— (ed.) (2008), *Samtidsarkeologi—varför gräva i det nära förflutna?* Södertörn Archaeological Studies 6 (Huddinge: University of Södertörn).

—— (2009), 'Garbage or Heritage: The Existential Dimension of a Car Cemetery', in C. Holtorf and A. Piccini (eds.), *Contemporary Archaeologies: Excavating Now* (Berne: Peter Lang), 131–43.

—— Gustafsson, A., and Karlsson, H. (2006), 'The Air Torpedo of Bäckebo: Local Incident and World History', *Current Swedish Archaeology* 14: 7–24.

Byrne, D., and Nugent, M. (2004), *Mapping Attachment: A Spatial Approach to Aboriginal Post-Contact Heritage* (Sydney: Department of Environment and Conservation (NSW)).

Callon, M. (ed.) (1989), *The Laws of the Markets* (Oxford: Blackwell).

—— Law, J., and Rip, A. (eds.) (1986), *Mapping the Dynamics of Science and Technology: Sociology of Science in the Real World* (London: Palgrave Macmillan).

Campbell, F., and Ulin, J. (2004), *Borderline Archaeology: A Practice of Contemporary Archaeology-Exploring Aspects of Creative Narratives and Performative Cultural Production*, GOTARC Series B, Gothenburg Archaeological Theses 29 (Sweden: University of Göteborg).

Campbell, H. (2000), 'The Museum or the Garbage Can. Notes on the Arrival of Francis Bacon's Studio in Dublin', *Tracings* 1: 38–51.

Cappock, M. (2005), *Francis Bacon's Studio* (London: Merrell).

Certeau, M. de (1984), *The Practice of Everyday Life* (Berkeley and Los Angeles: University of California Press).

Chang, H. (2008), *Autoethnography as Method* (Walnut Creek, Calif.: Left Coast).

Clark, J., Darlington, J., and Fairclough, G. (2004), *Using Historic Landscape Characterisation* (London: English Heritage and Lancashire County Council).

Clark, K. (2001), *Informed Conservation: Understanding Historic Buildings and their Landscapes for Conservation* (London: English Heritage).

Clark, T. (2008), 'Can a Place Think? On Adam Sharr's *Heidegger's Hut*', *Cultural Politics* 4(1): 100–22.

Clarke, D. L. (1973), 'Archaeology: The Loss of Innocence', *Antiquity* 47: 6–18.

Clavé, S. A. (2007), *The Global Theme Park Industry* (Wallingford: CABI).

Cleghorn, P. L. (1981), 'The Community Store: A Dispersal Center for Material Goods in Rural America', in Gould and Schiffer (1981), 197–212.

Clifford, J. (1988), *The Predicament of Culture: Twentieth Century Ethnography, Literature and Art* (Cambridge, Mass.: Harvard University Press).

—— (1997), *Routes: Travel and Translation in the Twentieth Century* (Cambridge, Mass.: Harvard University Press).

CLUI (1996), Around Wendover: Centre for Land Use Interpretation Newsletter, <http://www.clui.org/clui_4_1/lotl/lotlsu96/around.html>, accessed 10 June 2009.

—— (2009), American Land Museum, <http://www.clui.org/clui_4_1/alm/index.html>, accessed 15 June 2009.

CNN (2000), 'Preparation pays off; world reports only tiny Y2K glitches: 1 January 2000', <http://archives.cnn.com/2000/TECH/computing/01/01/y2k.weekend.wrap/index.html>, accessed 22 February 2008.

Cochran, M. D., and Beaudry, M. C. (2006), 'Material Culture Studies and Historical Archaeology', in D. Hicks and M. C. Beaudry (eds.), *Cambridge Companion to Historical Archaeology* (Cambridge: Cambridge University Press), 191–204.

Cocroft, W. D. (2006), 'The Spadeadam Blue Streak Underground Launcher Facility U1', *Prospero: The Journal of British Rocketry and Nuclear History* 3: 7–14.

—— (2007*a*), 'Defining the national archaeological character of Cold War remains', in Schofield and Cocroft (2007), 107–127.

—— (2007*b*), *The High Down Test Site, Isle of Wight, Rocket Test Site Survey Report*, English Heritage Research Department Report Series 90/2007 (London: English Heritage).

—— and Alexander, M. (2009), *Atomic Weapons Research Establishment, Orford Ness, Suffolk: Cold War Research and Development Site, Survey Report*, English Heritage Research Department Report Series 10-2009 (London: English Heritage).

—— and Thomas, R. J. C. (2003), *Cold War: Building for Nuclear Confrontation, 1946–1989* (London: English Heritage).

—— and Wilson, L. K. (2006), 'Archaeology and Art at Spadeadam Rocket Establishment (Cumbria)', in Schofield, Klausmeier, and Purbrick (2006), 15–21.

—— Devlin, D., Schofield, J., and Thomas, R. J. C. (2006), *War Art: Murals and Graffiti—Military Life, Power and Subversion* (York: Council for British Archaeology).

Coffey, A. (1999), *The Ethnographic Self: Fieldwork and the Representation of Identity* (London: Sage).

Cohen, S. (1994), 'Identity, Place and the "Liverpool Sound" ', in M. Stokes (ed.), *Ethnicity, Identity and Music: The Musical Construction of Place* (Oxford: Berg), 117–34.

—— Lashua, B., and Schofield, J. (2010), 'Dig the Music', *British Archaeology* 110, 22–7.

Collins, P. (2002), 'British Car Factories since 1896—Lessons Learned from the First Complete Survey of the Remains of a 20th Century Industry in the United Kingdom', in D. Jones (ed.), *20th Century Heritage: Our Recent Cultural Legacy*, Proceedings of the Australia ICOMOS National Conference 2001 (Adelaide: University of Adelaide/ICOMOS), 166–75.

Connerton, P. (2009), *How Modernity Forgets* (Cambridge: Cambridge University Press).

Connor, M. A. (1999), *Archaeological Testing of the World War II Prisoner-of-War Camp (5EP1211) at Fort Carson, El Paso County, Colorado* (Lincoln, Nebr.: US Dept. of the Interior, National Park Service, Midwest Archeological Center).

Coombes, A. (2003), *History after Apartheid: Visual Culture and Public Memory in a Democratic South Africa* (Durham, NC: Duke University Press).

Cooper, T. (2008), *Laying the Foundations: A History and Archaeology of the Trent Valley Sand and Gravel Industry* (York: Council for British Archaeology).

Costall, A. (1995), 'Socialising Affordances', *Theory and Psychology* 5: 467–82.

Cox, M. (2001), 'Forensic Archaeology in the UK', in Buchli and Lucas (2001*e*), 145–57.

—— Flavel, A., Hanson, I., Laver, J., and Wessling, R. (2008), *The Scientific Investigation of Mass Graves: Towards Protocols and Standard Operating Procedures* (Cambridge: Cambridge University Press).

Cresswell, T. (2004), *Place: A Short Introduction* (Oxford: Blackwell).

Cribb, R. (1991), *Nomads in Archaeology* (Cambridge: Cambridge University Press).

Crossland, Z. (2000), 'Buried Lives: Forensic Archaeology and Argentina's Disappeared', *Archaeological Dialogues* 7(2): 146–59.

—— (2002), 'Violent Spaces: Conflict over the Reappearance of Argentina's Disappeared', in Schofield, Johnson, and Beck (2002), 115–31.

Crystal, D. (2001), *Language and the Internet* (Cambridge: Cambridge University Press).

Csikszentmihalyi, M. (1990), *Flow: The Psychology of Optimal Experience* (New York: Harper & Row).

—— (1996), *Creativity: Flow and the Psychology of Discovery and Invention* (New York: Harper Perennial).

David, B., and Wilson, M. (2002), 'Spaces of Resistance: Graffiti and Indigenous Place Markings in the Early European Contact Period of Northern Australia', in B. David and M. Wilson (eds.), *Inscribed Landscapes* (Honolulu: University of Hawaii Press), 42–60.

David, N., and Kramer, C. (2001), *Ethnoarchaeology in Action* (Cambridge: Cambridge University Press).

—— Sterner, J. A., and Gavua, K. B. (1988), 'Why Pots are Decorated', *Current Anthropology* 29: 365–89.

Davis, S. (2008), 'Military Landscapes and Secret Science: The Case of Orford Ness', *Cultural Geographies* 15: 143–9.

Dawdy, S. L. (2006*a*), 'In Katrina's Wake', *Archaeology* 59(4): 16–21.

—— (2006*b*), 'The Taphonomy of Disaster and the (Re)formation of New Orleans', *American Anthropologist* 108(4): 719–30.

Dawson, B., and Cappock, M. (2001), *Francis Bacon's Studio at the Hugh Lane* (Dublin: Hugh Lane Municipal Gallery of Modern Art).

Dawson, L., and Jessop, O. (2007), 'Archaeological Building Recording of Student Residences, Fulwood Road, Endcliffe Crescent, Endcliffe Vale Road and Oakholme Road, Sheffield, South Yorkshire', unpublished report (University of Sheffield: ARCUS).

DeFazio, K. (2002), 'Designing Class: Ikea and Democracy as Furniture', *The Red Critique: Marxist Theory and Critique of the Contemporary*, Nov./Dec. 2002, <http://www.redcritique.org/NovDec02/designingclass.htm>, accessed 6 May 2009.

Deleuze, G., and Guattari, F. (1981), *A Thousand Plateaus: Capitalism and Schizophrenia* (Minneapolis: University of Minnesota Press).

Dench, G. (1975), *Maltese in London: A Case-Study in the Erosion of Ethnic Consciousness* (London: Routledge & Kegan Paul).

Dewilde, M., Pype, P., de Meyer, M., Demeyere, F., Lammens, W., Degryse, J., Wyffels, F., and Saunders, N. J. (2004), 'Belgium's New Department of First World War Archaeology', *Antiquity* 78(4), <http://antiquity.ac.uk/projGall/saunders/index.html>, accessed 9 June 2009.

Dingwall, L., and Gaffney, V. (2007), *Heritage Management at Fort Hood, Texas: Experiments in Historic Landscape Characterisation* (Oxford: Archaeopress).

Dion, M. (1999), *Tate Thames Dig* (London: Tate Gallery).

Dobinson, C. (2001), *AA Command: Britain's Anti-Aircraft Defences of the Second World War* (London: Methuen).

—— Lake, J., and Schofield, J. (1997), 'Monuments of War: Defining England's 20th-Century Defence Heritage', *Antiquity* 71: 288–99.

DoCoMoMo (2008), 'General information', <http://www.archi.fr/DOCO-MOMO/index.htm>, accessed 23 September 2008.

Doretti, M., and Fondebrider, L. (2001), 'Science and Human Rights: Truth, Justice, Reparation and Reconciliation, a Long Way in Third World Countries', in Buchli and Lucas (2001*e*), 138–44.

Dougherty, J. W. D. (ed.) (1985), *Directions in Cognitive Anthropology* (Urbana: University of Illinois Press).

Douglas, M., and Isherwood, B. (1979), *The World of Goods: Towards an Anthropology of Consumption* (London: Routledge).

Dublin City Gallery The Hugh Lane (2008), Francis Bacon's Studio, <http://www.hughlane.ie/francis_bacons_studio.php?type=About&heading=Studio-+ Relocation&rsno=7>, accessed 26 February 2009.

Du Gay, P., Hall, S., Jones, L., Mackay, H., and Negus, K. (eds.) (1997), *Doing Cultural Studies: The Story of the Sony Walkman* (London: Sage).

Dunlop, G. (2008), 'The War Office: Everyday Environments and War Logistics', *Cultural Politics* 4(2): 155–60.

Edensor, T. (2005), *Industrial Ruins: Aesthetics, Materiality, and Memory* (Oxford: Berg).

Edgerton, D. (2007), *The Shock of the Old: Technology in Global History since 1900* (London: Profile).

Edgeworth, M. (ed.) (2006), *Ethnographies of Archaeological Practice: Cultural Encounters, Material Transformations* (Lanham, MD: AltaMira).

Edmonds, M., and Evans, C. (1991), 'The Place of the Past: Art and Archaeology in Britain', in *Excavating the Present*, ii. *History* (Cambridge: Kettle's Yard), 16–18.

Eisenlohr, P. (2004), 'Language Revitalisation and New Technologies: Cultures of Electronic Mediation and the Refiguring of Communities', *Annual Review of Anthropology* 33: 21–45.

Elliott, P. (2003), 'Presenting Reality: An Introduction to Boyle Family', in P. Elliott, B. Hare, and A. Wilson (eds), *Boyle Family* (Edinburgh: National Galleries of Scotland), 9–19.

Ellis, C. (2004), *The Ethnographic I: A Methodological Novel about Autoethnography* (Walnut Creek, Calif.: AltaMira).

Emirzian, B. (2006), 'Google's Garage: Preserving a Legacy: Big Mouth Media', <http://www.bigmouthmedia.com/live/articles/google-buys-garage-where-it-all-started.asp/3235/>, accessed 9 June 2009.

English Heritage (2007*a*), 'Modern Times', *Conservation Bulletin* 56, <http://www.english-heritage.org.uk/server/show/ConWebDoc.12373>, accessed 9 June 2009.

—— (2007*b*), *Understanding the Archaeology of Landscapes: A Guide to Good Recording Practice* (London: English Heritage).

ESA (European Space Agency) (2009), 'Space Debris: History and Background', <http://www.esa.int/SPECIALS/Space_Debris/SEMQQ8VPXPF_0. html>, accessed 30 April 2009.

European Landscape Convention ([2000] 2008), European Landscape Convention: An Extract', in G. Fairclough, R. Harrison, J. H. Jameson, Jnr., and J. Schofield (eds.), *The Heritage Reader* (London: Routledge), 405–7.

Fabian, J. (2002), 'Virtual Archives and Ethnographic Writing: "Commentary" as a New Genre?', *Current Anthropology* 43(5): 775–86.

Fagan, B. (1991), 'Digging DeMille', *Archaeology* 44(2):16.

Fairclough, G. (2007), 'The Contemporary and Future Landscape: Change and Creation in the Later Twentieth Century', in McAtackney, Palus, and Piccini (2007), 83–8.

—— (2008), 'The Long Chain: Archaeology, Historical Landscape Characterization and Time Depth in the Landscape', in G. Fairclough, R. Harrison, J. H. Jameson, Jnr., and J. Schofield (eds.), *The Heritage Reader* (London: Routledge), 408–24.

—— (2009). 'n.d. Conservation and the British', in Schofield (2009*d*), 157–64.

—— and Rippon, S. (2002), *Europe's Cultural Landscape: Archaeologists and the Management of Change* (Brussels: Europae Archaeologiae Consilium).

Falconer, K. (2007), 'Cars and Chips: The Diet that Transformed Swindon's Industrial Landscapes', *Conservation Bulletin* 56: 17–19.

Ferguson, R., Harrison, R., and Weinbren, D. (2010), 'Heritage and the Recent and Contemporary Past', in T. Benton (ed.), *Understanding Heritage and Memory* (Manchester: Manchester University Press; Milton Keynes: Open University), 277–317.

Ferllini, R. (2007), *Forensic Archaeology and Human Rights Violations* (Springfield, Ill.: Charles C. Thomas).

Ferrándiz, F. (2006), 'The Return of Civil War Ghosts: The Ethnography of Exhumations in Contemporary Spain', *Anthropology Today* 22(3): 7–12.

Feversham, P., and Schmidt, L. (1999), *The Berlin Wall Today* (Berlin: Bauwesen).

Finn, C. A. (2001), *Artifacts: An Archaeologist's Year in Silicon Valley* (Cambridge, Mass.: MIT).

—— (2004), *Past Poetic: Archaeology and the Poetry of W. B. Yeats and Seamus Heaney* (London: Duckworth).

—— (2007), 'The "Sunrise Strip": The M4 Corridor', *Conservation Bulletin* 56: 20.

—— (2009), 'Old Junk or Treasure?' *The Guardian (Family)*, Saturday, 3 January 2009: 1–2.

Foley, R. A. (1981), 'A Model of Regional Archaeological Structure', *Proceedings of the Prehistoric Society* 47: 1–17.

Forsyth, P. (2007), Letter to the Editor, *British Archaeology* 93: 21.

Fowler, M. J. F. (2008), 'The Application of Declassified KH-7 GAMBIT Satellite Photographs to Studies of Cold War Material Culture: A Case Study from the Former Soviet Union', *Antiquity* 82(317): 714–31.

Frearson, C., May, S., Orange, H., and Penrose, S. (eds.) (forthcoming), *Heritage CHAT: Proceedings of the 2008 CHAT Conference* (Oxford: Archaeopress).

Frederick, U. K. (2009), 'Revolution is the New Black: Graffiti/Art and Mark-making Practices', *Archaeologies* 5(2): 210–37.

Freitas, L. (1999), 'Cultura material, prática arqueológica e genero: Um estudo de caso', in P. P. A. Funari (ed.), *Cultura material e arqueologia histórica* (Campinas: IFCH/Unicamp), 275–317.

Fuller, G., and Harley, R. (2004), *Aviopolis: A Book about Airports* (London: Black Dog).

Funari, P. P. A., and Zarankin, A. (eds) (2006), *Arqueología de la represión y la resistencia en América Latina (1960–1980)* (Catamarca: Universidad Nacional de Catamarca/Encuentro).

Garfinkel, S. (2000), *Database Nation: The Death of Privacy in the 21st Century* (Beijing: O'Reilly).

Gell, A. (1988), 'Technology and Magic', *Anthropology Today* 4(2): 6–9.

—— (1992), 'The Enchantment of Technology and the Technology of Enchantment', in J. Coote and A. Shelton (eds.), *Anthropology, Art, and Aesthetics* (Oxford: Oxford University Press), 40–67.

—— (1996), 'Vogel's Net: Traps as Artworks and Artworks as Traps', *Journal of Material Culture* 1(1): 15–38.

—— (1998), *Art and Agency* (Oxford: Oxford University Press).

Gibson, J. J. (1979), *The Ecological Approach to Visual Perception* (Boston: Houghton Mifflin).

Giddens, A. (1991), *Modernity and Self-Identity: Self and Society in the Late Modern Age* (Cambridge: Polity).

González-Ruibal, A. (2005), 'The Need for a Decaying Past: The Archaeology of Oblivion in Contemporary Galicia (NW Spain)', *Home Cultures* 2: 129–201.

—— (2006), 'The Dream of Reason: An Archaeology of the Failures of Modernity in Ethiopia', *Journal of Social Archaeology* 6: 175–201.

—— (2007), 'Making Things Public: Archaeologies of the Spanish Civil War', *Public Archaeology* 6: 203–26.

—— (2008), 'Time to Destroy: An Archaeology of Supermodernity', *Current Anthropology* 49(2): 247–79.

Gorman, A. C. (2005), 'The Cultural Landscape of Interplanetary Space', *Journal of Social Archaeology* 5(1): 85–107.

—— (2009*a*), 'Beyond the Space Race: The Significance of Space Sites in a New Global Context', in Holtorf and Piccini (2009), 161–80.

—— (2009*b*) 'The Gravity of Archaeology', *Archaeologies* 5(2): 344–59.

—— and O'Leary, B. L. (2007), 'An Ideological Vacuum: The Cold War in Space', in Schofield and Cocroft (2007), 73–92.

Gosden, C. (1999), *Anthropology and Archaeology: A Changing Relationship* (London: Routledge).

Gould, R. A. (1980), *Living Archaeology* (Cambridge: Cambridge University Press).

—— (1987), 'The Ethnoarchaeology of Abandonment in a Northern Finnish Farming Community', *Oulun Yliopiston Maantieteen Laitoksen Julkaisuja* 107: 131–52.

—— (2007), *Disaster Archaeology* (Salt Lake City: University of Utah Press).

—— and Schiffer, M. B. (eds.) (1981), *Modern Material Culture: The Archaeology of Us* (New York: Academic Press).

Gower, H. D., Jast, L. S., and Topley, W. W. (1916), *The Camera as Historian* (London: Sampson Low, Marston).

Graves-Brown, P. (2000*a*), 'Introduction', in Graves-Brown (2000*b*), 1–9.

—— (ed.) (2000*b*), *Matter, Materiality and Modern Culture* (London: Routledge).

Graves-Brown, P. (2007*a*), 'Avtomat Kalashnikova', *Journal of Material Culture* 12(3): 285–307.

—— (2007*b*), 'Concrete Islands', in McAtackney, Palus, and Piccini (2007), 75–82.

—— (2009*a*), 'The Privatisation of Experience and the Archaeology of the Future', in Holtorf and Piccini (2009), 201–13.

—— (2009*b*), '13 March 1993: The Library of Babel: Origins of the World Wide Web', in Schofield (2009*d*).

Green, D., and Kidd, A. (2004), 'Milton Keynes Urban Expansion Historic Environment Assessment: Historic Environment Considerations for the Milton Keynes & South Midland Sub-Regional Strategy' (unpublished report).

Green, L. F., Green, D. R., and Neves, E. G. (2003), 'Indigenous Knowledge and Archaeological Science', *Journal of Social Archaeology* 3(3): 366–98.

Guffey, E. E. (2006), *Retro: The Culture of Revival* (London: Reaktion Books).

Hakken, D. (1999), *Cyborgs@Cyberspace? An Ethnographer Looks to the Future* (New York: Routledge).

Hall, M. (2000), *Archaeology and the Modern World: Colonial Transcripts in the Chesapeake and South Africa* (London: Routledge).

—— (2001), 'Cape Town's District Six and the Archaeology of Memory', in R. Layton, P. Stone, and J. Thomas (eds.), *The Destruction and Conservation of Cultural Property* (London: Routledge), 298–311.

—— (2005), 'The Industrial Archaeology of Entertainment', in E. C. Casella and J. Symonds (eds.), *Industrial Archaeology: Future Directions* (New York: Kluwer/Plenum), 261–78.

—— (2006), 'Identity, Memory, and Countermemory: The Archaeology of an Urban Landscape', *Journal of Material Culture* 11: 189–209.

—— and Bombardella, P. (2005), 'Las Vegas in Africa', *Journal of Social Archaeology* 5(1): 5–24.

—— —— (2007), 'Paths of Nostalgia and Desire through Heritage Destinations at the Cape of Good Hope', in Murray, Shepherd, and Hall (2007), 245–58.

—— and Lucas, G. (2006), 'Archaeology at the Edge: An Archaeological Dialogue with Martin Hall', *Archaeological Dialogues* 13(1): 55–67.

—— and Silliman, S. (2006), 'Introduction: Archaeology of the Modern World', in M. Hall and S. Silliman (eds.), *Historical Archaeology* (Malden, Mass.: Blackwell), 1–19.

Hall, S. (ed.) (1997), *Representation: Cultural Representations and Signifying Practices* (London: Sage).

Hallam, E., and Hockey, J. (2001), *Death, Memory and Material Culture* (Oxford: Berg).

Harrison, I. (with Foreword by A. Marr) (2008), *Britain from Above* (London: Pavilion).

Harrison, R. (2002), 'Ngarranganni/Ngamungamu/Jalanijarra: "Lost Places", Recursiveness and Hybridity at Old Lamboo Pastoral Station, Southeast Kimberley', unpublished Ph.D. thesis, University of Western Australia.

—— (2003), 'The Archaeology of "Lost Places": Ruin, Memory and the Heritage of the Aboriginal Diaspora in Australia', *Historic Environment* 17 (1): 18–23.

—— (2004), *Shared Landscapes. Archaeologies of Attachment and the Pastoral Industry in New South Wales* (Sydney: University of New South Wales Press).

—— (2005), 'Dreamtime, Old Time, This Time: Archaeology, Memory and the Present-Past in a Northern Australian Aboriginal Community', in T. Ireland and J. Lydon (eds.), *Object Lessons: Archaeology and Heritage in Australia* (Melbourne: Australian Scholarly Publishing), 243–64.

—— (2006), 'An Artefact of Colonial Desire? Kimberley Points and the Technologies of Enchantment', *Current Anthropology* 47(1): 63–88.

—— (2009*a*), 'Excavating Second Life: Cyber-Archaeologies, Heritage and Virtual Settlements', *Journal of Material Culture* 14(1): 75–106.

—— (2009*b*), 'Towards an Archaeology of the Welfare State in Britain, 1945–2009', *Archaeologies* 5(2): 238–62.

—— (2009*c*),' "Three, Two, One . . . ?"; The Material Legacy of Global Millennium Celebrations', in Schofield (2009*d*), 147–56.

—— (2010*a*), 'Multicultural and Minority Heritage', in T. Benton (ed.), *Understanding Heritage and Memory* (Manchester: Manchester University Press; Milton Keynes: Open University), 164–201.

—— (2010*b*), 'What is Heritage?', in R. Harrison (ed.), *Understanding the Politics of Heritage* (Manchester: Manchester University Press; Milton Keynes: Open University), 5–42.

—— (2010*c*), 'Stone Artefacts', in D. Hicks and M. C. Beaudry (eds.), *Oxford Handbook of Material Culture Studies* (Oxford: Oxford University Press), 515–536.

—— and Linkman, A. (2010), 'Critical Approaches to Heritage', in R. Harrison (ed.), *Understanding the Politics of Heritage* (Manchester: Manchester University Press; Milton Keynes: Open University), 43–80.

—— and Schofield, J. (2009), 'Archaeo-ethnography, Auto-archaeology: Introducing Archaeologies of the Contemporary Past', *Archaeologies* 5(2): 185–209.

—— Fairclough, G., Jameson, J. H. Jnr., and Schofield, J. (2008), 'Heritage, Memory and Modernity: An Introduction', in G. Fairclough, R. Harrison,

J. H. Jameson, Jnr., and J. Schofield (eds.), *The Heritage Reader* (London: Routledge), 1–12.

Harrison, R., McDonald, J., and Veth, P., (eds.) (2005), 'Native Title and Archaeology', *Australian Aboriginal Studies* 2005(1) (Canberra: Aboriginal Studies Press).

Hart, D., and Winter, S. (2001), 'The Politics of Remembrance in the New South Africa', in V. Buchli and G. Lucas (2001e), 84–93.

Harvey, D. (1990), *The Condition of Postmodernity: An Enquiry into the Origins of Cultural Change* (Oxford: Blackwell).

Hayden, D. (2004), *A Field Guide to Sprawl* (London: W. W. Norton).

Hebdige, D. ([1979] 1988), *Subculture: The Meaning of Style* (London: Routledge).

Hegarty, C., and Newsome, S. (2007), *Suffolk's Defended Shore: Coastal Fortifications from the Air* (Swindon: English Heritage).

Hewison, R. (1987), *The Heritage Industry: Britain in a Climate of Decline* (Methuen: London).

Hicks, D. (2005), ' "Places for Thinking" from Annapolis to Bristol: Situations and Symmetries in "World Historical Archaeologies" ', *World Archaeology* 37(3): 373–91.

—— and Beaudry, M. C. (eds) (2010), *The Oxford Handbook of Material Culture Studies* (Oxford: Oxford University Press).

—— and Horning, A. (2006), 'Historical Archaeology and Buildings', in D. Hicks and M. C. Beaudry (eds.), *The Cambridge Companion to Historical Archaeology* (Cambridge: Cambridge University Press), 273–92.

Highmore, B. (2002a), *Everyday Life and Cultural Theory* (London: Routledge).

—— (ed.) (2002b), *The Everyday Life Reader* (London: Routledge).

Hine, C. (2000), *Virtual Ethnography* (London: Sage).

Hodder, I. (1982), *Symbols in Action: Ethnoarchaeological Studies of Material Culture* (New York: Cambridge University Press).

—— (1987), 'Bow Ties and Pet Foods: Material Culture and Change in British Industry', in I. Hodder (ed.), *The Archaeology of Contextual Meanings* (Cambridge: Cambridge University Press), 11–19.

—— (1999), *The Archaeological Process: An Introduction* (Oxford: Blackwell).

Hoggart, R. (1969), *Contemporary Cultural Studies: An Approach to the Study of Literature and Society* (Birmingham: University of Birmingham Centre for Contemporary Cultural Studies).

Holtorf, C. (2004a), 'Doing Archaeology in Popular Culture', in H. Bolin (ed.), *The Interplay of Past and Present* (Huddinge: Södertörns högskola), 40–8.

—— (2004b), 'Incavation–Excavation–Exhibition', in N. Brodie and C. Hills (eds.), *Material Engagements: Studies in Honour of Colin Renfrew,*

MacDonald Institute Mongraphs (Cambridge: Cambridge University Press), 45–53.

—— (2005*a*), 'Can Less be More? Heritage in the Age of Terrorism', *Public Archaeology* 5: 101–9.

—— (2005*b*), *From Stonehenge to Las Vegas: Archaeology as Popular Culture* (Walnut Creek, Calif.: AltaMira).

—— (2007), *Archaeology is a Brand! The Meaning of Archaeology in Contemporary Popular Culture* (Walnut Creek, Calif.: Left Coast).

—— (2008), 'Zoos as Heritage: An Archaeological Perspective', *International Journal of Heritage Studies* 14(1): 3–9.

—— (2009), 'Imagine This: Archaeology in the Experience Economy', in Holtorf and Piccini (2009), 47–64.

—— and Piccini, A. (eds.) (2009), *Contemporary Archaeologies: Excavating Now* (Berne: Peter Lang).

Hoskins, J. (1998), *Biographical Objects: How Things Tell the Stories of Peoples' Lives* (London: Routledge).

Hunter, J., and Cox, M. (2005), *Forensic Archaeology: Advances in Theory and Practice* (London: Routledge).

Huyssen, A. (2003), *Present Pasts: Urban Palimpsests and the Politics of Memory* (Stanford: Stanford University Press).

Hyatt, M. S. (1999), *The Y2K Personal Survival Guide* (Washington, DC: Regnery).

ICOMOS (2001), *The Montreal Action Plan*, <http://www.international. icomos.org/20th_heritage/montreal_plan.htm>, accessed 23 September 2008.

IKEA Group, The (2008), Facts and Figures, <http://www.ikea.com/ms/ en_GB/about_ikea_new/about/read_our_materials/ff08_gb.pdf>, accessed 9 June 2009.

Ingold, T. (2000), *The Perception of the Environment: Essays in Livelihood, Dwelling and Skill* (London: Routledge).

Jameson, F. (1984), 'Post-modernism or the Cultural Logic of Late Capitalism', *New Left Review* 146: 53–93.

—— (1989), 'Nostalgia for the Present', *The South Atlantic Quarterly* 88(2): 527–37.

—— (1991), *Postmodernism, or, The Cultural Logic of Late Capitalism* (Durham, NC: Duke University Press).

Jameson, J. H., Jnr., Ehrenhard, J. E., and Finn, C. A. (eds.) (2003), *Ancient Muses: Archaeology and the Arts* (Alabama: University of Alabama Press).

Jarvis, H. (2002), 'Mapping Cambodia's "Killing Fields" ', in Schofield, Johnson, and Beck (2002), 91–102.

Jensen, R. (1999), *The Dream Society: How the Coming Shift from Informa-tion to Imagination will Transform your Business* (McGraw-Hill).

Johnson, W. G. (2002), 'Archaeological Examination of Cold War Architec-ture: A Reactionary Cultural Response to the Threat of Nuclear War', in Schofield, Johnson, and Beck (2002), 227–35.

Jones, Q. (1997), 'Virtual Communities, Virtual Settlements and Cyber-Archaeology: A Theoretical Outline', *Journal of Computer Mediated Com-munication* 3(3): 1–24.

Joy, J. (2002), 'Biography of a Medal: People and the Things they Value', in Schofield, Johnson, and Beck (2002), 132–42.

Karlsson, H. (2004), *Försummat kulturarv. Det närliggande förflutna och fotbollens platser* (Mölnlycke: Bricoleur).

Keeffe, G. (forthcoming), 'Compost City: Underground Music, Collapsos-capes and Urban Regeneration', *Popular Music History*.

Keesing, R. (1985), *Cultural Anthropology: A Contemporary Perspective* (3rd edn.) (Melbourne: Harcourt Australia).

Keller, C. M., and Keller, J. D. (1996), *Human Cognition and Tool Use: The Blacksmith at Work* (Cambridge: Cambridge University Press).

Kohl, P. L., and Fawcett, C. (eds.) (1995), *Nationalism, Politics and the Practice of Archaeology* (Cambridge: Cambridge University Press).

Kopytoff, I. (1986), 'The Cultural Biography of Things: Commoditization as Process', in A. Appadurai (ed.), *The Social Life of Things: Commod-ities in Cultural Perspective* (Cambridge: Cambridge University Press), 64–91.

Kroeber, A. (1919), 'On the Principle of Order in Civilisation as Exemplified by Changes of Fashion', *American Anthropologist* 21(3): 235–63.

Küchler, S. (2002), *Malanggan: Art, Memory and Sacrifice* (Oxford: Berg).

Kuletz, V. (1998), *The Tainted Desert: Environmental and Social Ruin in the American West* (New York: Routledge).

Kuper, A. (1996), *Anthropology and Anthropologists: The Modern British School* (3rd edn.) (London: Routledge).

Lake, J., and Hutchings, F. (2009), 'The Enigma of Place: Reading the Values of Bletchley Park', in N. Forbes, R. Page, and G. Pérez (eds.), *Europe's Deadly Century: Perspectives on 20th Century Conflict Heritage* (Swindon: English Heritage), 87–96.

Lake, J., Monckton, L., and Morrison, K. (2006), 'Interpreting Bletchley Park', in Schofield, Klausmeier, and Purbrick (2006), 49–57.

Latour, B. (1987), *Science In Action: How to Follow Scientists and Engineers Through Society* (Cambridge, Mass.: Harvard University Press).

—— (1993), *We Have Never Been Modern* (Cambridge, Mass.: Harvard University Press).

—— (1996), *Aramis, or The Love of Technology* (Cambridge, Mass.: Harvard University Press).

—— (1999), *Pandora's Hope: Essays on the Reality of Science Studies* (Cambridge, Mass.: Harvard University Press).

—— (2000), 'The Berlin Key', in Graves-Brown (2000*b*), 10–21.

—— (2005), *Reassembling the Social: An Introduction to Actor–Network Theory* (Oxford: Oxford University Press).

—— and Woolgar, S. (1979), *Laboratory Life: The Social Construction of Scientific Facts* (Beverly Hills: Sage).

Law, J. (ed.) (1992), *Sociology of Monsters: Essays on Power, Technology and Domination* (London: Routledge).

—— (1993), *Organizing Modernity: Social Order and Social Theory* (Oxford: Blackwell).

—— (2002), *Aircraft Stories: Decentering the Object in Technoscience* (Durham, NC: Duke University Press).

—— (2004), *After Method: Mess in Social Science Research* (London: Routledge).

—— and Bijker, W. (1992), *Shaping Technology/Building Society* (Cambridge, Mass.: MIT).

—— and Hassard, J. (eds.) (1999), *Actor Network Theory and After* (Blackwell: Oxford).

Leach, E. (1982), *Social Anthropology* (Oxford: Oxford University Press).

Leach, J. (2007), 'Differentiation and Encompassment: A Critique of Alfred Gell's Theory of the Abduction of Agency', in A. Henare, S. Wastell, and M. Holbraad (eds.), *Thinking Through Things: Theorising Artefacts Ethnographically* (London: Routledge), 167–88.

Legendre, J. (2001), 'Archaeology of World War 2: The Lancaster Bomber of Fleville (Meurthe-et-Moselle, France)', in Buchli and Lucas (2001*e*), 126–37.

Lemonnier, P. (1986), 'The Study of Material Culture Today: Toward an Anthropology of Technical Systems', *Journal of Anthropological Archaeology* 5: 147–86.

—— (1992), *Elements for an Anthropology of Technology*, Anthropological Paper 88 (Michigan: University of Michigan Museum of Anthropology).

Leone, M. P., Potter, B. P., Jnr., and Shackel, P. A. (1987), 'Towards a Critical Archaeology', *Current Anthropology* 28(3): 283–302.

Lewis, E. (2008), *Great IKEA! A Brand for All the People* (London: Marshall Cavendish).

Lilley, I. (ed.) (2000), *Native Title and the Transformation of Archaeology in the Postcolonial World* (Sydney: Oceania).

Lipovetsky, G. (2005), *Hypermodern Times* (Cambridge: Polity).

Lucas, G. (2001), *Critical Approaches to Fieldwork: Contemporary and Historical Archaeological Practice* (London: Routledge).

—— (2004), 'Modern Disturbances: On the Ambiguities of Archaeology', MODERNISM/*modernity* 11(1): 109–20.

—— (2006), 'Historical Archaeology and Time', in D. Hicks and M. Beaudry (eds.), *The Cambridge Companion to Historical Archaeology* (Cambridge: Cambridge University Press), 34–47.

Ludlow Collective, The (2001), 'Archaeology of the Colorado Coal Field War 1913–1914', in Buchli and Lucas (2001*e*), 94–107.

Lyotard, J. F. ([1979] 1984), *The Postmodern Condition: A Report on Knowledge* (Manchester: Manchester University Press).

McAtackney, L. (2005), 'Long Kesh/Maze: An Archaeological Opportunity', *British Archaeology* 84: 10–15.

—— Palus, M., and Piccini, A. (eds.) (2007), *Contemporary and Historical Archaeology in Theory: Papers from the 2003 and 2004 CHAT conferences*, BAR International Series 1677 (Oxford: Archaeopress).

Majewski, T., and Schiffer, M. B. (2001), 'Beyond Consumption: Towards an Archaeology of Consumerism', in Buchli and Lucas (2001*e*), 26–50.

Manzo, K. A. (1996), *Creating Boundaries: The Politics of Race and Nation* (London: Lynne Reinner).

Marin, L. ([1984] 1990), 'Utopic Degeneration: Disneyland', in L. Marin (ed.), *Utopics: The Semiological Play of Textual Spaces* (Atlantic Highlands, NJ: Humanities International), 339–58.

Marshall, Y., Roseneil, S., and Armstrong, K. (2009), 'Situating the Greenham Archaeology: An Autoethnography of a Feminist Project', *Public Archaeology* 8(2–3): 225–45.

Mason, M. (2009), 'Housing: Then, Now and Future', <http://www.moyak.com/papers/house-sizes.html>, accessed 6 May 2009.

May, S. (2009), 'Then Tyger Fierce Took Life Away: The Contemporary Material Culture of Tigers', in Holtorf and Piccini (2009), 65–80.

Merriman, P. (2004), 'Driving Places: Marc Augé, Non-Places, and the Geographies of England's M1 Motorway', *Theory, Culture and Society* 21 (4/5): 145–67.

Meskell, L., and Scheermeyer, C. (2008), 'Heritage as Therapy: Set Pieces in the New South Africa', *Journal of Material Culture* 13(2): 153–73.

Miller, D. (1984*a*), 'Appropriating the State from the Council Estate', *Man* 23: 353–72.

—— (1984*b*), 'Modernism and Suburbia as Material Ideology', in D. Miller and C. Tilley (eds.), *Ideology, Power and Prehistory* (Cambridge: Cambridge University Press), 37–49.

—— (1987), *Material Culture as Mass Consumption* (Oxford: Blackwell).

—— (ed.) (1995), *Acknowledging Consumption: A Review of New Studies* (London: Routledge).

—— (1998*a*), *A Theory of Shopping* (London: Polity).

—— (ed.) (1998*b*), *Material Cultures* (London: UCL).

—— (2001), 'Behind Closed Doors', in D. Miller (ed.), *Home Possessions: Material Culture behind Closed Doors* (London: Berg), 1–22.

—— (2005*a*), 'Introduction', in S. Küchler and D. Miller (eds.), *Clothing as Material Culture* (London: Berg), 1–20.

—— (2005*b*), *Materiality* (Durham, NC: Duke University Press).

—— and Slater, D. (2000), *The Internet: An Ethnographic Approach* (London: Berg).

Miller, J. (2007), 'Afterword', in Penrose (2007), 187–90.

Minnis, J. (2007), 'The Car: An Agent of Transformation', *Conservation Bulletin* 56: 11–13.

Mitrašinović, M. (2006), *Total Landscape, Theme Parks, Public Space* (Aldershot: Ashgate).

Moore, G. E. (1965), 'Cramming More Components onto Integrated Circuits', *Electronics* 38(8): 114–17.

Moore, H. L. (1986), *Space, Text and Gender: An Anthropological Study of the Marakwet of Kenya* (Cambridge: Cambridge University Press).

MORI (2000), 'Attitudes towards the Heritage: Research Study Conducted for English Heritage', April to July (privately circulated report).

Morris, D. (2006), *Corsair KD431: The Time-Capsule Fighter* (London: History Press).

Moshenska, G. (2008). 'Ethics and Ethical Critique in the Archaeology of Modern Conflict', *Norwegian Archaeological Review* 41(2): 159–75.

Murray, N., Shepherd, N., and Hall, M. (eds.) (2007), *Desire Lines: Space, Memory and Identity in the Post-Apartheid City* (London, Routledge).

Myers, A. (2009), 'The Small Finds', in Bailey, Newland, Nilsson, and Schofield (2009), 4–13.

New Economics Foundation (2004), *Clone Town Britain: The Loss of Local Identity on the Nation's High Streets* (London: New Economics Foundation).

Newland, C., Bailey, G., Schofield, J., and Nilsson, A. (2007), 'Sic Transit Gloria Mundi', *British Archaeology* 92: 16–21.

O'Connor, B. (2008), 'UCD Scholarcast: Dust and Debitage—an Archaeology of Francis Bacon's Studio', <http://www.ucd.ie/scholarcast/scholarcast10.html>, accessed 3 October 2009.

Olivier, L. (2000), 'L'Impossible Archéologie de la mémoire: À propos de "W" ou le souvenir d'enfance de Georges Perec', *European Journal of Archaeology* 3: 387–406.

Olivier, L. (2001), 'The Archaeology of the Contemporary Past', in Buchli and Lucas (2001*e*), 175–88.

Olsen, B. J. (2001), 'The End of History? Archaeology and the Politics of Identity in a Globalised World', in R. Layton, P. Stone, and J. Thomas (eds.), *The Destruction and Conservation of Cultural Property* (London: Routledge), 42–54.

Orser, C. (2004), *Historical Archaeology* (2nd edn.) (London: Pearson Education).

Page, R. (2007), 'Where the Action Was: Recording Music Clubs and Venues', *Conservation Bulletin* 56: 36–7.

Palahnuik, C. (1996), *Fight Club* (New York: W. W. Norton).

Paterson, A. G., Gill, N., and Kennedy, M. (2003), 'An Archaeology of Historical Reality? A Case Study of the Recent Past', *Australian Archaeology* 57: 82–9.

Pearman, H. (2007), 'Good old Billy: Design Week Online', <http://www.designweek.co.uk/opinion/good-old-billy/1133894.article>, accessed 9 June 2009.

Pearson, M., and Shanks, M. (2001), *Theatre/Archaeology* (London: Routledge).

Penrose, S., with contributors (2007), *Images of Change: An Archaeology of England's Contemporary Landscape* (Swindon: English Heritage).

Perec, G. (1997), *Species of Spaces and Other Pieces* (Harmondsworth: Penguin).

Perry, T., and Glinert, E. (1996), *Rock & Roll Traveller USA* (New York: Fodors).

Pfaffenberger, B. (1992), 'Social Anthropology of Technology', *Annual Review of Anthropology* 21: 491–516.

—— (1998), 'Mining Communities, Châines opératoire, and Sociotechnical Systems', in A. B. Knapp, V. C. Piggot, and E. W. Herbert (eds.), *Social Approaches to an Industrial Past: The Anthropology and Archaeology of Mining* (London: Routledge & Kegan Paul), 291–300.

—— (2001), 'Symbols Do Not Create Meanings—Activities Do: Or, Why Symbolic Anthropology Needs the Anthropology of Technology', in M. Schiffer (ed.), *Anthropological Perspectives on Technology* (Tucson: University of Arizona Press), 77–86.

Piccini, A. (2009), 'Guttersnipe: A Micro Road Movie', in Holtorf and Piccini (2009), 183–200.

—— and Holtorf, C. (2009), 'Introduction: Fragments from a Conversation about Contemporary Archaeologies', in Holtorf and Piccini (2009), 9–29.

Pinch, T. J., and Bijker, W. E. (1989), 'The Social Construction of Facts and Artifacts: Or How the Sociology of Science and the Sociology of

Technology Might Benefit Each Other', in Bijker, Hughes, and Pinch (1989), 17–50.

Pine, B. J., and Gilmore, J. H. (1999), *The Experience Economy: Work is Theatre and Every Business a Stage* (Cambridge, Mass.: Harvard Business Press).

—— (1992), *Mass Customization: The New Frontier in Business Competition* (Boston, Mass.: Harvard Business School).

Pinsky, V., and Wylie, A. (eds.) (1989), *Critical Traditions in Contemporary Archaeology: Essays in the Philosophy, History and Socio-Politics of Archaeology* (Cambridge: Cambridge University Press).

Pinto, R., Bourriaud, N., and Damianovic, M. (2003), *Lucy Orta* (London: Phaidon).

Piotrowski, C. M., and Rogers, E. A. (2007), *Designing Commercial Interiors* (New York: John Wiley & Sons).

Rassool, C. (2007), 'Memory and the Politics of History in the District Six Museum', in Murray, Shepherd, and Hall (2007), 113–28.

Rathje, W. L. (1979), 'Modern Material Culture Studies', *Advances in Archaeological Method and Theory* 2: 1–37.

—— (1981), 'A Manifesto for Modern Material-Culture Studies', in Gould and Schiffer (1981), 51–6.

—— (2001), 'Integrated Archaeology: A Garbage Paradigm', in Buchli and Lucas (2001*e*), 63–76.

—— and Murphy, C. ([1992] 2001), *Rubbish! The Archaeology of Garbage* (New York: HarperCollins).

Read, P. (1996), *Returning to Nothing* (Cambridge: Cambridge University Press).

Reed-Danahay, D. E. (1997), *Auto/Ethnography: Rewriting the Self and the Social* (Oxford: Berg).

Reid, E. O. F. (1999), *Why 2K?—A Chronological Study of the (Y2K) Millennium Bug: Why, When and How Did Y2K Become a Critical Issue for Businesses?* (Singapore: Universal).

Renfrew, C. (2003), *Figuring It Out* (London: Thames & Hudson).

Rheingold, H. ([1993] 2000), *The Virtual Community: Homesteading on the Electronic Frontier* (2nd paperback edn.) (Cambridge, Mass.: MIT).

Ritzer, G. ([1995] 2004), *The McDonaldization of Society: An Investigation Into the Changing Character of Contemporary Social Life* (rev. New Century edn.) (London: Sage).

—— (1998), *The McDonaldization Thesis: Explorations and Extensions* (London: Sage).

—— (2003), *The Globalization of Nothing* (London: Pine Forge).

—— (ed.) (2006), *McDonaldization: The Reader* (London: Pine Forge).

Robertson, A., and Kenyon, D. (2008), *Digging the Trenches: The Archaeology of the Western Front* (Barnsley: Pen and Sword Military).

Rothschild, N. A. (1981), 'Pennies from Denver', in Gould and Schiffer (1981), 161–81.

Roux, V. (1985), *Le Matériel de broyage: étude ethnoarchéologique à Tichitt (R.I. Mauritanie)* (Paris: Éditions Recherche sur les Civilisations).

—— (1989), *The Potter's Wheel: Craft Specialization and Technical Competence* (New Delhi: Oxford & Ibh).

—— and Bril, B. (eds.) (2005), 'Stone Knapping: The Necessary Conditions for a Uniquely Hominin Behaviour' (Cambridge: McDonald Institute for Archaeological Research).

—— —— and Dietrich, G. (1995), 'Skills and Learning Difficulties Involved in Stone Knapping: The Case of Stone-Bead Knapping in Khambat, India', *World Archaeology* 27: 63–87.

Russell, L. (2001), *Savage Imaginings: Historical and Contemporary Constructions of Australian Aboriginalities* (Melbourne: Australian Scholarly Publishing).

Samuel, R. (1994), *Theatres of Memory: Past and Present in Popular Culture* (London: Verso).

Samuelson, T., and Peters, J. (1995), 'Landmarks of Chicago Blues and Gospel: Chess Records and First Church of Deliverance', in D. Slaton and R. A. Shiffer (eds.), *Preserving the Recent Past* (Washington, DC: Historic Preservation Education Foundation:), ii. 117–22.

Saunders, N. J. (2001), 'Matter and Memory in the Landscapes of Conflict: The Western Front 1914–1999', in B. Bender and M. Winer (eds.), *Contested Landscapes: Movement, Exile and Place* (Oxford: Berg), 37–53.

—— (2002), 'Archaeology and the Great War, 1914–2001', *Antiquity* 76: 101–8.

—— (2003), *Trench Art: Materialities and Memories of War* (Oxford: Berg).

—— (ed.) (2004), *Matters of Conflict: Material Culture, Memory and the First World War* (London: Routledge).

—— (2007), *Killing Time: Archaeology and the First World War* (Thrupp: Sutton).

Saunders, R. (2002), 'Tell the Truth: The Archaeology of Human Rights Abuses in Guatemala and the Former Yugoslavia', in Schofield, Johnson, and Beck (2002), 103–14.

Saxon, E. (1965), 'The Street that Shames Hero Island', *Titbits*, 6 March 1965, 30–1.

Schiffer, M. B. (1987), *Formation Processes of the Archaeological Record* (Albuquerque: University of New Mexico Press).

—— (1991), *The Portable Radio in American Life* (Tucson: University of Arizona Press).

—— (2000), 'Indigenous Theories, Scientific Theories and Product Histories', in Graves-Brown (2000*b*), 172–96.

Schnapp, A. (ed.) (1997), *Une archéologie du passé récent?* (Paris: Fondation Maison des Sciences de l'Homme).

—— Shanks, M., and Tiews, M. (2004), 'Archaeology, Modernism, Modernity', *MODERNISM/modernity* 11(1): 1–16.

Schofield, J. (1999), 'Now We Know: The Role of Research in Archaeological Conservation Practices in England', in P. McManamon and A. Hatton (eds.), *Cultural Resource Management in Contemporary Society: Perspectives on Managing and Presenting the Past* (London: Routledge), 76–92.

—— (2000), 'Never Mind the Relevance? Popular Culture for Archaeologists', in Graves-Brown (2000*b*), 131–54.

—— (2002), 'The Role of Aerial Photographs in National Strategic Programmes: Assessing Recent Military Sites in England', in R. Bewley and W. Raczkowski (eds.), *Aerial Archaeology: Developing Future Practice* (Amsterdam: IOS in co-operation with NATO Scientific Affairs Division), 269–82.

—— (2005), *Combat Archaeology: Material Culture and Modern Conflict* (London: Duckworth).

—— (2006), *Constructing Place: When Artists and Archaeologists Meet*, <http://diffusion.org.uk/?tag=art>, accessed 8 June 2009.

—— (2007), 'Angus Boulton, Archaeologist', in A. Boulton (ed.), *Restricted Areas* (Manchester: Manchester Metropolitan University/MIRIAD).

—— (2008), 'The Office: Heritage and Archaeology at Fortress House', *British Archaeology* 100: 58–64.

—— (2009*a*), 'Peace Site: An Archaeology of Protest at Greenham Common', *British Archaeology* 104: 44–9.

—— (2009*b*), *Aftermath: Readings in the Archaeology of Recent Conflict* (New York: Springer).

—— (2009*c*), 'Office Cultures and Corporate Memory: Some Archaeological Perspectives', *Archaeologies* 5(2): 293–305.

—— (ed.) (2009*d*), *Defining Moments: Dramatic Archaeologies of the Twentieth Century* (Oxford: Archaeopress).

—— (2010), ' "Theo Loves Doris": Wild-Signs in Landscape and Heritage Context', in T. Neal and J. Oliver (eds.), *Wild Signs: Writing in the Margins* (Oxford: Archaeopress), 71–79.

—— and Anderton, M. (2000), 'The Queer Archaeology of Green Gate: Interpreting Contested Space at Greenham Common Airbase', *World Archaeology* 32: 236–51.

Schofield, J. and Cocroft, W. (eds.) (2007), *A Fearsome Heritage: Diverse Legacies of the Cold War* (Walnut Creek, Calif.: Left Coast).

—— and Morrissey, E. (2005), 'Changing Places—Archaeology and Heritage in Strait Street (Valletta, Malta)', *Journal of Mediterranean Studies* 15(2): 481–95.

—— —— (2007), '*Titbits* Revisited: Towards a Respectable Archaeology of Strait Street, Valletta (Malta)', in McAtackney, Palus, and Piccini (2007), 89–100.

—— Beck, C. M., and Drollinger, H. (2003), 'The Archaeology of Opposition: Greenham Common and Peace Camp Nevada', *Conservation Bulletin* 44: 47–9.

—— Johnson, W. G., and Beck, C. M. (eds.) (2002), *Matériel Culture: The Archaeology of Twentieth Century Conflict* (London: Routledge).

—— Kiddey, R., and Lashua, B. (forthcoming), 'People and Landscape', in J. Carman, C. McDavid, and R. Skeates (eds.), *The Oxford Companion to Public Archaeology* (Oxford: Oxford University Press).

—— Klausmeier, A., and Purbrick, L. (eds.) (2006), *Re-mapping the Field: New Approaches in Conflict Archeology* (Berlin: Westkreuz).

Second Life Wikia (2009), 'Hippos', <http://www.slhistory.org/index.php/Hippo>, accessed 9 June 2009.

Shanks, M. (1992), *Experiencing the Past: On the Character of Archaeology* (London: Routledge).

—— (2004), 'Three Rooms: Archaeology and Performance', *Journal of Social Archaeology* 4(2): 147–80.

—— and Tilley, C. ([1987] 1992), *Re-constructing Archaeology* (Cambridge: Cambridge University Press).

—— Platt, D., and Rathje, W. L. (2004), 'The Perfume of Garbage: Modernity and the Archaeological', *MODERNISM*/modernity 11(1): 61–83.

Sharr, A. (2006), *Heidegger's Hut* (Cambridge, Mass.: MIT).

Shepherd, N. (2002*a*), 'Heading South, Looking North: Why We Need a Post-Colonial Archaeology', *Archaeological Dialogues* 9: 74–82.

—— (2002*b*), 'The Politics of Archaeology in Africa', *Annual Review of Anthropology* 31: 189–209.

—— and Ernsten, C. (2007), 'The World Below: Post-Apartheid Urban Imaginaries and the Bones of the Prestwich Street Dead', in Murray, Shepherd, and Hall (2007), 215–32.

Sherman, W. R., and Craig, A. B. (2003), *Understanding Virtual Reality: Interface, Application and Design* (San Francisco: Morgan Kaufmann).

Smith, D. (2002), 'Dodge-Tide: A Rusting Rural Legacy', in D. Jones (ed.), *20th Century Heritage: Our Recent Cultural Legacy. Proceedings of the*

Australia ICOMOS National Conference 2001 (Adelaide: University of Adelaide/ICOMOS), 161–5.

Smith, L. (2004), *Archaeological Theory and the Politics of Cultural Heritage* (London: Routledge).

Sontag, S. ([1977] 2002), *On Photography* (Harmondsworth: Penguin).

Sorkin, M. (ed.) (1992), *Variations on a Theme Park: The New American City and the End of Public Space* (New York: Hill & Wang).

Squires, W. (2006), 'Open Mic: The American Adventure', <http://www.s104638357.websitehome.co.uk/html/magazine_21_openmic.htm>, accessed 10 June 2009.

Stager, C. (1995), 'Graceland and Sun Studio', in D. Slaton and R. A. Shiffer (eds.), *Preserving the Recent Past* (Washington, DC: Historic Preservation Education Foundation), ii, 115.

Stamp, G., and Powers, A. (2008), 'The Twentieth Century Society: A Brief History', <http://www.c20society.org.uk/docs/about/history.html>, accessed 23 September 2008.

Stauffer, E., and Bonfanti, M. (2006), *Forensic Investigation of Stolen–Recovered and Other Crime-Related Vehicles* (London: Academic Press).

Steele, C. (2008), 'Archaeology and the Forensic Investigation of Recent Mass Graves: Ethical Issues for a New Practice of Archaeology', *Archaeologies* 4(3): 414–28.

Sterenberg, J. (2008), *Forensic Archaeology, Anthropology and the Investigation of Mass Graves*, International Forensic Science and Investigation Series (London: Taylor & Francis).

Stevenson, G. (2001), 'Archaeology as the Design History of the Everyday', in Buchli and Lucas (2001*e*), 51–62.

Stocking, G. W. (1985), *Objects and Others: Essays on Museums and Material Culture* (Madison: University of Wisconsin Press).

Strathern, M. (1988), *The Gender of the Gift* (Berkeley: University of California Press).

—— (2004), 'The Whole Person and its Artefacts', *Annual Review of Anthropology* 33: 1–19.

Stratton, M., and Trinder, B. (2000), *Twentieth Century Industrial Archaeology* (London: Spon).

Sundbo, J., and Darmer, P. (2008), *Creating Experiences in the Experience Economy* (Cheltenham: Edward Elgar).

Sun International (2009*a*), 'The Magic Company', <http://www.suninternational.com/Destinations/Casinos/Grandwest/Family/Pages/TheMagic-Company .aspx>, accessed 30 April 2009.

Sun International (2009*b*), 'Bars/Night Club', <http://www.suninternational.com/Destinations/Casinos/Grandwest/DiningBars/Pages/Bars-NightClub.aspx>, accessed 30 April 2009.

Sutherland, P. (2008*a*), *Community: The Elephant and Castle* (Elephant and Castle: London College of Communication).

—— (2008*b*), *Home: The Elephant and Castle* (Elephant and Castle: London College of Communication).

Symonds, J. (2004), 'Historical Archaeology and the Recent Urban Past', *International Journal of Heritage Studies* 10(1): 33–48.

Talbot, G., and Bradley, A. (2006), 'Characterising Scampton', in Schofield, Klausmeier, and Purbrick (2006), 43–8.

Taussig, M. (1992), *The Nervous System* (London: Routledge).

Thomas, J. (2004), *Archaeology and Modernity* (London: Routledge).

—— (2009), 'Sigmund Freud's Archaeological Metaphor and Archaeology's Self-Understanding', in Holtorf and Piccini (2009), 33–45.

Thomas, N. (1998), 'Foreword' to Gell (1998).

Thomson, D. (1999), *In Nevada: The Land, The People, God and Chance* (London: Abacus).

Tiffin, J., and Terashima, N. (eds.) (2001), *HyperReality: Paradigm for the Third Millennium* (London and New York: Routledge).

Tilley, C. (1989), 'Archaeology as Socio-political Action in the Present', in Pinsky and Wylie (1989), 104–16.

—— (ed.) (1990), *Reading Material Culture: Structuralism, Hermeneutics and Post-structuralism* (Oxford: Blackwell).

—— (1999), *Metaphor and Material Culture* (Oxford: Blackwell).

—— (2004), *The Materiality of Stone* (Oxford: Berg).

—— (2006), 'Introduction', in Tilley et al. (2006), 1–11.

—— Keane, W., Kuchler, S., Rowlands, M., and Spyer, P. (eds.) (2006), *Handbook of Material Culture* (London: Sage).

Tomlinson, J. (2007), *The Culture of Speed: The coming of Immediacy* (London: Sage).

Townsend, C. (2008), Lecture by Chris Townsend, <http://www.boylefamily.co.uk/boyle/texts/index.html>, accessed 26 February 2009.

Trigger, B. G. (1996), *A History of Archaeological Thought* (Cambridge: Cambridge University Press).

Tuck, C., and Cocroft, W. D. (2005), 'Digging up the Space Age', *British Archaeology* 81: 6–31.

Ucko, P. (1969), 'Penis Sheaths: A Comparative Study—The Curl Lecture 1969', *Proceedings of the Royal Anthropological Institute*, 27–67.

Udder Creative (2009), 'The American Adventure Theme Park: History', <http://www.theamericanadventure.moonfruit.com/> accessed 9 June 2009.

Uhel, R. (2006), *Urban Sprawl in Europe: The Ignored Challenge*, EAA Report 10/2006 (Copenhagen: European Environment Agency).

Ulin, J. (2009), 'In the Space of the Past: A Family Archaeology', in Holtorf and Piccini (2009), 145–59.

UNESCO (2008), White City of Tel Aviv: The Modern Movement World Heritage listing Description, <http://whc.unesco.org/en/list/1096>, accessed 10 December 2008.

Urry, J. (2008), 'Leisure Places', in N. Hazendonk, M. Hendriks, and H. Venema (eds.), *Greetings from Europe: Landscape@Leisure* (Rotterdam: 010 Publishers), 21–7.

Virilio, P. (1994), *Bunker Archaeology* (New York: Princeton Architectural Press).

—— (2000), *A Landscape of Events* (Cambridge, Mass.: MIT).

Wagner, R. (1992), 'The Fractal Person', in M. Godelier and M. Strathern (eds.), *Big Men and Great Men: Personifications of Power in Melanesia* (Cambridge: Cambridge University Press), 159–73.

Walshe, K. (2002), 'Protest, Peacekeeping and Resistance: Assessing the Heritage Significance of 20th Century Activist Sites', in D. Jones (ed.), *20th Century Heritage: Our Recent Cultural Legacy. Proceedings of the Australia ICOMOS National Conference 2001* (Adelaide: University of Adelaide/ICOMOS), 290–3.

Webmoor, T. (2007), 'What About "One More Turn After the Social" in Archaeological Reasoning? Taking Things Seriously', *World Archaeology* 39(4): 547–62.

—— and Witmore, C. L. (2004), Symmetrical Archaeology, <http://humanitieslabs.stanford.edu/Symmetry/Home>, accessed 9 June 2009.

—— —— (2008), 'Things Are Us! A Commentary on Human/Things Relations under the Banner of a "Social" Archaeology', *Norwegian Archaeological Review* 41(1): 53–70.

Whyte, J. (2002), *Virtual Reality and the Built Environment* (Oxford: Architectural Press).

Wilkie, L. A. (2001), 'Black Sharecroppers and White Frat Boys: Living Communities and the Appropriation of their Archaeological Pasts', in Buchli and Lucas (2001*e*), 108–18.

—— and Bartoy, K. M. (2000), 'A Critical Archaeology Revisited', *Current Anthropology* 41(5): 747–77.

Williams, E., and Costall, A. (2000), 'Taking Things More Seriously: Psychological Theories of Autism and the Material–Social Divide', in Graves-Brown (2000*b*), 97–111.

Williams, R. (1966), *Culture and Society, 1780–1950* (New York: Harper & Row).

Wills, H. (1985), *Pillboxes: A Study of UK Defences 1940* (London: Leo Cooper).

Wilson, L. (2009), 'Notes on a Record of Fear: On the Threshold of the Audible', in Holtorf and Piccini (2009), 113–28.

Wilson, S. M., and Peterson, L. C. (2002), 'The Anthropology of Online Communities', *Annual Review of Anthropology* 31: 449–67.

Winner, L. (1980), 'Do Artifacts Have Politics?', *Daedalus* 109(1): 121–36.

Witmore, C. L. (2004), 'On Multiple Fields: Between the Material World and Media, Two Cases from the Peloponnesus, Greece', *Archaeological Dialogues* 11: 133–64.

—— (2006), 'Vision, Media, Noise and the Percolation of Time: Symmetrical Approaches to the Mediation of the Material World' *Journal of Material Culture* 11(3): 267–92.

Wolf, W. (1996), *Car Mania: A Critical History of Transport* (London: Pluto).

Woolgar, S. (1991), 'The Turn to Technology in Social Studies of Science', *Science, Technology and Human Values* 16(1): 20–50.

Wylie, D. (2004), *The Maze* (London: Granta).

—— (2007), *British Watchtowers* (Göttingen: Steidl).

Yellen, J. E. (1977), *Archaeological Approaches to the Present* (London: Academic Press).

Young, D. E., and Goulet, J. G. (eds.) (1998) *Being Changed by Cross-Cultural Encounters: The Anthropology of Extraordinary Experience* (Ontario: Broadview).

Zarankin, A., and Funari, P. P. A. (2008), ' "Eternal Sunshine of the Spotless Mind": Archaeology and Construction of Memory of Military Repression in South America (1960–1980)', *Archaeologies* 4(2): 310–27.

Zimmerman, L., and Welch, J. (2006), 'Toward an Archaeology of Homelessness', *Anthropology News* 47(2): 54–5.

Žižec, S. (1997), *The Plague of Fantasies* (London: Verso).

Zongming, Z. (2005), 'Living on the Cyber Border: *Minjian* Political Writers in Chinese Cyberspace', *Current Anthropology* 46(5): 779–803.

Index

Made in the USA
Coppell, TX
04 January 2023

10430251R00198